SOUTH AMERICA

EXPLORATION

BY THE SAME AUTHOR

NON-FICTION

MY JOURNEY TO AFRICA

RUSSIA AND THE SILK ROADS

SOUTH AMERICA ENCHANTMENT

FICTION

THE RED CARPET COLLECTION

THE RIVER OF LIFE

POEM COLLECTIONS

SONGS OF HONOUR

THE COLORS OF LIFE

THE BEST POEMS AND POETS OF 2005

SOUTH AMERICA

EXPLORATION

robert f. edwards

www.trafford.com

North America & international
toll-free: 1 888 232 4444 (USA & Canada)
phone: 250 383 6864 ♦ fax: 250 383 6804
email: info@trafford.com

The United Kingdom & Europe
phone: +44 (0)1865 722 113 ♦ local rate: 0845 230 9601
facsimile: +44 (0)1865 722 868 ♦ email: info.uk@trafford.com

10 9 8 7 6 5 4 3 2

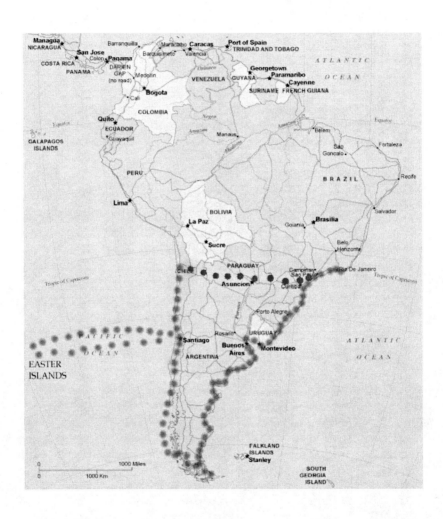

Table of Contents

Table of Contents

About the Author

Robert F. Edwards is presently living in Burnaby, British Columbia, Canada with his wife of thirty-two years. He maintains a close connection with his daughter and grandson, also living in the Lower Mainland. After a successful career in the business arena, he now has the time to pursue his driving ambition of world travel and has been on every continent. He enjoys sailing, trekking, and mountain climbing. In later years, he took on the challenging sport of fencing, and is proficient with all three weapons. He also writes poems, and fictional stories. He partakes in the arts in the various forms; painting in acrylic and water-color, and clay sculpturing, along with photography.

His Credo;
The difficult is done at once, the impossible takes a little longer.
If a job is worth doing, it is worth doing right.
Don't abuse your friendships, and you will always have friends.

INTRODUCTION

Like so many adventures, I have always tried to focus on three important parts of that global community. I am always grateful if these moments can be accomplished, or these regions I am able to enjoy a first-hand experience.

My wishes on this particular adventure of 2001 were to see the Easter Islands, which again in my boyhood thirst for adventure on the pages of others knowledge was fascinated by the statutes that are scattered throughout the island in such a remote part of the world. Number two, was to go around the Cape, that was not only presented to me, but to sail through the Strait of Magellan and the Beagle Channel, I was more than fortunate to feel the wind as a true sailor with canvas. These demanding waters have the highest respect of sailors' folklore and definitely my admiration. On a much lighter note, I hoped to accomplish by spending time in Rio de Janeiro, at the famous beach of Copacabana. It was everything that I believe the tourist information provides and far, far more. Rio de Janeiro is a very exciting city in a remarkable country. So, the three wishes were given to me, and I received them with awe and admiration.

But there is so much more, like the Iguazu Falls, the Patagonians, the Torres del Paine, the freight ship from Punta Arenas to Puerto Montt, the volcano in the lake area of Chile, and on and on it goes. The people and their lifestyles, anything from the tango in Argentina to the samba in Brazil, to the delicious fish dishes that the Chileans have enhanced this journey far beyond any of my expectations. I am more than grateful for having this experience.

R.F.E.

**February 1st, Thursday
Vancouver, British Columbia**

My adventure begins. I got up; or rather I got out of bed, as I had been up most of the night, unable to sleep. I had to confess not from excitement, but lack of concentration on dropping off to sleep. However, as the alarm beckoned and it was time to commence this journey, now 4:45 a.m., I jumped up out of bed and prepared myself for the day ahead. My good wife was up and prepared some coffee before driving me to the airport. It was a process which both of us had gone through many times before. Goodbyes were never easy and this one was no exception, no matter how many times this ritual had been performed before. We were both trying to put on a good face, and to our credit, I believe we had done our best effort yet.

We arrived at the airport in good time and we had prearranged that my wife would say goodbye without going in and for both our sakes it seemed to be better that way. The airplane was scheduled to leave on time, and the first leg was with Alaskan Airlines to Los Angeles, where I got off but my luggage continued its journey to Santiago, Chile. I spent a bit of time in the airport trying to get an e-mail to my beloved but was unsuccessful so I continued on to the designated spot before the long flight ahead.

I managed to get an aisle seat instead of a window seat which I'd requested but it was a full flight, and non-eventful. The flight took its natural course in reaching its altitude, and we continued with periodic updates. The only real criticism I had was it was extremely hot and unfortunately the area that I was in seemed the worst. This was a bad attitude, to complain over such a minor inconvenience; however, it prevented me from getting the much-needed sleep that I had been counting on.

I won't say goodnight, because I'm not sure when one day has ended and the other one has started, but that does conclude my first day of traveling.

SOUTH AMERICA EXPLORATION

February 2nd, Friday
Santiago, Chile

We arrived in Santiago, Chile on time, without any hang-ups. I was surprised to learn that Canadians had to pay the highest entrance fee. The Australians paid $30, the Americans paid $45 and the Canadians paid $55, all in U.S. dollars. With that out of the way, my first priority was to check on my flight to the Easter Islands tomorrow. The airport was modern and well laid out, so it was easy to find the information required, and the Domestica Airport was the one that I would leave from. It was within walking distance, an older airport but still well organized. I decided to leave the majority of my luggage in a service compartment in the international airport for the next 3 or 4 days, which saved me carrying it around to the Easter Islands.

I was impressed with the politeness of all the attendants and taxi drivers, and it was a good fare (24 km to the core of the city), still I found the Chilean people mild-mannered and helpful. I couldn't say with any authority at that point, but I felt they were honest with their information. I met a gentleman named John that helped interpret with the taxi driver and the hotel and, again, not the pressure that I had experienced in so many other countries throughout the world. Helpful, obviously wanting to achieve a conclusion to his efforts, but not overly distraught if it didn't come to pass. Once we established a price for the fare of back and forth to the airport tomorrow and the hotel, I was accompanied by a Japanese gentleman from Osaka, much younger than myself but then who isn't these days!

The journey into Santiago was my first experience of Chile. It was quite arid and the mountain ranges, which John pointed out, were the Andes. My desire to see all the major

3

mountain ranges in the world had now been fulfilled. They reminded me of the mountain ranges that I had experienced in Mongolia and also the Sierra Madres along California and into Mexico. The journey was enjoyable, as the highways were excellent. The traffic flows were heavy, even though it was only 6:30 a.m. local time (to the best of my knowledge, it was approximately five hours different). The sun was just rising over the Andes and it was warm, not hot.

When we arrived at the hotel, the first thing that I noticed about the city was the cleanliness and the layout; it was a beautiful city. As the day progressed I kept realizing this to the fullest degree. My hotel was modestly priced, more than adequate for my needs. The room was very small, a single bed and I had to share a bathroom; but again, in compliance with what I had witnessed in the short time I had been here, was the cleanliness and the general respect for the property of one and all. Some of the buildings had graffiti, but were still in good condition. There was a pride that prevailed. The proprietor was polite and apologized for his limited English; such a difference compared to some of the adventures that I had been on in the past. The straightforward, business-like manners and the lack of haggling prevail, which seemed to have been abandoned in North America under the same conditions.

They quoted a lot in U.S. dollars, and once I explained that I was Canadian and was carrying Chilean currency, I asked if there was a difference, or a black market preference. They said, "No, it's just absolutely the same, whatever you want to pay," so accommodating, and easygoing. After I had checked in, my next quest was to try and get an e-mail off to my beautiful wife. I set off walking down the city boulevards, which were massive, park-like settings between the traffic on either side. It made my city, Vancouver, also a beautiful city, feel squashed together. The forefathers had put a lot of thought into the buildings and transportation accesses in a logical way. Even with the traffic congestion, there was still greenery and lots of benches, giving it a European flavour.

SOUTH AMERICA
EXPLORATION

I walked for the better part of an hour, just enjoying myself, before stopping to get a beverage, which was something like pop with a fruit flavour. I started my trek again to send an e-mail and found a place with ease. To my surprise I not only was able to get an e-mail done, but also was able to log into 'Explorer' with ease, which happened to be just one of the servers I was using.

I was struck by the city's abundance of beautiful facades and ornate structures, which were well maintained. The people were modestly but well dressed and there seemed to be an air reminiscent of the 50's in Canada...of order, continuity and satisfaction. I stopped into a small café and the gentleman and young girl (who could be his daughter) were polite and pleasant. That was the other thing – so pleasant to be around. The transportation was interesting. There seemed to be a colour code for the local transportation, which was yellow, whether it was a cab or bus, so lots of yellow around, but again in good shape. The tourist buses, from what I had read about, sounded like they were state of the art.

It was a city of parks, or places of leisure, and there didn't seem to be any particular class or period of time that people took advantage of them. The shops were smaller than what I was accustomed to. I went into a grocery store, well stocked with all the facilities and my first purchase was bread. It was delicious, fresh and probably no additives either!

The people seemed to be more Indian, with less noticeable difference or homogenizing of ethnic backgrounds. They appeared to be of a similar race or origin, probably a blend of Spanish and European with Natives long ago. The dress was more conventional, and even the young people were taking pride in their appearance, rather than the 'Charlie Brown baggy look' back home. That afternoon, jet lag had caught up with me so I returned to the hotel for a rest, knowing that all was well and I felt very comfortable and safe in that city.

After a few hours rest, I returned to the parks, so enjoyable and manicured. In front of one of the administration buildings, the grounds were open to the public, and I found people like myself just sitting and enjoying the evening, which now was about 7:30 p.m. and young lovers practising lip to lip contact. There was a sense of tranquility, even with the heavy traffic, which I could hear in the background in the downtown core of this large city of over four million. Though it was extremely hot, with the gentle breezes blowing it was comfortable to be outside. I hadn't seen so many pigeons for a long time, preening, and waiting their turn for something to drop their way on these manicured boulevards.

Back in the downtown core, I strolled past stores, which were well displayed, and there were tiles on the streets as well as in the corridors linking the streets. By now I had covered an area of about four blocks by five blocks with lots of facilities to sit down and enjoy myself, but I was looking for a restaurant rather than fast food. I located a great deal of the latter, even to the good old McDonald's and Burger King, also there were a lot of fried chicken places and pizzas. I spent a great deal of time walking before I finally gave up on trying to find a nice restaurant before choosing one of the more expensive hotels. The restaurant was at the top, on the 17th floor, and the waiters (most of them middle-aged men) were all dressed in clean grey aprons. When I asked what would be a good Chilean dish, the waiter without hesitation strongly recommended the bass, as famous in this region of Chile. I was going to order a red wine and the disapproval on his face made me return to the white vintage he suggested, which was an excellent choice. The bass was exquisite, accompanied by baby carrots, brussel sprouts and cauliflower.

I had the good fortune of walking the perimeter upstairs and there was a pool just outside the restaurant. It was about 9:00 p.m. and the sun was just starting to set behind the Andes. Such a beautiful experience for my first night in Chile. The mountains had a glow to them as the sun set, and the city lights appeared. I had enjoyed conversation with a German lady and we both returned to our table for a few glasses of wine and talked about each other's country and the country that we were now visiting. She was returning home in a day or two and I was on my way to the Easter Islands.

After spending a few hours with her, I tried making my way back to the hotel, but got a little twisted around, so I took a cab. The driver was very pleasant and apologetic; when they don't speak English it seems to be that it was their fault, not my lack of conforming to their culture. Before long it was the better part of 12:30 – 1:00 and tomorrow was another day.

Good night, one and all, and good night, little honey bun.

Robert F. Edwards

I got up with a bit of a dry taste in my mouth, probably one too many glasses of wine last night. I had to be ready for the taxi to take me to the airport at 7:00 a.m. and this was one morning that I certainly could have slept in. Without dwelling on the subject, I prepared myself and the taxi driver was waiting for me. Another quality that I have to add to the many Chilean ones I had noticed, and that was reliability.

We drove to the airport and I booked into the flight to the Easter Islands. The flight itself was uneventful, for the better part of four thousand kilometers and five hours long. However, we headed into time rather than away from it, and I picked up two hours of extra time as a bonus. I was one of the first off the airplane and the flight must have had a hundred people plus on it. Of course I was looking for my contact, Lucille, and being the first off with little or no luggage I bypassed her. As I started to get a little concerned, this wonderful woman appeared and was really excited, hugged and kissed me. She was definitely part of the island, wide in girth, to say it politely, and had a warm, loving disposition. She showed me the paper that someone had written for her, and my name was spelled correctly in big block letters so I would be able to identify her. These people were organized, and the good fortune that I had experienced on my previous journeys seemed to be holding true.

She got a bus and arranged to drop people off to different hotels, and the last four remaining passengers were all going to her place. Besides myself, there was a couple from Puerto Rico and a young lady from Chile. We started to make conversation, and these people were more than accommodating to speak English for 'guess who'. Lucille showed us our rooms, and explained that her home was ours, and if we wanted to cook it was fine. Whatever we wanted, she would look after us; she had a real motherly concern about our well being. She was concerned about the short time I would be here, in order to see the entire island and have a pleasant experience.

The first observation I made of the island; it reminded me a lot of Moshi, in Tanzania. However, the people were a happy bunch and this island has a tropical appearance. It felt extremely hot, although the temperature was only in the 70 degrees F range; it was the humidity. At first, I thought it was my lack of acclimatizing, but no, my three new companions were experiencing the same thing. I even noticed that Lucille had some perspiration. She served us watermelon and explained a bit of the island, and then showed us her tropical garden, which I had taken some pictures of. There were bananas, limes and papayas, even the more conventional produce that Canadians were familiar with, like lettuce.

There was a general consensus that this island could be self-sufficient for food products, also they were famous for their sweet potatoes and different types of yams.

We were just about to stroll down to the village when Francisca, the Chilean young lady discovered that she had the wrong luggage. With a few phone calls, the airport said that the fellow had returned her luggage and would be there shortly to retrieve theirs. We all hopped in a taxi that Lucille had ordered and off to the airport. The taxi dropped us off in the downtown core and took the luggage back to Lucille's place. It was refreshing to find that people exist in this world with honesty and integrity and were truly accommodating to our problems. I laughed and said that anywhere in North America you would have said goodbye to the luggage forever, but here it was no trouble, and I mean, really no trouble.

We got dropped off at the art bazaar, where the local artists congregated making souvenirs of the little statues that were so famous on this island. They came in every size, shape and material, from wood to the original volcanic stone. If I found space in my luggage, I would take some with me. We continued on down to the dock in the main harbour and talked to some people about scuba diving and snorkeling. The waters were very pleasant, and with the amount of perspiration that was pouring off us, we all wished that we had bathing suits on, to jump in.

By now, the afternoon had found its way into early evening and by 6:00 p.m., we were starting to head back to Lucille's place. I was enjoying my newfound friends' company, even though all three of them were speaking Spanish. When we were unsure of which fork in the road to take, a taxi came along and told us which one to take. I had to give Francisca full points; she seemed to have a very good idea of the island and where we were. In all fairness to the other three of us, this was not her first trip here, so she had a good command of the island.

Once back at Lucille's place, we freshened up a bit and I met a Frenchman staying with her also. Daniel and I talked for some time; he was a very charming man and spoke English fluently. When Francisca and the rest joined us, it was dinnertime at approximately 9:00 p.m. Our meal consisted of fresh tuna and pumpkin (which was absolutely delicious and I had more than one helping), sweet potatoes, Roma tomatoes and avocados. For dessert we had papaya and pineapple, all healthy and delicious. Along with this, we had a drink they make, like a milkshake, with different fruits in it, like bananas or papaya. Francisca said you could even put avocados in.

By the time dinner was over, we had been told that this was the period of a great feast on the island, and the celebrations ended that night with the crowning of the new queen. The queen carried this honour of her coronation for one year, a symbolic and emotional feast, if not the biggest feast of the island. Daniel had a vehicle and offered to take us down there, which was most considerate and all of us took advantage of it, to see the coronation of the new queen. The costumes were not quite as traditional as the original ancestors' wardrobes, but still an enjoyable experience. All the island people seemed to participate, and it was their festival, not put on for the benefit of tourists. Although they welcomed us with their hospitality, we were a minority compared to the island people. Most of the island people were inter-related in some way, with Polynesian overtones and were a very close-knit community. For those needing stress therapy, either physical or mental, just come down here and enjoy the laidback attitude, this was 'Island Time'. We enjoyed the evening, listening to the music, which was not as traditional as I thought it would be, and the band was more electronic than their ancestors' ever were.

The queen was crowned. I gathered that she had just lost a relative, and the whole group took a moment in silence, for remembrance and prayer for this passing soul. The barbecues were absolutely gigantic, as they spread the meat out, a full "rack" cooked over the coals, and also in shish kebab type. By midnight, we had all exhausted our physical resources, since we had done a fair amount of walking that day, and my feet were sore. We walked back to Lucille's place and said goodnight to one and all.

So, on that note, I'll say goodnight also. Goodnight, my little loved one.

Robert F. Edwards

At 6:00 in the morning, I could hear tremendous downpours. My first recollection when I went to the window was some of the monsoons I had been in. I had been told that on the island, you could have heavy rains and then blue skies shortly thereafter. However, this rain was quite persistent and the overcast skies prevailed. Around 9:00 a.m., people started to surface from their beds and we proceeded with breakfast, which was included. It was an impressive layout, with an abundance of different types of fruit, cheese, meats, fresh buns, and juices and of course, coffee. This coffee sufficed my needs, but unfortunately it was only instant coffee along with powdered milk, so for those connoisseurs who demand the real thing, it was lacking somewhat, but an excellent spread of food.

The rain was continuing, not with the torrential requirements of a rainforest, but still persistent. We were all starting to feel it might be one of those lazy Sunday days, but the four of us decided to try and get a vehicle and see the island. Lucille phoned a group of people, but because of the large amount of tourists that had arrived here, there were no vehicles to be found. Along with myself, Lucille, her young son and a friend, we literally did a door-to-door search asking for a car, or a little Suzuki jeep to be more precise. As it became more and more doubtful, at the last place, they had a vehicle for tomorrow but only a very expensive car. So I said no, and by now I was reconciled to not being able to see much of the island today. Lucille was not defeated yet, and now she had abandoned the idea of rental cars, but was going to ask her friends.

SOUTH AMERICA
EXPLORATION

We entered a little grocery store and no, they didn't have a vehicle, but here was my first introduction to a very popular Chilean snack. It was like a Cornish pastie, either with meat, fish or cheese, and it was baked in pastry, with the ingredients inside, and neatly twisted at the ends before being placed inside an oven and baked. It was just scrumptious; even after my large breakfast, I thoroughly enjoyed my first empanada.

After contacting many of Lucille's friends and relatives, as a last ditch effort she called on one of her in-laws, and was ecstatic when she saw their Suzuki parked in the garage. She tracked them down and lo and behold, yes, we had a vehicle. These were wonderful people, on this remote island, with an ancestry to the Polynesians. There was a strong sense of cooperation with each other, and of course, we were their main source of income, the touristas! They were just a very kind, easygoing, helpful bunch of people and Lucille had to be close to the top of the pyramid of those great qualities.

Now, with a vehicle in hand, even the weather started to improve. It was still overcast, but the four adventurers decided that we were going to at least see how the roads were. Because of the volcanic base this island was on, the water had dissipated and even though some of the potholes contained puddles, the roads were acceptable to drive on.

To the Easter Islanders, better known as Rapa Nui, the statues were Moai and they were primarily made of different types of volcanic ash. The base of the Moais was grey or black ash, but the head or hat was red and quite a distinguished combination. A few of the Moais still had the eyes in place, and those that did

were made out of coral. A lot of thought had gone into these
ancient monuments, and the island itself was an archeolo-
gist's delight. The statues were cut in quarries and then
dragged great distances over steep, rugged terrain. The coastline was formidable, with few natural harbours. Even the two
little beaches were just small pockets of sand. However, the
island was beautiful and lush, fitting all the criteria of a tropical paradise.

Like so many places in the world, even though this was one
of the most remote islands with inhabitants on it, there had
been conflicts. It was about 2000 km. from any other land
mass and 3700 km. from the South American coastline. I saw
one of the cargo vessels en route to New Zealand, and when
standing on the hilltops, the sea looked endless.

In historical tradition, there were some theories of two cultures or tribes of people, known as the Long Ears and the
Short Ears, or as the 'corrupt people' and the 'thin people'.
Some of the theories have it that as they had a population ex-
plosion, the natural food supply dwindled, and the scarcity of
food caused the conflicts that arose.

Francisca, the young Chilean lady, was acting as our own
private tour guide, as she had visited the Island before, and
was knowledgeable about all the historical sites. One of the
first places we visited was Maunga Orito. This was where a lot
of the tops or head pieces were, and to the unfamiliar eye you
could easily drive by this first without realizing the significance. As I looked around, I noticed the different parts of the
Moais lying down, just incomplete pieces of them. We continued along the south coast to Ahu Vaihu. There are eight large
Moai statues here, overturned and lying face down. For some
unknown reason during one of the conflicts, a lot of these
statues were pulled down. Also, on this particular site, there's
a headless Moai with short legs, unlike most of the other
Moais that are larger. This resembled the Pre-Incan statues in
the Andes, which again added to more archeologists' myster-
ies. There was a lot of rubble and destruction in this area. We
were very close to the coastline here, and there was a cave

along this rocky shore which none of us went into. I would have had to be much thinner than I was, probably one of the Thin People's places! We spent some time looking around and Francisca was able to point out some of the statues lying down. Because of the erosion and many years of salt from the ocean, there was deterioration.

Our next stop is Ahu Akahanga. This area contained the quarries where they formed these great statues out of the faces of the mountains. In the broadest sense of the term they were volcanic mountains, but now more like rolling hills, still quite a vigorous walk up. In these quarries I saw some of the Moais that for whatever reason weren't completed, and they were carved at different angles, whatever the stone would permit. I took pictures of ones that were very large. In fact, Francisca said that one of them was the largest known on the island and it was lying face down, incomplete. Only the face was finished and the long body, others were lying vertical, almost in state, and in a giant's tomb literally carved into the faces of the mountains.

When completed, they hoisted these huge structures and moved them down the very steep incline before erecting them in different areas. Just climbing this terrain had produced a lot of perspiration on all of us. We walked down to a volcanic basin, with a small lake in it. This probably served as a fresh water reservoir, and around this basin there was another group of Moais standing. I would not stake my reputation on it, but I believe there were about 600 of these statues on the island. I had no intentions of doing a count, nor did I have the opportunity to see each and every one of them, but as I became more familiar with what I was looking for, I started to notice them at different levels. One of them I almost stepped on. All that was left was just a face, that time and erosion had taken its toll on, leaving only a lasting memory of that particular one. We went down a different route on this hillside and arrived in a marsh area. These were quite prevalent and during the rainy season, Francisca told us that it was typically marsh.

Robert F. Edwards

The next place along our way was Ahu Hanga Tetenga and it was probably "the" place. There was a huge row of Moai statues and again I took more pictures of these ones. They were very impressive in different shapes and sizes, but they were all in a row. I wondered if this wasn't an inland road that they were stored on before being put on rollers or trees to move to their final position. These particular ones weren't facing the sea, as the other ones were. Some religious theories claimed they were looking out to sea for guidance, or strangers to rescue them.

We moved on to Ikos Trench. The theory here was that the "haves" and the "have-nots" were separated by this great divide, allowing the priests to have more control over their quality of life. Legend holds that this great trench was built for defense filled with wood and set on fire to prevent invasion. There was evidence of this that archeologists were confirming by carbon data.

As we progressed, we arrived at the first beach, (Francisca's favourite) which was quite small. Further along we came to a larger beach and it was surprising that for a Sunday, there weren't more people about, although it was still intermittent rain and overcast. This park area was very well done, with picnic tables, and small concessions available. The grounds outside the sandy beach were clean and well manicured and the trees provided a first-class location for picnics.

Along with all this natural beauty were the historical monuments of the Moai and there were quite a large row of them. Often standing alone was a much larger one, many metres high in this area of Anakena & Ahu Ature Huki.

We returned to the only main highway on the island and saw one of the Moais at Vaitea, but by this time it was getting late so we returned to our little homestead quite fulfilled. Our group consisted of Francisca, the Chilean lady which I had found out was 19 years old, and Karina and Pedro, she was 30 and he was a few years older, and then there was the real old guy, me! However, we all seemed to be enjoying ourselves and I found all three of them very compatible. Everybody was accommodating me by speaking English.

After a short rest, we ventured into the city and found a small restaurant. The ladies had French fries and chicken, Pedro ordered pasta and I had a hamburger and milkshake. Yes, I traveled to the middle of nowhere, better known as "The Navel of the World" to have a hamburger. But it was good and I enjoyed myself very much.

We discovered that we had lucked out again, as this was a great feast day, when the locals selected a princess for the year. Legend said that for the person selected, there were usually 3 or 4 deaths in the family, not exactly a celebration of events. By now it was dark, about 10:00 p.m. and the celebration took place with a large group of the islanders. This was the second day of the feast, where they relived the heritage of the island, with traditional costumes of the island. With the aid of modern technology, a large video screen displayed pictures of the island in different quarters. It was well done, almost like a mini-documentary.

Along with that, the islanders appeared on stage, wearing the progression of historical garb. The first period was very scantily dressed, then the next period depicted the plantation occupation by the slave traders, then the Chilean military period, and Lucille appeared in that part, so all of us gave a big hand and that group was well-received. From there, they moved into the current era, and finally the queen was elected for the year and was presented. The rain started to come down and we were all ready to call it a night, but the word was out that the coronation was still to take place over by a large Moai.

The four of us decided that we were going to be adventurous in the dark. I wished I had brought my camera or better yet, my flashlight, as we were crossing a field in the dark, but there were enough locals ahead of us to follow the trail. When we arrived at the location, they had placed flaming torches to outline the perimeter of the event and all the young people participating were dressed in the original attire. The men wore a grass loin cloth, in some cases almost a g-string, and grass strips wrapped around the calf of their legs, and they all had different wooden paddles.

I watched these men dancing, there didn't seem to be any particular style, but a lot of rhythm. One man fascinated me; he danced across fairly rugged terrain with beaten-down grass, so their feet must be very strong. He moved like a mystical god with his legs going sideways, back and forth, probably symbolic of some kind of animal. The other men danced in different forms, but the rhythm was consistent. I noticed, even in this darkness with just the torches for light, that their legs were very muscular. The women danced also, but were more in the background. As in so many cultures, the male is more dominant. The performance with chanting and dancing continued for the better part of an hour. Then, a bamboo carriage was brought out for the new princess, and carried by her new subjects. That concluded the ceremony, and it was a grand finale of this feast. It was my good fortune to be able to witness this event, as it wasn't planned on my part. Once back at Lucille's, we said good night to each other.

And goodnight my beautiful little wife, Marietta.

18

SOUTH AMERICA
EXPLORATION

February 5th, Monday
Hanga Roa, Easter Islands

Let the day begin! My compadres were not quite the early riser as myself, and it was 9:30 a.m. before the shuffling of life began. Lucille served a delicious breakfast of fresh fruits, juices, bread, cheese and meat if one desired, with coffee or tea. Gradually, the hustling and bustling of the day commenced as one member surfaced to greet another.

Lucille asked me a favour, if I would mind having a roommate today, and since it would be my last night, I agreed. After all that she'd done for me, it was a small favour.

Francisca was determined to show me, if not the others, everything that there was to see on the island. We started our day off by going to the caves, and there were a lot of volcanic caves here. Some of them were quite deep, others were fairly shallow. The young couple agrees to join me, although Francisca prefers to stay above. We venture in, combat ready! With my flashlights, we are able to penetrate quite a distance into the caves; I even meet up with another Chilean gentleman that wishes to go further in. There aren't any stalactites like other caves I have been in, as the mineral content is not the soft limestone of the mainland.

I have noticed when it rains here (and there are some very heavy downpours) that due to the volcanic composition of this island, it doesn't retain the water except in very limited areas. This holds true with the caves, they are wet but don't contain a lot of moisture. I saw no evidence of nesting of either birds or bats, and very few insects. There was a growth in one spot of algae forming near an opening, almost a natural sunroof! We explored the caves quite extensively and it is said that if you had the time, you're supposed to be able to come out at a different part of the island.

Robert F. Edwards

After being in the underground part of the island, we've chosen to be at the highest point of the island, Ahu Tepeu. This is a remarkable climb, but we chose to do it by the jeep. We stopped at different intervals and I've taken some pictures along the way. The view is absolutely breathtaking, with long grassy plains and the village itself. As we approach the top of this summit, you can literally see from one end of the island to the other.

Once up at the summit, none of us can believe the wind. It is so strong. Lucille has warned Francisca and us to be careful  up here. These winds are almost a gale force. Kite flying is out of the question, and for hang-gliding; I think all you'd have to do is open your shirt and run like heck and you'd be out of control! We're fascinated not only by the strong winds, but also the view, as you can actually see the curvature of the earth.

We then make our way to see the largest Moai ever erected. It is at Ahu Te Pito Te Kura, along the northern coast. There's a group of the Moai in good shape, probably restored through archeologists or government programs. I'm finding a lot of the original ones have either fallen over, or been torn down, and show the effects of erosion, being surrounded by sea and salt and high winds, but they're beautiful and mystical. When they were first built they were conceived with eyes, which give them a more foreboding appearance. The one at the ceremony last night had eyes in it and these are large pieces of coral that are white with a blue background, most impressive.

20

SOUTH AMERICA
EXPLORATION

We start to make our way to a very interesting part, where the ceremony of the birdman takes place. During the development of the first civilization here, probably in the later 1800's/1900's, the tradition began. The young men would scale down this treacherous cliff, dive into the crashing waves, to swim a formidable distance to one of the three small islands offshore, scramble up to find a nest with an egg of the Sooty Tern bird and return the same route, carrying the egg back before anyone else. To me the cliffs look impregnable, but they were able to do it, as the first rock-climbers. The fellow that got the egg back first without breaking it received favours from the chief and was granted numerous concessions as a chosen person of the island. In modern society's context, this must have been the first Ironman contest.

The ceremonial village of Orongo is about 400 meters above the crater lake of Rano Kau. They've reconstructed a lot of the housing in this area which were built out of stone or shale rock. They're tiered up and because the walls are so very thick they support the heavy-earth covered arched roofs, and the doors are very small crawlspaces. I mentioned to Francisca that I was going to try to go in and she started to laugh and said, "You'll get stuck!" and I agreed, "Yes, they must have been very thin people." I had seen some woodcarvings that depict a skeleton-type form, maybe these were known as the Thin People? It must have been difficult to live in this dramatic area of the island, as all of the houses face directly out to sea and would have taken the full impact of the high winds that I've experienced here.

21

Robert F. Edwards

We continue on to another very impressive area, a large extinct volcano. It has now developed into a shallow, marshy lake. There's a deep crevice in the side of this crater, a v-shaped window to the nearby sea. It's a picturesque part of the island and a natural for the cameras to be brought out. We all agreed this is where we'd like to build our homes to enjoy the perfect view.

I've exhausted most of the day, and again exhausted my fellow travelers. Karina's hip is bothering her considerably, and good-natured Francisca is saying that her feet are sore. Plus, Pedro, even though he does a lot of running, looks a little tired! I feel like the Energizer bunny commercial, pounding the little drum. These accommodating people have moved to the beat of my drum! I can't say enough about their companionship and the enjoyment that I've felt being with all three of them.

Now we head back to town for something to eat. I had my heart set on that delicious Chilean pastie, the empanada that I had before, but I've gathered it's more of a morning dish. Out here on the island, they don't microwave food, they actually cook it. Francisca, with her determination, contacts one of her friends that have some, but it's cold and if we wait a little bit they'll warm it. The three main ingredients are some kind of meat, fish or cheese. Her friend doesn't have any made with cheese, Pedro is a vegetarian, and Karina abstains, so it's just Francisca and myself that enjoy them. They're not as good warmed up, but still delicious, and my mouth waters just thinking about them.

By now, it's about 7:00 p.m., and later this evening Lucille has planned a special feast with her family, and she's invited us to participate if we want. Lucille is such a wonderful person, and your happiness is her reward. I feel a better person for knowing her. While we are waiting, we do what normal tourists do, and that is shopping.

We wearily get back into the little jeep to head back to Lucille's place to clean up, and are we dirty! We had all laughed ourselves into hysterics from the high winds that left our clothes just filthy, and our faces looked like we had been dragged through a dirt pile, we were literally black! We all rushed to have the first showers. Francisca and I go first, while Karina and Pedro have taken the opportunity to wash the jeep, which also badly needs it.

While the others enjoy a few relaxing moments, I took advantage of the break to get caught up on some of my notes. I met an interesting couple traveling together, Daniel and Christina, and talked to them for a while. With them, I experienced my first taste of a Chilean alcoholic drink, a pisco sour. With all due respect, it's not what my taste buds enjoy, but it is the most popular drink here. The strong grape brandy is served with lemon juice, egg white and powdered sugar. I took a small sip, but it's something that I would have to develop an acquired taste for.

I met my new roommate, Giuseppe; a young man that has just arrived. He works in a hospital in Milan, with computer programming and luckily for me, he speaks English. Dinner is ready about 9:00 p.m., and it is definitely a feast, to say the least! There are 3 or 4 different types of meats, and kumara, a sweet potato, which the Islanders prefer to wheat products.

Robert F. Edwards

There's different types of squashes, tomatoes and taro root, plus many foods that I don't recognize, but all scrumptious. Lucille's put a lot of work into this and her sons have also gone that extra mile for us.

It was a large group, there must have been close to 20 visitors and family together. I sat beside one of Lucille's relatives, a professor, and though he didn't speak much English, we communicated well enough for me to appreciate his great humour. We were all in the party mood, and before the evening's finished, I had taken lots of pictures of the group. It is a grand feast and what a great last night. If this is an omen of how my trip is going to continue, it is going to be awesome.

By 1:00 a.m. I excuse myself and go to my room. Even though I don't leave until tomorrow afternoon, it's going to be an exceptionally long day. God knows how long the party did last; I just know that this party animal enjoyed it immensely.

Good night one and all, good night my little true love. I miss you.

SOUTH AMERICA
EXPLORATION

February 6th, Tuesday
Hanga Roa, Easter Islands

I am up with the sun this morning, as it is my last day on the Island, and I don't want to miss a moment. After Lucille has provided us all with a nourishing and delicious breakfast, we discuss a few plans for the day. My main concern is to return our vehicle promptly, but for the locals, this does not seem to be such an issue. They have a laissez-faire attitude with time, and do not seem to be worried about it. Where I am concerned about returning the jeep punctually, they seem to have little or no concern if it does come back. At $50 a day, it was a good investment.

This morning, the group of us head down to the one and only village, Hanga Roa to check out the shops for souvenirs, as your typical tourists. Myself, not as in tune with this type of shopping as the others, find the prices very high. They quote in U.S. dollars and the little moais start at $10 to $15 and range up to many hundreds of dollars for the large size replicas. The one I really liked was a bit big to be packing around, and they quoted $80 U.S., and I wasn't able to budge them down, and in this open-air market, Visa payment was not accepted. I purchased a few postcards, and bought some representations of Captain Cook's first visit with the Long Ears. I settled on a small Moai, and bartered it down from $25 to $15, as a small memento of this remarkable island, the navel of the world.

Hanga Roa is spread out, space not being an issue here on the island. For the size of the population that supports it, it is not an easy centre to walk around in, and the villagers use vehicles to get around in.

Back to Lucilles' and then on to the Internet station, it's a favourite spot for me now. I have really welcomed the ease of

25

communication on this trip so far, although the prices seem to vary considerably at different locations. Here on the Island, it costs 5000 Chilean pesos per hour, but I have paid as low as 1000 pesos/hour. My previous traveling experiences depended on telephone or fax for communication, and if this was all that was available, the expense is cost prohibitive. ($20 to $30/minute) The Internet is a great boon that modern technology has provided, at least for this traveler. I got caught up on the few emails that Marietta had sent, and now the liquid sunshine, so prevalent on tropical islands, is once again upon us.

Karina and Pedro decide to continue shopping, so Francisca and I venture off together. She shares with me a rather romantic story, that on her last visit here with her parents, she met a young man and they have kept in touch. This lovely young lady did not wish to impose upon him, nor have the Islanders whisper their secrets, so she left a note, spelled out in stones, "I am here", and a picture of herself, and is now waiting in hope that he will respond.

The clock is ticking down the hours on my last day here, and I asked if we could see a bit more of the island to get some last pictures. She took me to a signpost that reflects the distances, showing Australia and Chile and other points north, and I get a picture taken of it, as well as myself. This trip I'm going to make an effort to have myself included in some of the pictures, which I usually forget to do, and end up with postcard views rather than personal mementos.

There's a beautiful tall square-rigger ship that is anchored in the outer harbour along with a catamaran, which I couldn't pass up the opportunity of taking a picture of this nautical setting. We returned back to the park of the coronation ceremony last night, since it had one of the best Moais with eyes still intact. Also, there was an unusual graveyard, which I took some pictures of. It's interesting when you travel to observe the different cultures and their views. This graveyard is not only very colourful in its tombstones and plots, but it's well-maintained and demonstrates the respect these people have for all things, both present and past, and a good attitude towards the future.

Francisca and I returned to Lucille's, as it was close to 1:00 p.m., and I needed to get to the airport soon. I had purchased some cigarettes as a going-away present, not exactly what I wanted to get Lucille, but she smokes and it's probably as good a gift as any for a person that enjoys that habit. Lucille asks us to wait a few moments, because she wants to change and come with us. I'm honoured and grateful. It might be a small thing, but these moments of kindness are the things that I remember most as I make my way through life.

When I had been planning this trip, I was quoted 1000 pesos for a ride to the airport or into town, and these taxis don't have meters. Lucille's generously picked me up, and now dropped me off, inclusive in the price. We get to the airport and the many wide-bodies airbuses on the runways are full. Already the new wave of touristas is getting off, and just as many of us are getting on.

I said my goodbyes to Lucille, and Francisca had asked me to leave my last goodbye for her. I thought it a remarkable thing; I was almost three times her age and yet, I think there was a friendship and feeling of enjoyment that we had spent this short time together. I told her I would always remember her as my little Chilean guide and she laughed, and I promised her that I would keep in touch with e-mail.

It was an emotional moment for all of us, and I had not realized how much I had touched both of them, and Lucille was hugging me and stroking my hand. She placed a small little necklace with a Moai around my neck, I gave them both a hug and a kiss on the cheek and with that, I was on the plane to Santiago, Chile.

It arrived on time and I picked up the balance of my luggage. I managed to get a taxi to take me to the other bus station, smaller and more in the core of the town. Without too much difficulty, I purchased a ticket to La Serena for tomorrow morning at eight-thirty. The cab driver then drove me to a hotel, and I checked in with no problems whatsoever. Back

Robert F. Edwards

on the street, I found an Internet place but unfortunately it closed at ten-thirty.

I spotted a Chinese restaurant and had a meal, not Chinese food by my standards. I order wontons, in the broadest sense of the term, beef with onions chopped in it, more of a "broth" stew and rice. I was very thirsty and drank four bottles of diet Pepsi. The gentleman serving me, after the third one, started to look at me and said something in Spanish.

I went back to my hotel room satisfied. It is a pleasant evening, although a little humid. And so, concluded another long day.

Goodnight, my little beautiful wife, my little Marietta.

SOUTH AMERICA
EXPLORATION

February 7th, Wednesday
Santiago, Chile

I had a wake up call at seven o'clock. I had a very restless night. I don't know whether it is just I couldn't sleep or I was just unable to get used to the time differences. However, for whatever reason, I had a very restless night and like so many times, when I could sleep, it was time for the day to commence. With that, I heard the knock on the door and got myself prepared for the long day ahead on the bus. I had packing to do and rearranging and I thought I had an awful lot of time, but before too much ado, it was quarter to eight.

I was able to flag down a cab driver person and showed the gentleman the ticket to the bus station. He started driving and I tried to explain it was north, he said "si", and I was quite sure he was taking me to the wrong bus station. By the time we got to the bus station, it was now about ten after eight and I knew that I was at the first bus station close to the railroad station, but he insisted that this was where the bus to La Serena was to depart from. I walked through this large bus depot, and this was really the first time that I realized not all Chileans were bilingual. In fact, a minority was probably bilingual. Nobody spoke English and I did find a bus that was going to La Serena. However, it was the wrong bus line. Everybody was trying to help me and finally, one man explained to me what I knew in the first place, I needed to be at the other terminal. It was now quarter after eight. The buses leave punctually and the bus that I had a ticket for was at eight.

In another taxi, I was heading through the streets of Santiago to the other bus terminal. I was trying to be optimistic, but it looked impossible to get through all that morning traffic. But this amazing taxi driver knew what he was doing and whenever there was an opening became a credit to his profession. Somehow, he got me on the bus only minutes before the bus-driver took off.

I could hardly believe how this had been successful. It had taught me a great deal. One; was to do my homework, which I had; and then follow through regardless of who wanted to change it. Two; because the bus transportation was so popular throughout not only Chile but also South America, there were many bus lines that competed for traveling and be sure to get on the right bus at the right terminal.

We were soon heading out into the country. It had a similarity to any country that has arid drying winds that suck up moisture. I saw the first cactuses and yes, they actually did look just like the pictures, these big armed banditos standing tall and foreboding on the rocky hillsides, in all shapes and sizes and heights. There were literally hundreds within my view as we made our way along this first leg of my inland journey of about five hundred kilometers. The roads were exceptionally good, in many cases, four-lane highways with a good divider.

Also, the bus seats were as comfortable as anything that I would hope to find on a first-class airline and to my pleasure, they served coffee and a small box of cookies. It was a pleasant ride and now that my heart was back pounding normally and I had about seven hours to sit and be comfortable, I was enjoying the surroundings that prevail. There were at least two bus drivers that would alternate at different intervals, and a lot of tollbooths on this well-maintained highway.

About noon, I started noticing people on the side of the road, all dressed in white aprons. They waved what looked like little pompoms to flag people and my first observation was that they were boxed-lunch people to serve travelers. The driver stopped and my basket had two pastries, a hundred pesos each. The one pastry consisted of a caramel filling, dulce de leche, which was very popular, and a cinnamon bun.

We did not stop other than for tollbooths and to change drivers. The scenery was endless and I wouldn't say monoto-

nous, but consistent. Some areas showed a little more vegetation than others and the valley areas were agricultural. The
area was fertile, but on the mountain ranges it was quite barren, like Nevada. Right on time, about three- thirty, we rolled
into La Serena.

It was founded in 1544, with a history of silver and copper
mining. But as the forties rolled around, the economy
changed drastically and a local boy made president. His
name was President Gabriel González Videla. He turned La
Serena into one of the premier beach areas, and I noticed a lot
of camping along the beaches. Some of the beaches had derelict ships that washed ashore under great storms that prevailed on this coastline. I had been told that some of the
ocean currents on the beaches were very strong and should
be addressed with caution.

The city itself had a colonial façade and they had restored
some of the buildings of the periods of the fifteenth and six-
teenth centuries into functional first class accommodations
for trade and commerce. Once off the bus, I made arrangements for my next leg of the journey tomorrow, to Calama. It
was about a thousand kilometers away, and would leave
around four o'clock tomorrow afternoon. I asked a cab driver
if he knew of a cheap hotel and he said "si". So, I checked
into Hotel Casablanca. I had a little chuckle because only two
years ago, I was in the city of Casablanca in Morocco. No,
this did not have much similarity to Morocco. However, the
room was adequate and the accommodations would suffice. It
was now getting to be very obvious to me that my Spanish
was very limited and I was right back to being the way I traveled in so many other circumstances, totally on my own and
isolated from communication with the majority of the people.
I was glad that my experiences of the past benefited me in the
present. I decided that the next step on the agenda would be
to get some Chilean money. La Serena is a major center compared to some of the other ones that I would be going to further north, and before I crossed over into Argentina, I would
like to, if possible, get some Argentine currency. I was start-

ing to realize that I was going through a lot of Chilean pesos and my ability to do the conversion to Canadian, had now seemed to become null and void. Chile was not a cheap place to visit.

My first priority was the Internet. After probably the better part of two kilometers, I saw the Internet and it was a nice building, done up in a sort of a Polynesian type atmosphere with only eight or ten computers. To my amazement, the gentleman spoke some English and they had a special for an hour and fifteen minutes, nine hundred pesos. I got an e-mail from Marietta with a complete update.

I wanted to check out the super grocery store that I had been told was nearby, and true to their word, it was. As I looked around, to my disappointment, the layout and size was very similar to the Great Canadian Superstore, a large discount food store in British Columbia. Even the yellow signs and banners were the same. It did not bring back homesickness, because this is not one of my favorite stores to shop in. However, they gave me an idea about prices for the average consumer products. To my surprise, they were pretty much the same prices as what we would pay in Canada for equivalent products. Obviously the local items such as watermelons and other produce are available year round, rather than seasonally imported as in Canada.

I made my way back to the core of the city, which is laid out in a grid-type form, so it's not difficult to get around in. Many of the historical buildings have been turned into modern day facilities. There were certain franchises familiar to me, such as 'Radio Shack' and 'Bata Shoes', and a big box merchandiser of home supplies that looked similar to Home Depot. Obviously, a lot of American chains are trying to penetrate this lucrative market. I am not aware of what the average income in Chile is, but I have observed a comfortable standard of living. A computer shop had some displays in the window, quite sophisticated looking equipment, at approximately fifteen hundred Canadian dollars, which speaks well for it.

SOUTH AMERICA
EXPLORATION

I wasn't successful with trying to exchange to Argentine currency, since most of the banks were closed. After spending a few hours walking around this city and through some of the piazzas, I found a restaurant that accepted Visa. I ordered clam chowder and in all sincerity, it was the best clam chowder I've ever had, although quite different from the only two I am familiar with, Manhattan or Boston clam chowder. For those that are not conversant with the two, the Manhattan clam chowder has a red tomato sauce in it, and the Boston clam chowder has a white creamy base. I enjoy them equally, but this was quite unique. Yes, it had clams in it, but it also had shrimp and other types of shellfish in a light broth. The soup was similar to a bouillabaisse, but steaming hot with diced green onion tops on top. The main dish was eel, the catch of the day, which is something I have not eaten before. Pickled eel is popular in the cockney areas of London, and that is the only previous encounter I have had with eel. However, it was very good, and served with French fries.

Feeling well nourished, I returned to the piazza, which was filled with little kiosks of every type of souvenir that could be obtained. By eight o'clock, I was beginning to feel tired, so returned to the hotel, thinking I would have a short rest. But once I finally fell into bed, I was just too tired to get back up again. Of course, I woke up periodically through the night, a customary habit of mine. I did sleep well into the next morning, but I don't have to worry about it, for my day starts when I want it to.

With this in mind and an early evening, I wish to say goodnight to one and all. And goodnight, my little treasure bee, Marietta.

Robert F. Edwards

I slept until eight o'clock in the morning, and shaved in cold water. I was apprehensive about having a shower, but I did see two nozzles. This room is adequate for my needs, but I wouldn't recommend it other than fitting my price range. I turned on the water, and the pressure started off well, only to trickle away. I had to use my own soap, and toilet paper, grateful for the homemade supply I brought with me. And there's no towel, so I'm glad I brought a towel. So, with the trickle of cold water still persisting, I abandoned the idea of having a shower this morning.

After getting dressed, I spent some time catching up on my notes so that I wouldn't forget too much of this adventure that was still in the cradle of infancy. With that completed, I then started my quest around ten or eleven o'clock to have break-fast. I found a nice coffee shop and had a cappuccino, and a toasted ham and cheese sandwich, adequate but not overly exciting.

Now, the day's ahead of me and I started to explore some of the churches, and of course, my continual quest of banks. After going to three or four different ones, I realized that my Spanish must improve on this trip, or it's going to be very lim-ited in conversation. However, everyone was polite and help-ful, but no Argentine currency available, so I probably will have to wait until I cross over the border, which is no major handicap at this point in time.

I spent quite a few hours wandering in the park, watching men perform puppet shows, and taking it all in. There was a lot of street vendoring going on, and a bit of begging also. It was here, for the first time that I came in contact with a group of rough-looking men, and decided they would be better to

SOUTH AMERICA
EXPLORATION

avoid, which I did. I strolled past many public buildings (the department of justice, the department of education) and beautiful parks in this area. Also, you can go to a different beach everyday if you so wish, but this wasn't part of my itinerary. Some of the back streets reminded me of other Latin countries, such as Cuba and Mexico. The sidewalks were clean and very narrow, almost elevated platforms. The buildings are usually closed, and even the houses have large wooden doors so there is very little that you can see from the streets.

One of the interesting things that I witnessed was the delivery of propane, which is the main fuel for cooking. To make life competitive, I saw two trucks from different companies, but each had the same system. On top of the truck was a large propane cap with a chain attached. As they drove through the streets banging this, it made a bell-like sound indicating to the people that if they need propane, the deliveryman is at hand. It reminded me of my childhood with the bread man and milkman. And even, once upon a time, we had an iceman who did the same thing (just to show my age). These men, when I was at the ripe old age of four or five, actually delivered with horses.

I enjoyed my stroll, listening to the many musicians. One young man, well dressed, was playing a bass fiddle in an archway for donations. In the bazaar, a group of young men were playing modern music, but were using some very unique instruments. The construction of these used different types of animal horns and a large piece of bamboo for blowing through. I saw three or four circular-type horns, perhaps trying to mimic the French horn in style. Their music did not really appeal to me. However, in another part of town near the cathedral, two men were playing harps, electrical harps, believe it or not, using a small Honda generator. They were dressed up in gaucho outfits with black striped pants, white boleros and the flat sombreros. Theses entrepreneurs looked good and were selling tapes and CDs, but unfortunately they had run out of their own music, otherwise I would have bought one.

35

Robert F. Edwards

I returned to the bazaar and ordered one of the empanadas that I had enjoyed so much on Easter Island. Well, Lucille's relatives have the corner on this market, as theirs was so scrumptious. This one was what you'd call ... fast food. The same identical ingredients, just different quality. You can't get a hamburger at McDonald's and call it good. In this fast food restaurant, you can't get an empanada and call it great.

I returned to get my luggage, then patiently waited for the bus to arrive. I would now start my fifteen-hour journey to La Serena, which will take me right through the night; and by eight o'clock tomorrow morning, I will be in another part of South America. Well, like everything else, there is 'on time' and there is 'on time.' One of the things about traveling is the learning curve, no matter where you are. I manage to get to the right terminal, no problem there. I've now become accustomed to ask questions from at least two or three other people, and if they all confirm the same answer, I'm pretty sure that I've got the right information. This happens to be an Old Russian trick I developed when traveling in that part of the world.

Tour buses come and go, but mine still hadn't shown up. It's vital to get the number of the bus right, since they post the furthest distance rather than La Serena where I will be getting off. My bus finally does arrive, close to three-quarters of an hour late. Regardless, I was happy to get on, and get the right seat, but oh, what a difference! The one coming in from La Serena was like a Rolls Royce compared to this Volkswagen, and they have crammed in an extra row of seats down the middle, as there was a larger passenger list. I told myself, 'I'm not buying the bus, I'm just getting a seat on it.' Once on the road, it performed fine.

This form of bus travel was new to me, and I was learning that their buses only stop momentarily to regurgitate passengers off and accommodate new guests on, then proceed ever forward and onward to their destination. No stopovers or half hour breaks to accumulate food. There were first-class service buses that provide meals, but this wasn't one of them. In my description, this one said, "You hit the seat, be grateful it's yours."

The scenery hadn't changed much. The bus was working its way consistently along the coast; sometimes very rugged with jagged edges protruding out into the sea, other times there were small comforting beaches dotted with numerous camp-sites. I hadn't seen any motor homes or trailers that you normally see in North America. Here, tents and the form of camping that seems to be popular, and cabanas available for rent in different areas. The terrain was quite rugged, and the Andes were very prominent, with cactuses too numerous to mention.

As the hours moved forward, we passed small outposts. Most of the houses were wood construction and wouldn't be more than three hundred square feet, probably closer to a hundred, in many cases. By either farming or ranching, or whatever they could muster a living by, these people must be fairly poor judging by their living accommodations. They must be very communal, as the homes are closely congregated together. Like so many other countries in a warm climate, most of the hours are spent outside, even for cooking.

By nine-thirty, or quarter to ten, it was dusk and the bus kept on rolling. It was now a case of enduring the night in an upright position and as one hour gradually ticks its way through the minutes, I sat enthralled, looking at the full moon outside. If I wasn't on the bus, I would have enjoyed a bit of stargazing, and moon watching, for sure. The bewitching hour arrives at midnight and the new day has started.

There's no point in saying goodnight, because I'm still up.

Robert F. Edwards

So, I entered the new day still on the bus, and as we kept rolling through one city after another, I ended up in the Antofagasta Region. The city has a population of a quarter of a million, and Antofagasta is a very modern city. This area exports most of the Atacama's minerals, especially copper, now giving the highest tonnage in the South American area. At one time, it was nitrates.

When the sun came up around six o'clock, we had the coast-

line and had traveled further inland. The terrain was barren, very desert-like, with no vegetation, only the odd little tree as a real bonus. Like so many deserts that I've been in, once you have water, you have growth. But this terrain was similar to the outback of Australia, with dry riverbeds and erosion on the hills evident. When it rains, it must do so profusely, and with the clay soil, it probably doesn't take up much moisture and just runs off.

At nine-thirty, we managed to roll in to Calama. It's not a very large city, with a population of only a hundred and twenty thousand. I recalled what those young men on the Easter Islands were telling me when they said, "You really have to get outside of Santiago to get the full impact of Chil-

38

ean life." I would think the population here was the perfect size. Lots of stores, lots of activities, but it's a walking city. It was very easy to get around it, and tiles, I had never seen so many tiles. Actually, they were like a marble tile on the sidewalks and piazzas, and very slippery.

I got a cab to the Hotel Latina, which I could have walked to, but not knowing the distant, erred on the side of caution. Once established there, I returned to the bus depot to make arrangements to continue my journey on to Salta, Argentina. My concern was that buses don't run everyday across to this border, the next bus is Saturday and then there won't be another one until Wednesday. To my dismay, the bus line that I had just taken, the Tora Bus, is full for Saturday, which leaves me just two alternatives: One, to enjoy this area until Wednesday; or to try the other international bus line. I found it, but they were closed until ten o'clock.

My next conquest was to find an Internet source for e-mail. To my delight, I'm told that it is in a bank and when I get there, I see the Internet that brings such fulfillment to my life. As I hadn't eaten for the better part of eighteen hours, I contained my impatience and found something to eat. When I returned to the bank, it was to find out that they were promoting the Internet, but there was no place in this town that had the Internet yet. So, there will be no communication with my little true love. I was so excited, but it was not meant to be.

Now, my priority was accommodations at the hotel for an extra night, which was no problem. Then, on to the next bus terminal, which is on the opposite side of town. At first, 'no, they're full'; but 'yes, they do have one and it's on Sunday'. The big guy upstairs, as usual, is looking after all my requests, and all I have to do is put the order in and be patient, things will get done.

Knowing that I won't be leaving until around ten o'clock Sunday morning, I made arrangements to have some laundry done, which was long overdue. Between perspiration from the heat, and the winds blowing sand and dirt, my clothes were filthy.

Robert F. Edwards

I had heard about a place not far from here called the moon surface in a volcanic area, so my next quest is to try and see some of these regional spots. A taxi driver offered me a full day of enjoyment, for about two hundred and eighty dollars Canadian, and I politely told him if he could find more people to participate, I'd be happy to be one of them. After reading "The Lonely Planet" book, I now understood what the helpful ladies at the bus depot were trying to tell me. To see El Tatio pleasures and what I wanted to see, Valle de la Luna, (the Valley of the Moon) it was better to get a tourist bus from San Pedro than to try and organize a tour from Calama.

So, back to the bus depot. The good ladies said, "Yes, no problem," and gave me a list of the times for Saturday or mañana. I notice my Spanish is improving, and the people are very patient and helpful. After discussing various options, they said it would be better if I could have gone to San Pedro, stayed there overnight, and then taken the bus on Sunday to Salta, Argentina. I thought that was an excellent idea. Unfortunately, I didn't know how to get my clothes back in time. This meant - return to the hotel, I have spent a lot of time just running around today. Still, it has given me an opportunity to see this delightful place.

I noticed a lot of construction going on; streets were getting done, even garbage cans were being painted. Was there some kind of inspection happening? I found it very hot during the midday, and many people take a couple of hours off in the afternoon for a siesta. I was now hungry, and because I never seem to learn my lesson, I went to a fast food restaurant and had a chicken bun, French fries and a pop. The franchise business never lets you know what you're eating, no matter what country you're in, it might have been chicken when it started, but it sure didn't taste like that.

Later, in the evening, I had a bowl of soup that had a nice big potato in it, a piece of meat, rice, and a chunk of corn. They use a lot of corn here, which my wife would have enjoyed. I had also purchased some bread from a little pastry shop. Thanks to a lady in a small grocery store, when I told her what I wanted, instead of just saying, "Well, we don't have it," and that's the end of it, she took me to the road and tried to explain where to go. Then "un momento" and got someone to look after her shop and took me over there. I felt I was starting to get back into the swing of traveling without a language. After purchasing my bread, I returned to her store and got some yogurt, little juices, and cheese. This peasant was perfectly happy, sitting in front of a church, enjoying a wonderful evening with some music in the background.

There are women eating ice cream cones, children playing in the fountain, and dogs roaming free. I thought of my terrier at home, 'Yes, Buttons, there is a place in this world that you don't have to be on a leash, and could enjoying some freedom.' It's a beautiful evening and the sunset is giving the majestic skies pink clouds with a nice shade of blue for a background. Wish you were here, Marietta, to observe, so that in your next art class you could enjoy saying that this is reality. My thoughts were with her throughout the day, thinking that she wouldn't have survived this one, neither the bus trip, nor the heat. She's much better off with pictures, and I've taken quite a few pictures today. I'm going to return to my hotel room as it's starting to get dark, and call it a day, and wait for the adventures of tomorrow.

Goodnight, one and all. Goodnight, my little treasure bee, I love you dearly.

Robert F. Edwards

I'm very, very happy this morning. I had a good night's rest and I have to admit that I cheated a little bit. I watched CNN in Spanish. I haven't given up totally my quest for knowledge of the outside world. However, I feel rested and at peace with myself in this short time, in a more congenial atmosphere and concentrating on just doing the things that I want to get done.

The most important contribution to this state of mind is people helping me. I never realized how important it was when you depend on others for help. It has a very humbling effect and a rewarding one at the same time. These kind strangers continually reassured me of my faith in the homo-sapien. Anyway, without being too philosophical so early in the morning, all things are in place.

I got my laundry back, not only washed but also pressed. They came back in beautiful condition compared to what I had sent out; I was almost ashamed to own them. Anyway, it was three thousand eight hundred pesos. I had reverted back to writing on a piece of paper. It seemed to help bridge the gap between languages, and my pronunciation. Once they understood what I was trying to get across, they responded instantly.

The morning was pleasant, with soft breezes and a clear sky. I had the pleasure of enjoying this for two or three hours before I started my trip to San Pedro. I had a good breakfast of yogurt, buns and juice, all the compliments of Bob Edwards' shopping last night. Dogs wandered over to where I was sitting in the shade, wanting to be petted. I'm in, the animals like me.

SOUTH AMERICA
EXPLORATION

The main source of income in Calama is mining. In the piazza there was a statue representing this, a miner with a drill. People here are proud of their heritage and I think above all, they enjoy their lives. I wandered over to a church, and joined the other men that had come to pray, some to the Virgin Mary, others just praying. Of course, there are women as well. It was nice to see that first of all, the churches were open during the daytime; and second of all, people drop in to communicate with God.

Stores don't really open until ten o'clock or maybe ten-thirty, even if the signs say otherwise. But then, most of the shops stay open until ten o'clock at night. So, it's long hours and though their time schedules are different, their workload isn't. I checked with another young lady that spoke some English, and phoned somebody for me. Yes, my information yesterday was correct. There was no Internet in Calama.

I spent some time watching a man outside the church, with a bag of breadcrumbs feeding the pigeons. When I was a boy, I remember people keeping pigeons; it seemed to be in vogue. My mother used to say how dirty they were and yes, I've experienced the odd dropping walking through the streets of Vancouver as they fly from one window sill to another, cooing. It's quite nice to see a large flock of them, I forgot how accommodating these feathered friends of ours are, and how much I miss them in my city.

I've been figuring out the exchange rate between pesos and Canadian dollars, and value for value, I think these people make an annual income similar to a Canadian, in pesos. The

43

humor is that every Chilean working is at least a millionaire in pesos every year, compared to Canadians in our low thirty thousand dollar incomes.

I got to the bus station in lots of time, and was glad to see Anna Marie, the young lady that assisted me. By 12:30 or shortly thereafter, the bus arrived and I was glad she was there. I was getting used to the bus services, but this one didn't have the markings of the company on it and was a pretty old bus. However, it was for only an hour-and-a-half and I had ridden on considerably worse, so even this derelict didn't seem too bad. As soon as the bus was full, we were on our way to San Pedro de Atacama. This is an oasis village near a large saline lake. It's about one hundred and twenty kilometers southeast of Calama. This desert area is between two ranges of the Andes. It was hot, with drying sierra winds, and vegetation was almost non-existent. I witness the Andes for the first time, and the snowcaps with their majestic appearance reminded me of my familiar Rocky Mountains. On the lower level, rather than the rolling foothills of the Rockies, these are mounds of hard resin and the flatlands here are vast, equivalent to gravel pits. Maybe in some prehistoric time, these were large rivers, but that would be for the archaeologists to decide.

We must be coming very close to San Pedro. I now see in the valley below some green vegetation, always the first signs of an oasis, no matter where you are in the world. We pulled into the bus terminal, a very remote, sleepy little station. By now, it was well into midday; and even the taxi drivers (which numbered all of two) were lethargic about trying to get business coming off the bus. I asked a man where the main street was, and I showed him the list of hotels that Anna Marie provided me with. He pointed to an opening, a small portal surrounded by small kiosks. I walked through this collage of ponchos, wooden carvings and silver jewelry, carrying all my belongings for the months ahead and staggered around the crowds of people.

SOUTH AMERICA
EXPLORATION

I made it through this portal and into the opening of the piazza, there was no fountain here, not in this desert; water being too precious; but there were trees and shade.

To my right was the only church in town, a Catholic church. The entire city was made out of adobe. Some of the buildings were whitewashed, but it's definitely adobe; and even some of the roofs were of adobe rather than tile. The rest were flat, as they have no need to worry about rain or run-off here.

This village was an enchanting fantasy of illusions. I was sure that Clint Eastwood would have made more "Good, Bad, and the Ugly" movies if they'd known of this location. I had read that it was popular with young Chilean people to come up here for backpacking through the surrounding areas, including the Valley of the Moon, which I was determined to see. The appearance of the past in this ghost town of three hundred years ago is an illusion, as the present was here and vibrantly well. I easily found two Internet locations and their prices were better than the Easter Islands and Santiago. The three hotels that Anna Marie had recommended for me were full so I was forced to take a more expensive one. In fact, it was more expensive than what I had paid up until this time;

close to eighty dollars Canadian, but I was lucky to get it. People were still occupying it even though they were long overdue to have left. The town was packed, and I was probably, if not the oldest person here visiting, I was in the minority. The average age span was between late teens and mid-twenties, a tourist mecca of youth.

The main streets all had the appearance of the past, and the scarcity of wood. The doors were solid and some of the windows were made out of wine bottles, (fully intact) to provide light for the inner rooms. The thickness of the walls was more than commendable, being six to eight inches wide.

I went into a restaurant and ordered a diet Coke and broccoli soup or sopa as the Spanish call it. Even the seats were made out of adobe material. I had an instant recollection of a place in Tunis, where they filmed "Star Wars". Due to the heat, all the buildings were underground, and the hotels, bars and dwellings were actually semi-submerged into the ground.

These adobe dwellings are prevalent throughout South America and Mexico as well. The material is plentiful and in an arid country they provide longevity. The exteriors of these buildings are modest and misleading to the interiors, which

SOUTH AMERICA
EXPLORATION

were first class. I was amazed at how small these shops were; I would think less than three hundred square feet. They were very cool though, and comfortable in the midday sun. I was waiting to join a group to visit the attraction that drew me here, the Valle de La Luna, (Valley of the Moon.) I wish I had known the extent of what this place had to offer as I would have targeted it for three or four days, at least. I haven't been to the moon yet, but it's the next best thing. There was a place in the Outback of Australia called Coober Pedy with similar erosions from a period before Man.

The Valle de la Luna is fifteen kilometers west of San Pedro, an immense volcano area, now extinct. There were many interesting spots in and around San Pedro. Just a few other facts are, it's approximately twenty-four hundred to twenty-five hundred meters above sea level and most of the homes are adobe built. In romantic days gone by, it was a cattle drive station and that era came to an end when the nitrate mines of Antofagasta Railway ended this period. About three kilometers away, (a good walk) is Pukarā de Quitor & Catarpe. This was a twelfth century fortress on the Rio San Pedro River. El Tatio Geysers are twenty-five kilometers north of San Pedro. It is also the world's highest geyser field. I was not sure if I would be able to get there, but would like to compare notes on 'Old Faithful' in Yellowstone National Park versus this one, but destiny plots its own course and I will be grateful for what is given to me. A spot more feasible for me will be the volcanic hot springs, Termas de Puritama, which were only about thirty kilometers north of San Pedro.

The van tour started to organize for my trip to the Valley of the Moon. The driver/guide was wearing a Superman shirt. There is another couple, and then two women with a seven-month-old baby, and I made a comment, "We have Superman and Moon Baby," and everybody thought that was pretty funny. The first stop in the valley is impressive. As I gathered, it's a place of modern formations compared to the rest of the volcanic range prevalent in this area. There must have been some large floods and you could see the erosion by both

Robert F. Edwards

wind and water, which shaped unique clay formations. Some of them seem to be standing alone, independent of anything around them, and somewhat peculiar.

As we traveled further into this area, we started to enter some very narrow passages. Then, the canyons eventually opened up into a large plateau, and then into plains. On one side, was a vast sand bank, maybe 300 meters, and on the opposite side was a huge level plain. Far off in the distance I could see mountain peaks with snow on them. I had learned that there were only two volcanoes in this region.

Our mini van proceeded to another location, and this is where we walked quite a distance down into a narrow passage and had to go through caves. Some of them were so narrow that with my equipment on, it was rather difficult to get through. The guide told us there were two different types of salt mined in this area and I've taken a picture of the remains of the adobe buildings that the miners used.

It was about seven-thirty before we proceeded on to the main event, the moon basin and the sunset on it. By this time, I had become familiar with some of my group, a couple of Chilean university students. I had also met a school-

SOUTH AMERICA
EXPLORATION

teacher from England. Once we reached the last formation, we had to climb up a large sandbank.

I was reluctant to call it a sand dune, since I was conversant with the sea sands of the Great Sahara, and had climbed those dunes. It was probably not in excessive of 150 meters, but still exhilarating to walk along the ridge looking at the sunset. On the ridge there were very high gusty winds, and this seems to be one thing that's prevalent throughout the time I've spent in Chile. The continual winds gust, and then subside into gentle breezes and then gust back up again. There was another path I found, and I asked the school teacher if she'd like to come, and she said "why not, we're here", so without further ado, we broke away from the main group to start walking along this narrow corridor of rock. We had probably gone the better part of a kilometer before it became very narrow going in and quite precarious. I thought of my dear wife Marietta, and knew that I would never have gotten her to walk through this corridor, even at gunpoint. She would have been frozen stiff with fear. Out of a hundred people or so that are poised gingerly on the sand bank waiting for the sunset, there were less than twelve of us that made it to that point. It was perfect timing, the sun was just starting to make its final descent. The schoolteacher had her camera stolen in Bolivia, so I volunteered to take a couple of pictures for her. The scenery was breathtaking; the valleys and the odd anomalies of stone and terrain in this corridor, and the view beyond made this alone well worth the trip. I hoped I could

capture this sunset on film. There were such vivid colors; oranges, reds, greens and purples, colors that you wouldn't
think would be compatible with each other, let alone Mother
Nature producing them.

It was eight thirty before we got back to the van and headed
into town. I was at my hotel by nine-thirty and my room was
finally ready. It was adequate, but definitely overpriced. My
priority now was to get to the e-mail place before they closed
and lo and behold, I received the fifth one from Marietta. I
spent the better part of the hour catching up on my e-mail
correspondence. In a happy frame of mind, I pondered with
the idea of either having something to drink or going directly
to bed. I met up with two women staying in the same hotel,
they're both from Switzerland, but one is Swiss and the other
one is Chilean. We ended up going to a restaurant and having
a drink and just discussing the events that brought us here.
The Swiss woman and I exchanged email addresses and some
conversation before I returned to my room.

This is where things become rather unpleasant, to say the
least. I got into bed; only to find out that all the facilities that
were promised had been retracted. It was about eleven
o'clock; there was no air conditioning, the television didn't
work, there was no window, and the room was very hot. To
add to my further discomfort, the restaurant next door kept
playing loud music which continued well into the wee hours of
the morning.

*To conclude this evening, goodnight one and all, I love you lit-
tle honey bun and I miss you very much.*

SOUTH AMERICA EXPLORATION

February 11th, Sunday
Calama, Chile

I had a very poor sleep last night, only to find out when I got up during the night to go the washroom, that there was no power in the room. People were partying right up until three o'clock in the morning, along with the noise and the lack of air circulation in this room; I just cannot believe the horrendous price I paid for so little.

I started to prepare myself for the day, in the dark I might add, only to find out that there was no water as well. This was the straw that broke the camel's back; I was definitely going to ask for some kind of remuneration. I got my belongings together and went downstairs. The young lady at the front desk, after I had explained the situation, gave me a token of four thousand pesos, which was the best offer that she could do, and that she had taken upon herself. Feeling that four thousand pesos were better than nothing, I decided to do a reconnaissance on where to meet the bus.

One thing about traveling by myself and not being able to speak the common denominator of languages, I always like to give myself a generous amount of time, to find the right spot. Once feeling confident that I had at least got the location, I bought some supplies (water, juice, and a few buns) for the road. Returning to the lobby of the hotel, the desk clerk was in deep discussion with some French ladies that I met last night. After half an hour, nothing seemed to be resolved, as they thought they had reservations at this hotel, but didn't, and she had spent two hours last night phoning around, only to learn every hotel facility was full. She eventually phoned a woman that she had stayed with the very first time she had visited here, and was lucky to get rooms to put these four ladies up in. I suppose hindsight sometimes has the best directions, but I do believe, even with all the problems that I've had, I made the right choice by not sleeping under the stars.

There was still no power in the accommodations, or as far as that goes, in the town itself. Then, the reneging on the four thousand pesos because I paid by Visa, she can't give me the money, and they can't give me a credit, so we go round and round in circles. It was all part and parcel of traveling. With that I thought maybe I'd try and send Marietta another email, only to realize that there's no power, there's no computer, there's no email.

I worked my way back up to where I thought I was supposed to meet the bus and thank goodness that there was a couple of women from Paraguay that had been traveling on the same bus the previous day and were heading on their route back. I wasn't in the right spot; it was much further down. Still, I got there in plenty of time and was sitting waiting; of course, the bus was late, but eventually arrived. With a leap of enthusiasm, I charged merrily ahead, only to be told that I wasn't on the master form of that bus. The bus driver was polite and went through the agenda three or four times, but no, I wasn't on his schedule. With my heart leaping in my mouth, thinking what few alternatives I had left, he tried to explain to me that I was on Bus Three. I was about to think of alternative modes, when lo and behold, two more buses from the same company showed up. This is part of my enigma, when I am not able to communicate. Yes, I was on the third bus and to set my mind further at ease, my new friend Anna Marie was on the bus and helped me clear customs and immigration.

On the bus, I was sitting beside John, a gentleman from England. He was really into plants and had his own green house, gave lectures and no, it was not his profession, just a consuming hobby. He only travels in the winter because he wants to spend all his time in the summer nurturing his plants at home. It was nice to be able to talk to somebody fluently, rather than in a jagged conversation.

SOUTH AMERICA
EXPLORATION

We had been traveling for three hours before we arrived at the Argentine border, to clear immigration and customs. The landscape hadn't changed much, nor had the wind, but I had seen some guanacos, (like small llamas) they were very cute and running wild on the huge plains. The vastness and the aridness of this part of the country was impressive.

After the better part of an hour, I learned that this was only the first phase, Immigration, and then somewhere beyond was the Customs. The wind was blowing hard, and there was a convoy of three buses. We were bringing up the tailgate, so we had to wait what seemed endlessly to clear Immigration. Finally, it was our turn, and I will always remember that Immigration Officer as probably one of the more congenial, and amiable officials that I had passed through. The distance between the Chilean and Argentine stations was approximately forty to fifty kilometers, one of the largest unmanned borders that I've ever been on. Over the years my experience has been that Customs is either next door or beside. In this particular case we had gone for a couple of hours and I was at the point of questioning whether John had got the interpretation right. We rolled into what I thought was a village but no, it was Customs.

Robert F. Edwards

The place was busy with 'entrepreneurs' on either side of the narrow dirt road, but we had to stay on the bus until it was our turn. I was dreading this; I felt that they would probably dismantle my entire luggage, as everything had to come off the bus. After seeing some of the dogs sniffing out underwear, I worried that I was going to be forever and a day trying to put my belongings back in this compact luggage, in the dark.

But standing in queue, and watching the progress that was being made, the speed was amazing compared to the delay at Immigration. Once I got inside the building, it was obviously due to the fact that there were six people examining luggage, where there was only one poor amigo at Immigration. I was flagged over to a Customs Officer, casually dressed, wearing a baseball cap, a t-shirt, and of course the surgical gloves. They were all wearing them, I guess the word was out that people carry more than just illicit drugs, and by not declaring certain things, disease was probably transported from one country to another.

When my turn came, and I was ready to open up all of my belongings, this man said "passport", I showed him my passport, he asked "Canadian?" and I said "si", and that was it, move on. I don't know whether it was just the luck of the draw that foreigners got the royal treatment here, but John got the same preferential treatment that I did.

It was eleven o'clock at night before the bus rolled on and we were now deprived of the scenery, but John was a good conversationalist, and we hit it off. By two o'clock, we start to approach Salta, but the driver takes the wrong road. It was a gravel trail that turned into an asphalt highway, and then divided into a four-lane highway with a boulevard. Unbelievable, but we were on the wrong side of the highway, and a big transport truck flashed his signals to alert our driver, as he passed. As soon as possible, we crossed over the boulevard to get on the right side. These drivers were usually very good, it was just things really do look different in the dark, and even bus drivers can mistake the situation. To make matters worse, he took the wrong turn and got lost. Finally we found the right approach to Salta and it appeared like a phoenix rising out of nowhere on this highway.

My very first impression of Salta was that it was much larger than I had ever anticipated, with a population of five hundred thousand. John and I had already agreed to use the same hotel, and I'd looked up a few in my "Lonely Planet" with blurry eyes, since it was three o'clock in the morning. This was a time of day that I disliked the most for arriving anywhere, but to my surprise, not only were there taxi drivers, but some shops were open also. A big advantage I was having with my newfound relationship is that John is sociable, and bilingual with Spanish. We discussed which hotel and the cab driver "comprendes" and off we go. From first appearances, I had seen worse, and stayed at better, but the price of ten to fifteen dollars a night was in the range that both of us felt comfortable with.

It was an older classic building with high ceilings, but quite deserted. I was attempting to find somebody, but John said "let's go, we'll move on, it's a place for prostitutes." John asked the cab driver if he knows of any "residencials" or "pensións", similar to our "bed and breakfasts" establishments. The cab driver did, it was quite a distance but to my delight, it was right in the downtown core of Salta. We would never have found it on our own, as it was above stores that were boarded up for the night. After climbing up the hidden stairwell to the top, we asked the senorita if they had rooms and yes, I got a room without a bathroom for fifteen dollars a night. The place was immaculate, and with no hesitation, we checked in gratefully as by now it was close to four o'clock.

And after a long invigorating day, it is finally goodnight one and all, goodnight my beautiful little love bug. I know you would not have wanted to endure this day so you made the right decision, good night sweetheart.

Robert F. Edwards

February 12th, Monday
Salta, Argentina

John and I got up around eight o'clock and although we had the fan on all night and the window opened, it was still very hot and humid, since it rained hard during the night. I hoped it would be a day of rest and just lounging around and getting a few priorities addressed. One of course was getting to the Internet, two was getting some Argentine currency, and three was finding out a bus to the next leg of my adventure. John planned to look around and get a concept of the city.

We had a small breakfast, coffee and a bun and I put my entire Gore-Tex outfit on, including the trousers, due to the rain. I looked like I was ready to climb the Andes rather than patrol the streets of Salta. By 10 o'clock, the heavy rain had stopped, and it was a mild rain, quite pleasant and warm. The first step on the agenda was finding a bank, and I was pleasantly surprised to be able to get money out of the bank machine, so I drew out a couple hundred dollars in U.S funds, and the same in Argentine pesos.

With that challenge out of the way, we did a little bit of sight seeing around the city. It was impressive, well laid out, and a collage of both old historical buildings and new ones, all in excellent condition. The churches take precedence and I took a couple of pictures of the more impressive ones. We had chosen to do a city tour by walking. Both of us were in relatively good shape, and enjoyed walking rather than using a taxi. I was grateful to learn that John was a good map-reader and we found our way to the 16th century Convento de San Bernardo, for the Carmelite nuns, a nursing order. This being a hospital and a teaching institution as well, they were attracting young girls to the vocation and the religious order. At

one time, at its peak, it had over four thousand nuns and pa-
tients.

The beautiful carved algarroba wooden door is much admired here, so I took a picture
of that as well.

Salta is in a remote area of
Argentina, with vast distances
separating it from most of the
country. To find this
cosmopolitan oasis was just a
delight unto itself. On the way
to the bus depot, John and I
passed by a gondola, the Cerro
San Bernardo, said to provide
some wonderful views of Salta,
and we promised ourselves
that on our way back we
would go on it if time
permitted.

We found the bus "terminale"
well laid out and easy to understand. I found a bus and could
buy the ticket direct to my next stop, which is Resistencia and
the monasteries. There were actually two Jesuit monasteries
on the Argentine side and there's one that probably has the
better frescos in Trinidad, on the Paraguay side. The bus
would leave around four o'clock and at about nine o'clock,
idealistically, the following morning. So again, an all night
trip on the bus.

This one was comparatively expensive, and for the short distance it was over sixty-five dollars US, but it looked quite
luxurious. I got a feeling that I would be able to sleep on the
bus, or at least I was hopeful. Now the last and third priority
was the Internet, and to my good fortune the proprietor of this
"residencial" hotel has Internet and he said "yes go ahead, you
can use mine" so that evening I was looking forward to receiving some emails from my little treasure bee and getting one off
to tell her that the happy traveler had now made another leg

Robert F. Edwards

through this vast continent. With all three major requirements behind me now it was free time.

I had chosen to spend an extra day in Salta, and John and I
talked about renting a car to go out into some of the more remote areas of this region. To hire a taxi for the entire day
would be about a hundred and twenty to a hundred and forty
US dollars a day. We rented a nice car for seventy-five US
dollars a day and could have it delivered to our hotel that evening.

We spotted a little kiosk, and thinking we would just go
over and have a soft drink, once we spotted the hamburgers,
that was it. I've got to describe this hamburger in absolute
detail. Number one the bun was humungous, about six
inches in diameter, and the meat patty was hanging over the
side. What made it even more special; there was a fried egg
among the lettuce, onions, tomatoes, mayonnaise, and two or
three other condiments. And for this remarkable hamburger,
the price was one dollar US. Absolutely astounding. Obviously, both John and I ordered one, and they were not only as
good as they looked, they were delicious.

Now we approached the gondola, or teleférico to go up Cerro
San Bernardo. It was not fair to compare countries and regions to others, but everything here was so much cleaner
compared to the neighbors of the north, Mexico. This was not
with disrespect to Mexico, but more with admiration of Argentina. At the top is a good view of Salta and the Lerma Valley
below. We walked back down this mountain; it was like walking into a cosmopolitan area of an oasis, with wilderness all
around. I took some pictures of a great cathedral in red stone
that could be seen from the top of the mountain, a pretty good
landmark.

We decided Tuesday would be a day to explore the small
hamlets and villages, anywhere from a hundred to three hundred kilometers one way from Salta. Then, the following day
John wanted to go in the opposite direction. This was questionable for me, since I had to leave at four o'clock to start my
long journey overnight to the next port of call.

SOUTH AMERICA
EXPLORATION

During our walk, we passed through a residential district. In my fondest dreams, I wished that I could live in a home that equaled the sheer elegance of just the exterior of these; let alone what must prevail inside. I had been told that for an Argentine person, their home was their castle and some of these warranted that description. They had beautifully ornate iron works over the windows, carved wooded doors, and stucco, all in pristine condition.

By about six o'clock, we had literally walked the day away. We found the turismo information center and they were very helpful and informative. John was very involved in cacti, and gave lectures on this subject at home in Britain, and obviously had more of a quest for plants of the regions than I did. We decided to pick up some food for the evening meal and eat it back at the hotel rather than engage in going out for dinner. I bought a pizza-quiche dish, some yogurt, buns, tomatoes, cucumber, a green pepper, and lots of Sprite, sugar, a bottle of water, and other commodities for a grand total of eleven dollars. In Canada, it would've been at least double if not triple this. These supermarkets were very well merchandised, and I thought some of the prices were astounding. Something that you wouldn't see in Canada was a whole corridor of white smocks and uniforms. I noticed many employers had a dress code, and these white smocks, uniforms and jackets seemed to be a prevalent feature. I could quickly identify who was a customer and who was an employee, it made communication a lot easier.

With food in hand, we did a bit more comparison shopping on rental cars; Hertz was more expensive, so we finalized our arrangements with the original lady. John wanted to do a bit of shopping, as he needed a bag for carrying some of his articles, since the zipper on his old one had broken. I was also on a quest, as that morning during breakfast I noticed some young people drinking from what looked like a small goblet. They were putting tealeaves or some type of herb with sugar and hot water in it, and then sucking through a sieve type metal straw. John demonstrated for me by drinking about

Robert F. Edwards

four or five cups of this drink. It was very refreshing, and supposed to be good for medicinal purposes and stabilizes nausea. While looking in a bazaar, I managed to pick up both; an intricately carved cup and silver straw for sipping this beverage, mate. This would be a nice memento of the area and unique to this part of the world. Of course I haggled with this poor, ill-prepared trader; he wanted eight dollars for the cup and another three for the straw. By the time I finished with him, I got both of them for the price of the cup.

With success behind me, we returned to our hotel to prepare the evening meal. We made a bit of conversation with the proprietor's staff, friendly and good spirited women, and then prepared the evening meal. The proprietor with the key for the Internet office wouldn't be there until about ten-thirty. Fatigue and exhaustion came in waves, reminding me that I'd be burning the candle at both ends, and the torch in the middle was dwindling. I decided to lie down and asked to be woken when the Internet was available. At twelve-thirty I heard a knock at the door and quickly responded and got dressed. To my great delight, I had two emails from Marietta, one from Wendy, and one from an old friend Frank Kerr, along with all the general information that pops into my hotmail. I spent the better part of an hour-and-a-half reading and writing a few e-mails to my family before returning to my little bed.

Goodnight, one and all. Goodnight, Marietta; I sure love you, sweetheart, and I sure enjoyed reading your e-mails. You seem to be holding up so much better at least in written form than my last adventure. I love you, sweetheart. And Wendy, thank you very much for such a wonderful job of taking control over our family and looking after us. I'm so proud of my little family and I love you all very dearly. Goodnight, Marietta.

SOUTH AMERICA EXPLORATION

February 13th, Tuesday
Salta, Argentina

At seven o'clock, John and I had prepared ourselves for the day, and our car was parked outside the front door waiting for us to start our adventure. We both had a quick breakfast, and our confidence levels were yet to be proven. We started the adventure by first finding a petrol station and then filling up with a mere half tank of gas for twenty-seven dollars US. It was one of the first times I had ever driven a French vehicle, a Renault 19, not a performance vehicle but quite roomy, since it's a full sized car and rode considerably well.

The roads in Salta were one-way streets throughout the city. John was the navigator and I was the driver because he didn't drive at all. By eight o'clock we were heading out of town with the instructions from our helpful night clerk. The roads at this point were asphalt, until we got off the main artery and started heading towards the Andes, when the roads quickly turned into dirt trails. The day started with an overcast sky and the roads were still showing puddles from the previous rainfall. Our first destination is Cerrillos, it was only fifteen kilometers from Salta, and looked very much like any South American working class city. There was nothing there that enticed us to stop, so we continued on to the next location. La Merced was twenty kilometers from our original destination, larger than the previous one but again, with no real significance to our choice of events. The next one was El Carril, and this was where we got off the main highway and entered the Quebrada De Escoipe, a ravine valley. We could literally feel the grade of altitude as we started to climb into the Andes.

The scenery changed drastically and John was delighted to find so many different types of cacti. Once we got into Cuesta Del Obispo, which was sixty-two kilometers away, we started

61

to notice that the plants and vegetation were becoming lusher. John wanted to take a picture of some cacti, near a small little house that you wouldn't even know existed. The owner's attention was drawn to us because of his dog barking, a farmer, since we see a little cornfield, lettuce, squashes, plums and figs. Once he realized that all we were doing was taking pictures, crazy "turistas", he waved and made a few friendly gestures, and that was about the beginning and the end of that conversation.

The road had long ago changed from a relatively good asphalt road to dirt, a generous one lane with little or no shoulders. In addition to the washboard and potholes, I had to be cautious of streams that flowed across our dirt passage. They were not deep, but driving up to them I had no idea of their depth, or what conditions awaited me on this twisting, winding road that gained altitude continuously. John had an altimeter and every so often took a reading. We had gone up another thousand feet as we were working our way towards the summit.

We stopped often as John spotted different cacti that he wanted to examine growing among the alpine plants. He was quite surprised about the species he was finding and I was quite impressed with the majestic changing landscape that we were seeing. The rock formations must have a tremendous amount of mineral wealth in them.

From a distance, we thought the rocks on the hills were green, probably some kind of moss or lichen. However, when we got to them, it had to be the mineral content giving them a green color. Then, right alongside them would be bright orange colors. The mountains themselves were worth the trip through that winding snake-like road.

As we progressed, the sparse landscape of the arid terrain changed to a lush alpine with every twist and turn as we gained altitude. We were almost at the top of the summit when a fog formation came rolling in, or we rolled into it. It was extremely dense as we continued to gain altitude towards the summit.

SOUTH AMERICA EXPLORATION

I curtailed our speed and either John was not aware of how bad the roads were, or he was trying not to show any concern over it. As we reached the summit, and then started our gradual descent down, the fog dissipated and we were once again looking at breathtaking scenery. The valleys and mountain ridges were indescribable, and of all the pictures that I should have taken, (but didn't) was a range of mountains that looked like somebody cut the top off them, and in the foreground were electrical lines, quite a contrast. It looked like nature and mankind tried to outdo each other. As a backdrop were more beautiful higher ranges. Some were cut off by mist on their peaks, and throughout this winding, endless trail we stopped to take photographs.

One of the disappointing factors was of the many birds we saw; I wasn't able to capture them on film. One bird in particular that we tried to take a picture of was about the size of a small hawk, with a curved beak like a parrot and the colorings were very vivid. Bright yellows and reds, unfortunately it flew away before I was ready.

We passed a small village, Piedra Del Molina, more a hamlet really, on our way to Parque Nacional Los Cardones. This is the national park, and being totally naïve to the area, I wasn't aware that this region was famous for its cacti. To my limited eyes there were the ones that have an 'hombre' appearance with the arms held up high. Also there were cacti that looked like gigantic posts driven into the ground. These were large cactuses, thirty, maybe forty feet high, and a lot of them. After just visiting the Easter Islands, they resembled miniature Moais scattered along the hillside.

Robert F. Edwards

Another cactus quite prevalent was sort of flat, more a fern shape. Some were in bloom and really stood out, the large blossoms in white, vivid reds, and some yellows. Also, some of the miniature cacti in blues and yellows were equally impressive. With all these flowers in abundance, the landscape was breathtaking. Blended in amongst the cacti and thorny shrubs were heavy grasses, like pampas or reeds draping over the mountain ridges.

The next stop that we went to was Payogasta, about a hundred and forty-seven kilometers from Salta. It was a small village, with a nice church, and we walked around to try and get a perspective. It didn't seem to matter what size the city or hamlet was, there was always a church, a piazza with a fountain or statue, and in this area, the statue that prevails is the man that liberated Salta, he's very popular. From here we continued on to Cachi, just another ten miles down the road. The changing land formations are interesting, with various colored mineral layers in these mountains.

John was excited about the contrasting vegetation growing here, and was very animated with his findings, while I was certainly enjoying the scenic views of this trip. The clouds had cast many different shadows on the mountain ranges, creating their own majestic-looking landscapes. When observed with the eye of an artist, you see how wonderfully Mother Nature provides contrast. I don't think photographs can ever relay to what a painter's skill could do on canvas. The weather was very temperate as we drove up to higher altitudes; it was still pleasant to be outside.

By now it was well past mid-day, and we both agreed that the next place we came to, we would stop and have something to eat. This particular place was Laguna De Brealito, about twenty-two kilometers further along. We actually drove through it before we realized that we had passed by our opportunity to have something to eat. However, we asked some people in a little general store, and were directed three blocks in to this brand new accommodation. It was a hall-like setting, with immaculate tile floors, white walls, and a reed roof.

SOUTH AMERICA
EXPLORATION

It was a predominantly native village, from the appearance of the women serving here.

I ordered a dish that consisted of chicken and noodles, with some cheese and bread. What made this particular meal so unique was the little lady serving us, I would think probably in her mid forties. She was doing everything perfectly, and took her time, as if she didn't want to do anything wrong, and it must have been quite out of step with her normal day-to-day activity. There were about four women working in the back and only six tables that were being occupied, with locals drinking wine. As our waitress kept bringing out dishes, she was meticulous to make sure that she placed everything properly on the table. John asked her how much their rooms cost, which was eight dollars a night.

I think this was an example of the government trying to help integrate their native people and provide employment. In Canada, we've done a deplorable job on integrating our First Nations people. In Africa, they have reverted back to the original inhabitants, reclaiming land where Europeans had tried to change their cultural bases. In Australia, the aboriginals are misunderstood and some people think mistreated. Here, the Argentine government has tried to introduce tourism into this small Indian village by building some excellent accommodations, and training the locals to meet the standards of travelers such as us that were sitting at this table.

However, I don't believe that these Native people will carry on this advancement and although this project is beautiful right now in its infancy, it will probably falter and finally fall by the wayside. This is not because neither one is right, just that the natives and the government aren't communicating. The tour companies may push it for a while, and if the tourists get this far, the roads will be the Achilles' heel of this project. I commend all of the people for the effort, and it was a very enjoyable midday stop. There was not much to the rest of the village, other than a church and a few small adobe homes.

Robert F. Edwards

After lunch, we headed towards our final destination, which was Molinos. However, the roads seemed to take a turn for the worst. By the time we got to Seclantás, which is about a hundred and eighty-seven kilometers from Salta, it was four o'clock in the afternoon. A good portion of our time, and the main purpose of John's contribution to the car rental, was to see plants. I know he would've spent a lot more time examining, taking measurements and descriptions if he'd been on his own. Two reasons he would never have gotten this far, by any stretch of the imagination, was that he doesn't drive, and secondly there was no conceivable way that a bus would've logged in as many hours on these precarious roads as I had been able to do. So, he might not have spent as much time as required on his research, but he was able to acquire a much greater spectrum on the variety of cacti.

We spent some time in the village of Seclantás taking pictures and talking to the local artisans. One gentleman was very pleased to show us the work that he and his children were doing, on a reed instrument similar to the Peruvian flutes. I learnt how they could adjust the scale much by changing the height of the reeds on these flutes. He was quite talented, and the sounds that he produced were more than just music to my ears, the angels were blowing their horns. The young people also learn how to make mandolins and small string instruments in this region.

He told us that at five o'clock, the artisan building would be opened, but both John and I were starting to feel a little uneasy. We were not even at the midway point that we had chosen, and it was already four-thirty. We had left at eight o'clock in the morning, so we felt that we should take immediate action to try and get back at a reasonable hour, and avoid getting lost in these remote areas. We asked for instructions on how to get back, and were told that one road was quite a bit shorter, but not as good as the one that we had come on. We made a joint decision that we'd use that first road for two reasons; one is that it was new scenic opportunities, and second it was shorter. We couldn't imagine that the roads could be worse than what we had experienced on our way out here.

We made the right decision, the scenery was entirely different on that side of the valley, and John was delighted to have found more types of cacti. I noticed up on the summit there were clouds forming and seemed to be rolling in faster than I was driving. I brought this to John's attention, and we both got back in the car and headed in that direction. With the variety and color in the rock formations, from deep oranges to light pastels against the green backdrop, this was too good to pass up. The cloud formations had rapidly swept down the mountains, and we were lucky to get the opportunity to photograph these unique formations and color structures. We started to head up the trail that led to the summit and hadn't gone any great distance before the fog joined us. From thin mist it had now grown thicker until it was almost of pea soup. My concerns were two-fold: One – that I knew the road was both treacherous and narrow, and two - there was more traffic than what I had anticipated or had seen on the previous day when we were on the bus. Don't get me wrong, this was not five o'clock traffic in New York by any stretch of the imagination, but neither were the roads. So keeping this in mind, I was not overly concerned about driving in those conditions, but more about what was heading towards me. Visibility was reduced to no more than a car length, and some of the curves were almost a hundred and eighty degree turn.

There were a few moments with opposing traffic, but the Argentine drivers were highly courteous, which added to the safety that both John and I were seeking at that moment. There was one incident (and that was all it really consisted of), when a large truck approached and took up most of the road, but we both slowed to a crawl and passed each other without incident. We successfully reached the summit which seemed to be many steps to heaven in Gabriel's cloud formation, and then started our descent. As we got closer to the valley, the fog and sleet dissipated, and the roads returned to their normal condition of pot holes and streams to ford.

We had taken a shorter route back, and although the locals didn't think the roads were as good, we didn't notice any difference. We returned to the main highway without incident, until we got to the outer perimeter of Salta. Here, we took a wrong turn, but with a bit of driving through a residential area and asking a few times how to get to the core of the city, we were soon back on track. The Argentine people were most helpful.

Their driving style was a bit different for me, with not much signaling and in this particular city, mostly one-way streets. They have a weaving, "go if you can" attitude. At intersections, it was more or less courtesy, rather than traffic lights and stop signs. When I wished to pass a couple of times in narrow passages, the trucks would signal when it was safe, and the cars gave as much room as possible to make the transition.

Once back in the city, we had the same problem finding our hotel, but within due course we got there without too much concern. Amazingly, we got the car back half an hour before it was supposed to be picked up. I personally think that we got more than our value out of the car that day. We put some hard miles on, and it sure looked dirty, but all in all, it performed well.

I asked one of the staff to phone on my behalf to get the car returned, and then jumped into my email. It was about nine-thirty by then, and John had gone out to get some food at a "groceria", while I was busy answering my E's. I sent one off to Marietta and Wendy, and read a bit of news, with nothing too pertinent. I was enjoying the use of this machine that was considerably cheaper than if I'd gone to one of the Internet cafes. I have a sincere gratitude to these people for coming to my aid and assistance. Even this lady, Nora, that didn't speak any English, but still managed to give John and myself detailed, accurate descriptions of how to get in and out of town.

They're very conscientious people, and I found business easy to do in Argentina. The efficiency is good, and the pressure is absent. The car rental fellow came back with my credit voucher, and I gave him the payment in cash, no problems there. The gas was rather expensive, close to two dollars Canadian a liter, in this area. We had put twenty-eight US dollars into the car, and only got half a tank, but that was all that was required for our purposes. That day, I had put in ex-

Robert F. Edwards

cess of four hundred kilometers on it, and in rugged conditions.

John returned with his groceries, and we shared some buns with tomato and meat, and a couple of cups of tea. I had been driving for over twelve hours, and even the bus drivers here got rotation breaks and I hadn't, so I say my goodnights to everyone.

Goodnight my little treasure bee, I miss you very much and I love you dearly, sweetheart.

SOUTH AMERICA
EXPLORATION

February 14th, Wednesday
Posadas, Argentina

Today, I had decided to go to Posadas. It had a population of about two hundred thousand, located on the south bank of the Rio Parana. It was basically en route to the two areas that I wanted to see. One was San Ignacio Miní, one of the Jesuit monasteries about fifty kilometers east. My journey was to commence at around four-forty-five p.m., which translated into anywhere from five o'clock onward. That was one thing that buses seemed to delight in doing here, they gave you a schedule to follow, but they could arrive at any time and they were always late, some more than others, and always at the platform that you least expected.

I got up not knowing whether John had left or not, he was quite determined to catch a bus and go in another direction in search of more cacti. As I had just finished my toiletries and started to pack, there was a knock on the door and John asked "Would you like a cup of tea?" He had brought me a bottle of Sprite and some mate.

John was quite a chatterbox, and I hadn't thought anybody could outdo me but he had mentioned the same thing. He said, "You're a pretty good talker and I thought I was a good one". With all that conversation, I had learnt that he was fifty two years of age, never been married, worked for the Forensic Department in London and had done work for Interpol as well as Scotland Yard. He was an interesting man, and a good traveler, and had spent a lot of time in Ecuador on this trip. We said our goodbyes, and he was on his way to see more plants, and I was hoping to see more of Salta before I left on the bus later that day.

By the time I packed and got myself back in traveling mode, with all my things put into their rightful little corners of my traveling bag, it was the better part of eleven o'clock. I de-

Robert F. Edwards

cided to see some of the churches that had been suggested to me, and by the time I got closer to that area it was one o'clock. The siesta time was practised religiously so far in every area that I had been to and even in large centers, the majority of businesses honor this long tradition.

With that in mind, I felt that I probably should have a decent meal before I headed out on a journey that was going to be about twenty-two to twenty-four hours. I found a nice restaurant, and ordered cream of celery soup, and what I thought was a form of enchilada, but ended up to be a mixed salad. The salad was different than our western restaurants make, with very little lettuce, it had beets, cold peas, tomatoes, cucumbers and onions and a little bit of cheese on it. The waiter was very patient with me, and helped me learn the word for bread, 'pan'. I feel blessed to have this gift of people helping me in my stumbling ways, and it never ceases to amaze my friends. Even John had commented that he just couldn't believe that somebody could travel throughout a country, without some kind of command of the language. This waiter was no exception; he accepted my bumbling ways and my sincere approach of hoping that I was doing and saying it right.

I was amazed at the cost of food, compared to other things, and this meal was about fifteen dollars for a bowl of soup, salad and two pops. Not exactly bargain prices. I bought some postcards, which were reasonable, at fifty cents each. It was close to two o'clock before I headed back to check on any last minute emails. I knew it was Valentine's Day and I sent my beautiful wife a valentine email and another to my daughter.

I spent an interesting hour talking to the proprietor's son. This young man was eighteen years old and his father's fifty. His father started working when he was nine years old, his mother works also. At that time, the economy in Argentina was poor, with very high unemployment. They had just opened up this hotel recently. His father had a lot of experience in the hotel business as a manager with different chains in Argentina, and also in Europe. He lost his job not too long ago and like so many families, they were putting a last ditch effort of survival into being self-employed, and starting their own business. Throughout Argentina there were doctors, lawyers and other professional people that could no longer find work in their chosen field and were resorting to menial jobs of taxi drivers or delivering pizzas. The son's generation was saying "Why bother going to university, and spending seven or eight years only to end up sweeping sidewalks". He was telling me that just three years ago, most middle class families had a car, enjoyed regular holidays, and had a pleasant standard of living. Now they work at anything they possibly can, were losing their homes and fighting economically. They were very bitter about a hydro operation that the Americans had taken over. Much of the money paid was 'payola' to the government, which was felt to be corrupt and inept at that time. The Argentineans were very aware of the devaluation of their currency. At that time, it was pegged at par with the American dollar and unfortunately, was overvalued. This was causing a real problem with exports and their ability to improve their standard of living. But, if the peso dropped down, even par with the Canadian dollar, inflation would have a devastating effect on these people.

We talked about computers, and Argentina was very much on the cutting edge with technology. However, the Internet itself was quite expensive, with a flat fee and then so much per half hour. It was still reasonable compared to what they have to pay for telephones and chat rooms were very popular here. Talking to this young man, I learnt a lot about soccer; and he had the good fortune of traveling with his team to England. I understood that the difference between Argentinean and British soccer is that the British run extremely fast, this being their major thrust in the sport, whereas the Argentineans concentrate on passing. Once they've got the ball, they're almost sure to get a score because of their passing ability.

After all of this conversation, it was time to start my long journey to another part of Argentina. I got a taxi and the driver I picked didn't read too well, and I couldn't explain in Spanish what I wanted, even though I knew the word "terminale". I spoke to his dispatcher, and actually had quite a conversation with him on my way to the terminal. The driver didn't have the correct change so the tip was pretty good, but still only three dollars total to get there.

As I was waiting for the bus to arrive, I asked three different people which platform, and they all gave me the same answer; seventeen, eighteen or nineteen. When the moment of truth came, it was Platform Twenty that the bus arrived at. To this day, (other than the big guy upstairs looking after me) I don't know what made me go over and ask again, but anyway, I got on the bus. I suppose when I have finished this trip, I'll be able to write a thesis on buses in South America.

This one was huge, with precarious stairs to climb. It was the closest to a cargo hole that I had ever been in, and the seat was just a wooden bench. Considering I would be on it well into the next morning, this was not the luxury coach that I was hoping for. At least I was on the right bus heading towards Resistencia, where I would transfer over to another bus, supposedly a better one.

We lumbered along and between nine and ten we were served dinner, and I promised every airline in the world I would never ever make a poor comment on their selection of food. Buses have proven that the air traveler gets VIP treatment; this one served us a dry bun, a cookie in a wrapper, cold French fries and a greasy piece of chicken. I was thinking that "bring your own" would have been the better idea. However, the Argentineans were eating theirs with more grace than I was. After a small cup of Coca Cola to wash it down, that was the end of the food on a long extensive journey.

And with that, good friends and readers of this ongoing saga, and my beautiful little treasure bee, I'm going to say goodnight to one and all.

SOUTH AMERICA
EXPLORATION

I was still on the bus, and today I should celebrate that I have now been two weeks on the road. I had lost track of the kilometers, but even in a modest sense, if I included air miles, I would have at least circumnavigated the world once around the equator, or about twenty-five thousand miles. So, no jet setter, but for a ground troop movement I was logging a lot of kilometers.

At six-thirty, we arrived in Resistencia. It's a crossroads city, and other than changing buses, I didn't spend much time here. It is a city of sculptures, and is quite sprawled out. If you wanted to go to Paraguay or Santa Fe, it's a central location to head in different directions, exactly what I was doing. Across the Rio Parana is Corrientes, another city that doesn't have much to intrigue me, other than urban sprawl. Here in Resistencia, I was able to change buses, and though it was the same bus line, it was dramatically different. This was a newer bus and even though we were running late, the better part of an hour, this bus was waiting for us to make the connection.

Once all the human cargo is loaded, off we go, heading towards Posadas. In the daylight, I notice the terrain was much flatter, not quite as flat as the prairies or the Midwest as yet, but lush and green. The rivers are muddy, carrying a heavy red type of soil content. It was the first time I had seen buildings of wood, but very small and run-down. It looked like a poor area of Argentina, and I would've thought that higher up in the Andes, it would have been harder to carve out a living than in this agricultural base.

I spent the time on the bus reading about Posadas from my guidebook and bible of travel, "The Lonely Planet," and decided to take a chance on going directly to the monastery area, which was fifty kilometers from Salta, rather than wait-

Robert F. Edwards

ing and going the next day. When the bus rolled in and I went to get my luggage, this was the first time this happened to me: I had to pay the porter before he would turn over my bags. I didn't mind giving the fellow money, it was just I begrudged the way he approached the issue. However, I got my luggage and that was the most important thing.

I approached a taxi driver and explained where I wanted to go, as I thought I had to get to another terminal, but with his help I found that it was just on the other side of this very large bus terminal. With the luck of the Irish and Bob Edwards combined, the timing was perfect. It was ten after eleven and at eleven-thirty, the bus to San Ignacio Mini would leave. It was a local type of bus and the driver didn't speak any English whatsoever. I was realizing how hard it was to travel by myself without the language and how much support I needed from the locals. The driver was accommodating and some of my Spanish words were starting to make sense. I was starting to read more Spanish than when I first started this trip, but was still not conversant by any stretch of the imagination.

I got off at San Ignacio, and a young Spanish guy who spoke a bit of English gave me some good advice. I didn't stop at the first residential hotel; I went to the other end of town, where the camping site was. I somehow managed to communicate, and got a nice room for seven pesos. It was clean, with two small beds. I was ecstatic when I saw the list of things available here. There was cervesa for a dollar, and what got me so excited was email for two dollars. Even though I was greatly fatigued from being up for in excess of twenty-four hours, I was anxious to get the email. But, for whatever reason, at that time there was no email available there or anywhere else in town, so that was that.

I started to venture out to look at the general area about one o'clock, just in the heat of the midday sun. By now, most people have closed up for the afternoon. The town looked deserted and as I walked along, I did manage to find a couple of young fellows having a beer outside a "cantina" and with some of my garbled pronunciations, the proprietor guessed that I wanted some soup and I learned the word for bread is 'pan', and I had a beer. With that under my belt and my spirits up, I checked out the bus situation running to the Falls, about six or seven buses, for tomorrow. It looked like I was out of "no man's land" where buses only travel once or twice a week, if there is sufficient cargo to move. It was very lush there, the flowers were blooming; the bushes had beautiful red and pink flowers, amidst huge ferns. I wished Marietta was with me, as she would just salivate on all the different plants and trees that are around. Everything was so fresh and green in this little well maintained community.

With food under my belt, I thought maybe the ruins would be closed during the siesta and when in Rome, be a Roman. So, I went back to my room and did just that. At five o'clock, I had to struggle to get up, but I really wanted to get to the ruins before dark, if they were open. I had a pretty good idea of where they were, about twelve blocks from where I was staying. It was cooler; not quite as hot as the mid-day sun but still warm. The walkway to the monastery was pleasant and as I walked across the street, there were some little souvenir kiosks; a good sign that I was getting closer to the ruins.

As I rounded the corner, I saw a large white building and the admission fee was two dollars and fifty cents US. The building features a presentation of the general area. This is a rainforest, and one of the local birds, a small parrot with a big beak, long body and short legs was depicted in the woodcrafts popular in this area. There was information about the Jesuits, and a room with twenty mannequins dressed in the attire of that period. The black robe was traditional but the headgear was quite unique.

Being Roman Catholic myself and going to school with the Jesuit priests, I tried to remember what I had learnt about the origin of the order. It began with a young soldier serving in one of the Spanish Conflicts. He was seriously wounded which, in those days, could have been fatal. However, it did destroy his career and he turned to the faith of his region,

Robert F. Edwards

which was Roman Catholic. He became so fired with faith that he started to go out and preach his belief and his strong conviction to the reformation of the Roman Catholic faith, because at that time factions like Martin Luther and Henry VIII were challenging it. With this burning focus on reformation of the Church and the conviction of the Roman Catholic faith, he entered into the priesthood and was ordained. After he was ordained, he got permission to start a very vigorous order, which today is known as the Jesuits. The Jesuits were, and still are, primarily a teaching order, but what makes them so outstanding is their burning desire to convert pagans and to go where no orders had gone before. They accompanied most of the expeditions regardless where they were going. They suffered tremendous hardships and endured conditions that many soldiers in outposts never saw. These men were bound by faith and the vows that they took of obedience, chastity, and poverty and would often set up missions in the most hostile areas.

In my own country, Canada, the Iroquois Indians tortured and killed these men with a vengeance as they did not understand, but they admired the bravery that these men demonstrated. Another part of their history was here in Argentina. These dedicated men converted Indians and set up missions that were awesome, even by today's standards. Even when I went to a Roman Catholic school, the Jesuit priests were teaching and I found in my own life that they were more than fair, kind and tolerant of young teen-age boys in their most gregarious, obstinate ways and as one of those boys, I'm a better man for being under the direction of these dedicated men.

I entered the grounds of the monastery, now in ruins. I have seen Roman ruins in Libya and Morocco that were in better shape, and date back much longer. Fortunately for the Roman ruins, they were in arid deserts, which preserve things, and unfortunately these ruins are in an area where things quickly return to the soil. Most of the structures that are left are of stone. It's a very large complex and rightfully so, the church is the focal point of the mission. On both wings of the church there are smaller buildings which would have housed the Jesuit priests, and then in the outer surrounding walls were the rooms for converts and students. Traditionally, monasteries and nunneries took in refugees from all walks of life. The tranquility of life behind these closed walls drew not only young people to this way of life, but often those in conflict with the government of that time and that's where the word "sanctuary" or "sanctum" comes from: Protection.

In this complex is evidence of different walks of life. The large courtyards where the priests would have said their breviaries were well marked out. There were areas still evident where the wineries and vineyards were. This was a village or a city within itself, self-contained, and was run by the abbot who was the law and order of the community for all those within the walls.

I was told that the one in Trinidad, Paraguay, has better frescoes, and there are over thirty ruined Jesuit missions: seven are in the Rio Grande area of Brazil, there are eight in the southern region and there are fifteen in Argentina. I have no intentions nor do I have the time to see every one of them, though they played an important role in history. In 1808, Hernandarias, the governor of the Spanish province of Paraguay, ordered the leader of the Jesuits, Friar Diego De Torres, to send missionaries to convert all of the natives. The Jesuits were the preference of the Indians at the time, due to the fact that the alternatives were Spanish slave work on the estates or slavery by the hands of the Portuguese. Some of the missions grew in population to excess of four thousand, and held vast tracts of land. The Jesuits had a nation within a nation and it was getting embarrassing for the Spanish Prime Minister at the time. He convinced Carlos III to expel the Jesuits from Spanish lands and by the 1800's the villages were destroyed and many of the missions were abandoned.

The ruins that I was visiting did not have the craftsmanship or materials of the Roman temples and cities. Most of the stones are of a flat nature. There was no conformity in them, just whatever nature had provided and in many cases smaller stones were chipped to give stability or strength in the walls. The walls were about a half-meter in thickness. Most of the doorways were supported by a heavy piece of timber and their height was barely over two meters. This probably explained two things: one is that the Jesuits were aware of the structural stress of openings, and had to use whatever material that was available to them. It also hints that both the Spaniards and the local Indians were much shorter than we are today.

These missions, in addition to converting the local natives to Christianity, were self-supporting villages. There were vineyards for wine, and cultivation of many different crops, including the most popular corn, and probably yams and sweet potatoes that are predominantly grown in these areas. With the blend of the Indian's knowledge of vegetation and crop-bearing plants, and the Jesuits' knowledge of less worldly and religious beliefs, it was not a bad combination.

On my way back, I stopped at some of the kiosks, although the craftsmanship was not of any great quality. The toucan, a parrot-like bird, was predominant in their woodcarving. They had some of those drinking cups for mate that I had purchased in Salta, and a bit of leatherwork but other than just street souvenirs, there was nothing that I wished to buy. There were a few statues of Christ carved out of wood, reflecting the religious background of this community.

It was a pleasant night for walking and the village was a serene place to be. Some of the homes are exceptionally well built; the average one wouldn't exceed fifteen hundred square feet. The roads were wide, but not paved, and the main street had a large boulevard with benches to sit on. It was a conventional village for these parts and the people were exceptionally friendly.

As I'm now a grandfather, I noticed many young children, and all seemed very well behaved. Their mothers are usually full-time mothers, and their parents have time for them. Many of these families are poor, but there was still a contentment in these babies and young children. The old cliché "a child should be seen but not heard"', was evident here.

The evening was starting to see the first kiss of the sunset, and by the time I had got back to the campgrounds, the first shadows were replaced with darkness. This has been a most fulfilling day, granted a long one, and I was impressed at my stamina. Everything seemed to connect, and I saw and did a lot more than my fondest dreams. Also on the way back, I checked to make sure that I had the right time and location of the bus tomorrow. Most people rely on "tourista" information centers. I've found that if you check three times and you get the same answer from three different people, the odds are that that's the way it is. So, with that information behind me, I confidently returned to the campsite and my room. I tried sitting outside to do some taping, but the mosquitoes were taking their toll in the dark. It was well past the time to catch up on my overdue rest, and I was feeling some of the fatigue of being up all night on the bus.

So without too much rambling on at the midnight hour, I will say goodnight to one and all and I miss you dearly, my little love bug.

Robert F. Edwards

February 16th, Friday
San Ignacio, Argentina

I got up earlier than I anticipated, and had a relatively good sleep last night. Somebody literally was beating the drums last night, and unfortunately their musical ability was poor. I was quite generous with my application of insect repellant, even though I was not in the malaria belt; I was very, very close to it. With the amount of mosquitoes around, I felt it might be prudent to put 'off-limits' to my blood for these little vampires that leave a nasty bulge.

At about seven o'clock I was prepared for my trek to the other end of town, which was about a kilometer away, for the bus to pick me up at ten after eight. I wanted to settle up my bill but couldn't find anyone around. I did manage to wake up the dogs, their number and size was not a problem, but their determination for protecting the family and domicile was obvious. One little guy reminded me of my West Highland terrier 'Buttons', his ears were up, and tail was not showing any give, along with his heavy barking. I kept on talking to him, and he was beginning to mellow, when the woman woke up, still with sleep in her eyes. We settled the bill at eight pesos and I knew she'd be glad to get back to bed immediately with this foreigner out of her way.

Even at this early hour, with the sun just enjoying its first look at the day, I started to feel the perspiration down my back and my arms were starting to glisten. My luggage is starting to gather weight by the accumulation of bits here and there, already. That's one of the detriments of traveling. In due course, I got to the bus depot almost an hour early and stood there with the rest. At ten after eight, there was still no bus.

SOUTH AMERICA
EXPLORATION

I noticed something that brought a bit of déjà vu to my mind. I saw a young man walking by the church (across the street) and he made the sign of the cross as a gesture as he was passing. It brought to mind my aspirations to join a religious order as a youth. I took a few pictures of this community I was so impressed with. I think there's always a time and place where you find you could easily live, just because it's very peaceful and has tranquility that brings a contentment to your life. This place has done that for me.

My new destination is on the horizon due to the fact that the bus has arrived, for Puerto Iguazu. This is the Argentine side of the Iguazu Falls, which will take me the better part of six hours. The bus is a large, long-distance bus and I've got the front seat. The woman ticket-conductor was quite amazed that I didn't speak any Spanish, but she was a pleasant young lady, and managed to share a few words. As I watched her throughout the journey, she was highly efficient, very courteous and generous of her service to anybody that was on the bus.

As this bus was going to take the better part of six hours, I had lots of time to people-watch. One of the things that I noticed and my dear wife, Marietta always had a comment about was my observations of teeth. We often laughed and said that maybe in a previous life I had been a dentist. I don't think that the Argentine people go to orthodontists anywhere near like we do to have a perfect set of teeth. With a lot of the older people, when they have teeth missing, they don't replace them with partial dentures. This was different from when I was traveling through the Soviet Union, where people used a lot of gold to cap their teeth. Here, if it's bad, it comes out and the hole stays.

Also, the native women seem to have children at young ages, and fairly large families at that. Even in these small hamlets, the people are well dressed and well behaved. The one thing that has really impressed me in the short time that I've been in both these countries is the manners and the courtesy towards each other. North America could take a large page out of their book. Definitely, we have lost what they have kept.

This was a whistle-stop type of bus, and frequently stopped to let people off and on. My particular leg of the trip is the furthest point that this bus traveled. As the day continued, I probably saw more villages, hamlets and towns than most Argentine people have that live in the country. Each one is individual, with its own personalities and contribution to the community. Some consisted of only 'Main Street'; others were quite well laid out. For the first time on my visit, I've seen wood used extensively in one community, with corrugated metal roofs. Generally, it has been brick or adobe and tile roofs. Ironically, this wooden community was mostly rundown.

The landscape has changed from flat plains that produced crops like corn to more rolling hills; and very lush vegetation, anything from ferns to palm trees, and many picturesque flowers, anything from purples to deep reds, adorning the clematis vines. The grass is a prairie type, with wide blades; a tough coarse grass that probably can endure a lot of abuse. I recognized some pine trees in the higher altitudes, and logging trucks. Their logging procedure is different from ours, in that they cut their sections of wood not to the full length of the trees. Probably, their mills operate on a smaller linear base, as these lengths were less than six meters.

This was the first bus I had been on that actually stopped for little breaks. When I say "little", I mean ten minutes. The conductress knew that I only spoke English, and thankfully her English was very good. She would tell me, "ten minutes," and show ten fingers; the next time, "five minutes," with five fingers. I ran out and got a hamburger which, everybody was amazed at my ability to communicate, something I'd probably taken for granted. I don't fully comprehend how I am able to make myself understood, it's somewhat of a phenomena. When I'm at home and I speak the common language, no one listens, yet when in these far-reaching communities, people seem to understand what I need or want and even to the de-

SOUTH AMERICA EXPLORATION

tails, like whether I want mayonnaise or catsup on a hamburger. It never ceases to amaze me. I enjoy the courtesy, the understanding, and the good nature that not just these people, but other people that I've traveled with in their countries give me as a courtesy to a person that is trying to communicate. It's most rewarding and is getting easier all the time. I also find that I am able to read everyday more and more of the Spanish and actually comprehend a fair amount of what I'm reading.

As one hour found its way around the clock, another one took its place and before very long, I arrived at my designated port of call around 2:30, very tired. I had been traveling extensively and hadn't fully recovered from the previous bus rides. It was extremely hot, since I had arrived in this continent; I had probably perspired more than in all of the last year, with pneumonia included. However, I was in good spirits and actually felt physically a lot better than I had for some time. Still, dragging my luggage was not an attractive choice. I saw a nice hotel called St. John's Hotel near the bus terminal. Knowing full well that I was going to be taking a tour or something of that nature tomorrow, I felt that it was economical to spend a little more today to be close to the terminal and not have to commute back and forth from the hotel. By paying a little more I would save on taxis. Whatever my rationale, I was doing it and the hotel was a three-star hotel, with television, with real air-conditioning, and my own private bath. There was even a swimming pool and a restaurant beside it. All things being said and done, this was very much to my liking. Every so often, I treat myself to an upgrade, just to enjoy the luxury of traveling. A bonus in this particular situation, I had the pleasure of using my Visa credit card, which helps save on the immediate cash.

The next quest is, of course, getting the e-mail. After asking about four or five people, I was able to find the place. It was quite large, considering this was a small town and a border town as well, and happily, the price was very reasonable. I logged in and "la di da", some more e-mails from my little true love, and my nieces. All seems to be going well, except that they are getting snow and that was unusual for us. However, all spirits seem to be well on the home base and after I made contact and told them what has been transpiring, I signed off and took a stroll to the core of this community. I bought some groceries; cheese, buns, beer and orange juice and a bottle of water, all for ten dollars, which is what I spent the previous day for just one meal. My room had a fridge so I took advantage of this luxury and stocked it up for my stay.

The town was well laid out, and I managed to navigate through the twists and turns without getting lost. I had noticed a lot of leather shops, and I decided to come back and view them later on, as I was feeling fatigued and hot beyond all comparison. I kept thinking of the swimming pool in the complex and I knew my wife was going to chuckle at my obstinacy in life. Seldom do I eat salads and even more seldom do I ever go to a swimming pool. In all fairness, I'm not a swimmer, so water doesn't have a big priority in my life. However, on a hot day like today, anything to cool off would be rewarding. So, I get on my bathing suit and off I go to the pool, equipped with my tape recorder and even a bottle of beer. It was such a hot day; I was coasting through it with luck, rather than sharpness.

Some time during my earlier travels, the stem of my watch fell out, no surprise as I had trouble with this particular watch before. I was watching the progress of time, and I seemed to be mustering through it. I just barely got my hand in the water and I realized I still had my watch on. I quickly jumped out, dried it off, and hoped for the best. I was splashing around like a beached whale while the others swam by me like sharks stalking their prey. However, the water was warm and it was a picturesque setting, with palm trees around the pool, a real tropical paradise.

I enjoyed the time dictating some of my notes and some well deserved relaxation. When I got back to the room, I stretched out on the bed for about an hour and when I woke up, guess what? The watch wasn't working. I guess with the stem falling out, the water poured in this new reservoir and the watch finally decided that was it. Now I've got an immediate situation on my hands, to find another watch. I thought this would be an easy task, since every country I've been in before, there were always peddlers with their arms full of watches, and you could buy a watch just about anywhere. Of course, when I needed one, it was more than challenging to find. In due course, I found one, with the analog rather than the digital, but I didn't have many options as this was the only one she had and it was getting late. I was almost tempted to buy another leather bag, even though the quality was not the same as the one that I got in Morocco. Most of them ranged from rawhide at twenty dollars to nicer leather for thirty-five dollars, U.S. I didn't feel up to making any decisions, so just returned to the hotel.

I enjoyed having one of the beers that I had purchased and just relaxing. It was one of the few times that I had actually sat around without putting the pedal to the metal. I thought I would also treat myself to a good meal. Argentina is renowned for their beef and this seemed as good an evening as any to try it. In the restaurant (attached to the hotel) the first thing I ordered was an artichoke salad, with a dressing of oil and vinegar. One of the nicest artichokes I've ever had and I could see why people enjoy this particular delicacy. Also, it's a product of the region, so that was the main reason why I wanted to try it. The main course was steak, a filet mignon, accompanied by French fries, and wine. I ordered a dry red wine, it had a strong flavor, and not as pleasant as the Chilean wines that I've had. However, I don't think it's fair to make a judgment call on their wine at this point.

After the meal was when I experienced one of those differences when traveling. I said to the waitress, "I'm staying at this hotel," and she said, "Oh, that's fine." I said, "My name is Bob Edwards and I'm in Room 201," and I thought that she would get me a bill to sign and I would leave her a tip. Neither transpired and after a long period of waiting, they became

Robert F. Edwards

very busy. Around 10:00 p.m., I finally got up and walked out and I'm sure I'll be paying the bill when I prepare to leave.

With a good meal under my belt, I was hoping that I would be able to sleep in tomorrow.

With that in mind and my thoughts of my little honey-bun, and how grateful I was for all those e-mails that she was sending, I'm going to say goodnight. I love and miss you dearly. Goodnight.

SOUTH AMERICA EXPLORATION

February 17th, Saturday
Puerto Iguazu, Argentina

Yes, I slept in. Wow! It was seven o'clock. This was one of the few places that the shower worked, and there was an abundance of hot water. I thoroughly enjoyed the showers. I must have had at least four of them up to this moment. It was a bit early, so I watched television for a while, "Joan of Arc" with Peter O'Toole. It was funny; the subtitles were in Spanish and the English seemed to be hard to hear.

Breakfast was Continental-style; rolls, fresh fruit, coffee, lots of juices (two or three different types of juices), and some watermelon. Here again, just a point of comparison on different attitudes and behavior. In all the hotels that I had been in throughout the world, they usually asked for the room number or some form of confirmation. Here, it was just "help yourself", so I assumed that the hotel would just charge for it, whether you had breakfast or not. It was a very laissez faire, relaxed attitude, compared to the question and answer periods that North Americans go through for every transaction.

The front desk was another bonus at this particular hotel. The staff spoke English, which made it quite a bit easier for me, especially as I wanted some detailed information. I asked the young man about the Falls and he advised, "No, you can't do it in one day." He says, "It takes two days. One full day with the Argentine side and about the same on the Brazilian side." He recommended doing the Argentine side today and tomorrow, to take my luggage with me and go through Immigration and Customs. There was a place, I gathered, that you could have your luggage kept while you go and see the falls; and then proceed to catch a bus to Rio de Janeiro. He explained in great detail what had to be done; that you buy a Brazilian ticket on a local bus for four pesos and it's a round

Robert F. Edwards

trip; you go to the park, you have to pay another five pesos; and then once you're in the park, the bus stops there and they ran about every forty minutes right up until ten o'clock at night.

At the bus depot, it was fairly easy to understand their system, and the desk clerk spoke English. Of course, they were selling a packaged tour, and the fellow explained the deal; actually three boat trips, a safari through the jungle, and pretty well a complete day of activities for forty-five dollars. From what I had read about the Falls and what I wanted to achieve, I felt that forty-five dollars was modest for a full day of activity in such a remarkable site. So, I decided to take the full package, because if I piece-mealed it, it would have been twice as much.

I met up with some Israelis, six young men and women traveling together. One of the young men I spent a fair amount of time talking to while we waited for the bus. They were nice, clean-cut people, probably in their mid-thirties, from Tel-Aviv and Hebron. We didn't talk a lot about politics. It's not my style to bring up issues that are sensitive to people about their religion. But on the bus, the young man told me that when you finish High School, you have to spend three years in the Armed Forces. You can go directly into University; but then, when you come out, you have to spend your three years in the Armed Forces. So, you get three years, regardless what you do.

We entered the park, a lush, rainforest area. I got off the bus, and the tour group leaders were all wearing yellow shirts, very organized. I was carrying my backpack and one of the leaders approached me, to describe exactly what I would be doing for the rest of the day. She explained, "You are going to get soaking wet when you go to the Devil's Throat." At that, I was more than concerned because I had all my camera equipment in the bag with nothing to cover it. I wasn't prepared for this event, but I spotted a fellow with a big black garbage bag and to my good fortune, he shared one with me.

SOUTH AMERICA EXPLORATION

The first boat was a powerboat and it quickly took us to a section of the Falls where there is a boardwalk. I immediately thought of my dear wife, and as much as I wished she were here to see these fantastic Falls, I knew that with her dislike of heights, I would never have gotten her on this open-crate boardwalk. We walked for about a quarter of a kilometer, with different stop ways along the way to take photographs. Our tour group was well organized and kept the flow moving, but in leisurely manner, so everybody got a good chance to take their pictures. Again, my luck held and I met up with two Danish young ladies and as with many Europeans, they spoke several languages including fluent Spanish and they were on the same full day tour. Needless to say, this little Canadian air plant lodged itself on to these two women and they seemed to enjoy my company. From the boardwalk, you get a view of the rapids. The current is much stronger than one could comprehend, and once in the rapids, there was no turning back. Early sailors must have felt that they had found the edge of the world and flat as it was, went over, never to be seen again. The Falls were a majestic flow after the rapids, and then nothing but froth, foam and spray. In some ways, the best view of the Falls was from above.

Robert F. Edwards

From here we proceeded to our jungle expedition, on a small flatbed truck with wooden benches. We made our way through the jungle trail amidst lush vegetation, with an abundance of orchids about. These particular orchids were the ones that vanilla comes from. Folklore tales mention a governor of this area who believed this orchid had medicinal purposes for enhancing sexual prowess. Together with chocolate, (another locally grown product) he would have these every morning before visiting his wife to perform services that pleased him. Then, in the afternoon, more chocolate and vanilla before visiting his mistress, for the pleasures that he enjoyed the most.

The next part of this journey was through the river, partly by raft. Once we pulled away from the shoreline, I really hoped our guide knew these currents. Even though the water looked relatively calm, there was a strong current pulling the raft sideways. He was not struggling, but was keenly alert as

he paddled through these deceptively benign waters. More than once, I had my eye on the Falls. We did wear life jackets, but this would be of little comfort as you took a last look before going over the edge of the world. As he worked his way further away from the Falls, we started to enter an area of jungle similar to the everglades in Florida.

There were many tributaries on the river and one would have to be a seasoned rafter to know which fork to take. Sometimes, it was the narrow one used, rather than the one that seemed to be obvious to the inexperienced eye.

SOUTH AMERICA
EXPLORATION

In the jungle, there were three layers of vegetation. One of the major differences of jungle versus a forest is the collage of different types of vines. Many of these clinging plants require support from the higher-level trees. The one thing that seemed to be absent in this particular jungle was sound. It was perfectly silent. It was midday and maybe the animals and birds were taking shelter in the shade of trees. But, with the noise of the vehicle, I would have thought we might have disturbed a few of them.

We ventured down the waterway for the better part of an hour, before we got to a point where large trees had fallen over the narrow passage and from here we got back on land. Another trusty vehicle of the same vintage as its predecessor was waiting for us. With a bit of my Jungle Bob humour, I would have enjoyed using one of these big lorries to force my way through some of the forest trails in Canada. At two o'clock we were allowed a free hour to get something to eat and regroup before the next two events in the afternoon.

The girls ordered some empanadas. To best describe them, they were shaped like an oversized perogy, or miniature pasty, very universal. The inside of this turnover is available with many different types of filling, but the outside remains the same, pastry. These ones were crimped on both sides and deep-fried, frita. I thought I ordered chicken, but ended up with some form of hamburger. They also had salads and I ordered French fries. Yes, the old people eat poorly, the young people eat wisely. The restaurant was immaculate and the grounds of the park were in pristine condition, considering the amount of people that were here even today.

It was a popular place for visitors, as I have met people from Portugal, some Italians, and besides the two Danish girls and six Israelis, there was also a group of Japanese people. Quite a universal assembly. This lone Canadian stands neither small nor tall, but is "Uno" amongst the United Nations group that was forming that day in the park.

Robert F. Edwards

After we had completed our lunch, and did a bit of strolling around, we boarded the truck again and merrily, merrily go down the jungle trails. The guide on this particular venture was just delightful. He was probably in his late forties; but even the young ladies said that he really must enjoy his job because he was so outgoing, humorous, and ultra friendly. In addition to asking us questions, he also providing a lot of information. One of the facts that he enlightened a lot of people on, including some of the Argentine people was that the very first president of Argentina was a Negro. Also, they've had women presidents in Argentina. Their republic is usually remembered for the darkness of the Falkland Islands, or the political dictatorship of the Hunta regime, with the missing voice of Argentina. North Americans often question their democratic system and their recognition of equality. However, as far as their leadership qualities, Argentina accelerated the United States in having a black president, and also a woman president, but history tells the truth.

As we continued further into the jungle, our guide pointed out some of the unique hardwoods. The beautiful colors of these hardwoods, from purpleheart, to rosewood, ziricote, and many others that are in great demand globally for furniture were growing in this forest. We passed by a few people that were bold enough to walk the parameter trails. Either they were not versatile with map reading, or it was more difficult than what was implied, as they were lost with each turn. Our guide gave them directions on how to get through, as this was not a very pleasant place to spend the night; like any forest, it was damp. It would be better if they had more covering, since these people were only wearing shorts and tops.

We were approaching an area where the insect population was the only wildlife that I had witnessed any great abundance of, including the famous mosquito that likes to leave a little something behind. I had also seen gigantic spider webs; unfortunately my photo didn't turn out to any degree since spider webs are very transparent in the nature of their ability to capture prey. I had never seen spiders quite as large; some of them bigger than my thumb and webs that we were passing through were two meters in both directions. These creatures were determined to catch something more than just a mouthful to feast themselves on. None of our group was displaying any great affection for them, or wanting to spend anymore time cooing over them.

If I were a trophy collector, it would be the butterflies I would want. They were so abundant and talk about friendly; they would land on you and in many cases, just sit there and enjoy their new form of transportation. Their vivid colors and unique designs were so numerous that no artist's imagination could mimic the graciousness that Mother Nature has provided for these beautiful species. Some people were bothered by them, or not used to them would be a better word and tried flicking them away. I have to admit I did at first, but with the sheer number of them, it soon became a matter of course to look on your shoulder and see one or two sitting there, just enjoying the ride.

Because this area gets a lot of rain all year round, some of the trails were questionable, with heavy ruts in the roads. There was no way that an average vehicle, (even if they were permitted, which they were not) would be able to navigate these roads; as they would be high-centered all the time. As our truck rumbled through some of these soft spots, the guide pointed out different plants and vines, and was very helpful answering questions from the local passengers, in about three languages, I might add.

This leg of the safari concluded the rainforest tour, and we were now at the last part. At the beginning of the day, the first guide had asked me if I'd got a bag to protect my camera, and this was when I got a big Glad bag to protect my packsack. She said, "You're definitely going to get soaked." Our new guide also asked the same question, and handed out more plastic bags for cameras and passports. I had learned a long time ago that listening was probably the most important element when traveling, especially traveling alone the way I do. Most residents know what they're talking about, and they're also giving you the advice that is required to make the proper decisions. When he mentioned the passport, I thought of two things. One, by putting it in my backpack, it wouldn't serve much purpose to identify me if I did fall out of the boat, or got lost, so I tied a small plastic bag around my document pouch and secured it around my neck.

We boarded a rugged craft made of fiberglass, with an inboard outboard motor, and lots of power. Our launch point was below the Falls, directly opposite to earlier today, which was above the Falls. We worked our way up the gorge, and saw our first animal, a small deer. This region at one time had supported large cats, but there was no visual evidence of their presence at this time. We continued to work our way against the current, and I was grateful for the exceptionally powerful motor in this sturdy boat. We passed through turbulent rapids and the boat splashed and bobbed under their strength and might. I was sitting at the bow, getting the full impact of

the froth. I was taking a chance by having my camera exposed to take some pictures and lost track of the time while we were doing this. It was just too exciting to clock watch.

SOUTH AMERICA
EXPLORATION

At this point the falls divided into basically two sections. The first is larger than the other, but both are equally as impressive. We headed towards the area with the greater amount of spray and froth. As we got closer to it, the turbulence and the constant force of literally tons of water cascading over the cliff pushed the boat (strong as it was) backwards rather than forwards. We made our way as best as we could and I knew it was time to put my camera back in to the plastic bag. The spray was very intense and what we had been told to expect was coming true. A couple of Australian girls on the previous day had been told they would get wet, yet one didn't have her passport securely protected and it looked like shredded paper, one of the Danish girls said. As we got closer, the froth and spray was like a heavy rain. Being up front, I was watching one fellow taking a video. He was well prepared with rain gear on and his video protected with a cover also.

This was a very thrilling moment for me. As we got closer, it felt like a fantastic exhibition ride, and sure got my adrenalin pumping. Just as we were getting adjusted to this, the pilot made a sharp turn and we started to retreat. I, along with the

Robert F. Edwards

others, was thinking that the best is over and it was well worth it. But no, the best was yet to come and we headed towards the smaller Falls. As we got closer, there was a sequence of Falls, and the cascading effect was mesmerizing.

This section of the Falls had the same froth and turbulence, but because it was not as large, the boat had the power to get much closer. We were all holding our breath as we got closer and closer, and just before we hit the plundering cascade of water pounding unmercifully on the rocks below, the boat swerved at the last minute. One and all were drenched and soaking wet, but in good spirits amidst relieved laughter. It was definitely the ride of a lifetime!

The whole day had been a success, and worth the forty-five dollars they asked, but for me the experience of getting that close to the falls and feeling the might of water pounding down was priceless. One of the Danish girls thought the water had a salty taste to it, but I had so much water on me, I couldn't tell if it was the salt of the water, or my own perspiration.

We disembarked from the boat at another landing, and there was a large stairwell leading up to more walkways to different positions of the Falls.

In every aspect, the Argentine people have done an excellent job in maintaining a tourist facility, but without the pizzazz and overkill that North America often does. They have kept it in its natural state, yet provided the ability to take advantage of strategic areas for photography and experiences. For those that didn't get drenched on the boat, there was a point on the boardwalk that also felt the spray and might of the Falls. Since I was already drenched and couldn't be any wetter, I asked the girls to take a picture of me at this point: white hair, wet clothes, if possible, a smile. When we checked our maps, we realized that we had missed one spot. It was hard to believe, at that point in the afternoon that we could have left anything out. This boardwalk was on the other side from the vantage point we had in the morning, and gave a different view of the Falls as it cascaded over the rocks far below.

SOUTH AMERICA
EXPLORATION

From here, I recalled the legend of the Falls. As the story goes; a god was infatuated with a beautiful maiden and a great warrior also courted this maiden. Instead of complying with the god's wishes, she fell in love with the warrior and they set sail down this river. When the god found out that he had been abandoned for the warrior, he collapsed the maiden into a rock below the waterways and changed the warrior into a tree. Unfortunately, there were a lot of trees there, so I couldn't identify which one was the warrior.

At the bottom of the Falls, there would be no way of surviving those treacherous jagged rocks. Forceful waters pounded continuously, and if one had the misfortune of going over the falls, the rocks below would break you into pieces long before you got back into the rapids. The mythical god did not have a kind farewell for his deserted maiden. However, archaeologists have a better explanation. There was a fusion in the earth and this particular crack just collapsed conveniently where this "Rio Grande" or this great river was passing through, resulting in these magnificent natural Falls.

Concluding my visit in the park was a tall lookout point. It could pass for a lighthouse, but any boats in these waters

Robert F. Edwards

would be past the point of no return. As legend holds, 'beware of the Devil's Throat', and there actually, is where we got wet the most. It was around five o'clock when I said to the girls that I was prepared to go back. I was still soaking wet, but not uncomfortable due to the fact that the day was so warm. Still, I hoped to get out of those clothes and in some way dry them before I started my next journey to Rio de Janeiro.

I managed to get on the local bus with no trouble to the ter- minale and walked like a wet duck to my hotel. As if I hadn't got enough water already, I had a good shower and cleaned up, put on my shorts and my only other shirt. That morning, I'd taken my dirty socks, underwear and shirt and wrapped them up, and put on fresh clothes, which were now soaking wet. To my surprise, the dirty clothes had been laundered and neatly folded on the bed. I hadn't asked for this to be done, but I was grateful and more than willing to pay for it. Just different hotels, and events happen that you least expect.

With fresh, dry clothes on, I started to sort out my priori- ties. I needed to find out about transportation to Brazil, also send an e-mail to Marietta and wanted to try and return my watch. The new watch that I had purchased was difficult to read, and I had to put my glasses on to see where the hands were.

Priority one was the bus station. I found that the best al- ternative was to take the local transport to the border, then transfer to another bus at the main terminal to Rio de Ja- neiro. Even though it was Sunday, there would be at least six or seven buses throughout the day to Rio.

Next, the e-mail station, where they now recognized me. Two great e-mails where waiting for me, one from my nieces that were visiting with Marietta while I was away. I was surprised to hear they took an adventurous trip on their own to Victoria. For my dear wife, going from Vancouver to Victoria, taking a ferry and driving through a strange city is equally as coura- geous as these far-reaching outposts that I do in remote ar- eas, and I admired her for it. I gathered it was snowing again, and in the middle of February was quite unheard of in Van-

100

couver. The other e-mail was from my wife, and everything was going well, even the dog was back to being his healthy, vigorous self, so all is well on the home front.

So then it was back to where I had purchased the watch. After a lot of hand gestures and the lady talking in great depth in Spanish, the bottom line was "you own it, you've got it, you keep it, I have the money, adios." I was more than prepared to buy a more expensive watch, and pay the difference, but whether she didn't comprehend or whether she didn't want to is irrelevant. I did not accomplish my mission.

By now, it was around eight o'clock and I decided to try and finish off the last two beers I had rather than carry them around. I tried sitting by the swimming pool to record some of these events but couldn't find a quiet place. After an hour of dictating, I returned to my room, finished off the rest of my meager food supplies, and am ashamed to admit that I started watching television. The Argentine people have their own productions, but most of the shows were American sit-coms in English with Spanish sub-titles.

By eleven o'clock, I was not that tired, but I wanted to get as much rest as possible. Tomorrow, if I was successful could be a thirty-six hour day, which was long enough for anybody.

So, *"buenos dia, hasta la vista, adiós". That concludes today.*

Robert F. Edwards

February 18th, Sunday
Puerto Iguazu, Argentina

Well, I was up at about 7:30, with hopefully enough rest to endure the long overnight trip on the bus that I would be experiencing later that day. Downstairs for my Continental breakfast, I enjoyed a bowl of fruit and some bread, and real coffee, quite strong and most enjoyable. I settled up with the hotel and to my pleasant surprise, the laundry must have been included in the bill because sixty dollars is what was quoted and sixty dollars is what I paid. In Argentina, it was relatively easy to figure out the currency because of its parity with the U.S. dollar.

I now found out that the restaurant has its own bill and was expecting it to be an expensive meal, with the wine, steak and so forth. I had not yet figured out why restaurant food was so expensive. After paying for the restaurant bill, about twenty-nine dollars, I asked the young man about the buses. He told me that the bus would leave the terminal at nine-thirty. It was a quarter after nine then. The nice part is that I had a very short distance to make my way to the terminal, luggage and all. With that, I said my farewells and my appreciation for the service.

Just for interest, there was one thing about the room that was quite different from my previous experiences. Everybody in the world is basically the same. We all try to economize, and everybody has unique ways of doing it. This hotel has a switch at the front desk to turn off and on the air-conditioning in your room. There was free laundry, but a limited amount of free air-conditioning. If you're in the room, you get it; if you're not, they shut it off.

As I was patiently waiting at the bus terminal, I met an English woman from the Midlands and a gentleman from New Zealand. They mentioned that they had noticed me the previous day at the Falls, and they were going to spend the entire day perusing the Brazilian side of the Falls before returning back to the Argentine side. The transaction is very informal and as long as you have the proper documentation of re-entry into Brazil, there isn't too much formality with Immigration or Customs.

However, with all my luggage, when we reach the border, the Customs officer indicates that I have to get off the bus and go through proper Immigration which, with the number of times that I've done this, I probably could have given him instructions. I just needed to be told which building it was, and again being very helpful, they escorted me over to the building and wouldn't you know it, Bob Edwards went in backwards. It seemed I was trying to get my passport stamped by the Brazilian side before I cleared the exit stamp from Argentina, but the fellow was pleasant and explained it was a matter of maybe six meters at the most, to the right desk. I went over, the fellow smiled, looked at the passport, gave it a stamp, and then back over to the Brazilian side. The fellow looked at it, said, "Good, you have to fill out an entry form," and stamped both of them. He explained to me that I had ninety days, which I was aware of, and that really concluded both Immigration and Customs. Probably one of the simplest crossings that I had gone through and this seems to be the world over; one border was a formality and the other was a nightmare.

With this out of the way, I returned to the terminal, but my bus was gone. There was one thing about buses here; they don't have to be on time but if you're not there when they are, wait for the next one; and that was exactly what I had to do. With a little bit of help and the communication level being as good as ever, I found out that the next bus would be an hour. However, one of the attendants and a taxi driver tried to encourage me to take a taxi to the main bus terminal. They wanted ten dollars, but I had already purchased a ticket to go this route from the terminal at the Argentine side. It gave me a chance to catch up on the events of yesterday, at the Falls.

It was a nice day; a little overcast and cooler, which in some ways was a blessing for people like myself. I passed the hour quietly and enjoyably waiting for the bus. These local transport buses have a little turnpike gate up front where the conductor sits. I got somebody to help me lift my luggage over this little barrier, but with my supply belt on my waist, I found it challenging to squeeze through. After about ten kilometers, I got my first look at the Brazilian side of the Falls.

The Argentine side had stayed more of a village, while the Brazilian side is definitely a city; there was no mistaking it with numerous high rises. They stuck up like monolithic posts. There was no question that this was a very robust and aggressive city.

I was glad that I was able to, by luck rather than choice; stay on the side I had chosen because one town was a walking town, while the other was either a taxi or bus. There was no mistaking that you either would have to spend a great deal of time learning the bus routes or spend a great deal of money experiencing the same distance in cabs. It's a new city and you could almost feel the change on the mood of the people. It seemed that the Argentineans were generally having an economically hard time, while the Brazilians were very robust. I got the feeling, just by population density and the little I know about the economy of both countries, that Brazil could be likened to the United States of South America. Very well sustained on its own economy, and welcomes but doesn't really depend on others. The city, being a new one and large at the same time, was well laid out. There was a feeling of success and wealth. The buses were a little newer; the buildings were larger; and even the fast food places were more on the cutting edge.

We stopped in the middle of, literally it seemed nowhere except the bazaar. Most people were getting out and I managed to stumble out the word "terminale" and he pointed in the direction towards the bazaar. I thought, "Well, who knows? It's Sunday; all the little kiosks are closed and possibly on the other side is the terminal." As soon as I got off, a young man approached me and said something like "welcome". Sometimes travelers have a bad attitude, and I hate to admit it occasionally happens to me also. I had read that Brazil's crime rate was far in excess of other South American countries, and in Rio de Janeiro there was a catch phrase that "touristas" were filet mignon, like easy meat to digest. I had also read that robbery was at a rapid pace and they even robbed buses.

So, with all these preconceived notions, there was this young man who I was thinking was one of the people who are the middle men, who help you get your next mouthful of air and expected a large remuneration for telling you that you're still breathing, or that he was able to hail down a taxi with his arm better than yours. My assumption was completely wrong, he was an aid that the government had hired for those arriving from Argentina; and if you needed help, he was there to give you assistance.

I asked him, "the terminal?" He replied, "It's seven kilometers," and just as he said that, a big orange bus with metal seats popped out of nowhere to take me to the terminal. I had been on some hair-raising taxi rides through numerous cities and one that came to mind (besides the notorious New York drivers) was in Moscow. That was one of the most amazing high speed runs on main streets even with the pot holes, that taxi driver got up to ninety kilometers an hour. This bus

Robert F. Edwards

didn't reach that super sonic speed on the streets but being Sunday, traffic was at a minimum and his gas pedal was at a maximum. The people that had gotten on the bus were challenged trying to get their luggage over the turnpike gate, and the way this bus was traveling, the boat ride by the falls was more stable in your footing than standing trying to pass luggage through this small gateway.

In record-breaking time, we arrived. It was a first class terminal, new, and very well done. I have been impressed with the cleanliness in South America and the Brazilian side is, at this point, equally comparable to the other countries. Even on Sunday, I saw a crew of people in orange uniforms, sweeping the streets.

I was at the bus terminal by eleven-thirty, and though it wasn't raining at the moment, it was spitting. To go to the Falls, I would have to unpack to try to find my jacket. Sometimes, you can do a little overkill and that day, I felt that I had seen the best of the Falls and what I had seen in my memory was lasting. On the Brazilian side, it was more of a panoramic view of the entire phases of the Falls, which realistically were three or four cascades. What I enjoy about traveling alone is I can make a choice spontaneously, so I decided to at least find out when the next bus was leaving for Rio de Janeiro.

There were quite a few bus kiosks to choose from, and my Spanish was getting sufficient enough to read where I wanted to go; but quite a few of them didn't have any locations to Rio. A lot of them I recognized as being other directions to the south part of Brazil, but a larger portion were heading towards Argentina and Buenos Aires. True to their word, there were compartments to put your luggage in so that I wouldn't have to lug my bags around the Falls. I found the kiosk that said Rio de Janeiro and the luck of the Irish was with me again. I got the last seat on the bus. The reason I knew this was the woman kept asking me "uno?" (one) and I said "si".

A man came along while she was writing the ticket. He asked for the same privilege and he looked at her like "you know, I'm one of you; what the hell is he doing? Why does he get preferential treatment?" And she basically said, "Well, you know, I've started writing the ticket and he was here first." The fellow was quite indignant. He finally walked away and she continued writing my ticket up. There were no other buses leaving sooner than the one I was on for Rio. It was going to leave at two o'clock and would be "mañana," tomorrow, between 12:00 and 4:00 before it arrived. But I had my ticket and again, to my surprise, this was the first terminal where I had been able to use the Visa.

I prefer this method of payment as I find that by using the Visa, I always get the exact preferential exchange rate of the day since their currency is locked on an international basis with your currency. So, whenever possible, I do use the Visa for no other reason than getting the better exchange rate and plus a bonus. Like today, I have the privilege of waiting from twenty to maybe even forty-five days; depending on how progressive the system is, before I have to pay for it. Two small advantages, but well worth mentioning.

My next quest was to exchange some currency. It was my policy to always try and have some local currency. I was getting the best exchange rate, but also, with the same currency, I felt I got a better attitude from the locals and not quite as much of a "tourista". People don't give you the exchange rate that they've chosen rather than what it is. I talked to a fellow and he phoned for me, and almost before I hung up, another young man showed up and took me right to the exchange bureau. I was impressed with their tourist services, especially since this was Sunday and being a Catholic country and South America, they respect the Lord's Day a little more than in North America. I exchanged a hundred dollars for about a hundred and eighty "quesentas".

I had about two hours to wait, so took advantage of the time to catch up on recording some of the previous events. I also spent a little bit of time talking to a family that I met at the border waiting for the bus, (a father, mother, and two sons probably in their mid-twenties, and their daughter maybe

Robert F. Edwards

fourteen). The five of them were going to spend a month's holiday in Brazil. The young men were going surfboarding and the dad brought his fishing rod. The one young man had about three words of English; but somehow, the gift of the gab and the camaraderie of the global community just came out. I was surprised at the amount of words I was starting to comprehend. I've been given to understand that this is probably the first step of a true immigrant. You understand what the other person is telling you, you just can't say anything back.

I went to the restaurant and had a piece of chicken in a bun, and a coca-cola. With nourishment behind me and the day ahead of me, it was now about 1:30 as I sat at the platform, waiting for my bus. I have come to the conclusion that buses are like people. You can never judge them until you get to know them or that old cliché, "You cannot judge a book by its cover." The bus that showed up has definitely seen happier days behind it. However, as far as legroom and cushioning in the seats, it was far superior to anything I had ridden on, except the very first bus when I left Santiago. In the short time that I had been in Brazil, transportation seemed to move faster and the highways were in excellent condition, or at least this one that I was on.

The terrain is something that always has interested me. In some parts, it was quite flat and open sky; similar to Alberta or Montana in North America's mid-west. What I noticed there was rather than small independent farming, there seemed to be more collective communities. Besides a few big Brahma bulls, the area looked to be mainly agricultural. We had just passed a large cornfield, some of it just sprouting; other parts about midway through its growth cycle. The soil is much redder in pigment than most of the growing regions of North America, but it seems to yield a healthy crop. By the amount of rain that I had experienced today, together with the heat, these two ingredients will make any plant say thank you.

SOUTH AMERICA
EXPLORATION

Two hours into the trip, and the rain was still coming down extremely hard, a real prairie downpour. I was glad I wasn't out at the Falls getting soaked again by a different way.

The rain let up a bit as we stopped at a small terminal for a transfer break. Last night, I must have let some of the night raiders into my room because I wondered why my legs were so itchy under my socks. Lo and behold, I had the marks of the flying vampire, better known to society as the mosquito. With the heavy rains and the heat, not only do plants like this combination, but these flying insects that love to leave their venom behind, do as well. I certainly got my share of their marks to show they made contact last night.

The terrain was changing from flat plains to rolling hills and a lot of different types of vegetation; trees that have white leaves; on the hills I saw pine trees, and lots of colorful blossoms in purple, orange and red. Even though the bus was full, we continued to pick up passengers. I was sitting almost at the back of the bus, and there were some real chatterboxes aboard. Unfortunately for me, Brazilians speak Portuguese, which I don't understand. In the last couple of days in Argentina, I was starting to comprehend some conversation, but now I was right back to being totally isolated.

Anyway, the scenery was pleasant and I noticed it was getting dark earlier as we continued on our northern quest and would be close to the equator by the time we got to Rio de Janeiro. Every bus line in this country seemed to have its own rulebooks and system for feeding the passengers. The other ones handed something out in their floating palace, this one gave us a half hour or so in a stationary one. There was a buffet of reheated items, and I took what I thought was an empanada. To my horror, it contained a hot dog, which had probably been sitting since dawn under heat lamps, and now it was ten o'clock at night. I ate it for two reasons: one that I should have something in my stomach; and the other is that I paid for it. I took a bite, but it was just terrible and the only good part was the coca-cola that I was drinking. After settling up, I went outside with still some grease in my mouth, and saw a

Robert F. Edwards

little candy store. I felt, "Well, I've got some change left, I'll see if I can buy one little sweet or something to get this lard out of my mouth."

There was another young woman from the bus and she was buying something. Miracles never cease! She spoke English, and helped me buy some candies. Their chocolate tasted different, not as much sugar content, more of a European flavour, I thought. I got to talking to this young lady and one of her friends appeared. At first, I thought it was her husband, and she laughed. She said, no; they're both studying medicine. She had actually graduated, and was doing her internship at the age of twenty-two and her name was Evelyn. The three of us spent literally hours talking, both of them very nice people. His father and mother were working in Dallas, Texas doing domestic work to try and put him through university. Her parents, I gathered, were fairly well off. Her dad was a helicopter pilot and mechanic for an oil company. Also, her grandfather who was seventy years of age (and I met him when we arrived at Rio de Janeiro) was a military man. One of her great-grandmothers is a hundred and the other is ninety-eight or ninety-nine. Evelyn spoke exceptionally good English and could speak three or four other languages. She had a bubbly, outgoing personality and a genuine kindness for people. They were both Seventh Day Adventists and deeply committed to their faith. They really helped break the monotony and I felt very fortunate to have met them. I was apprehensive after reading some of the reports on Rio de Janeiro, and here a little miracle came popping into my life. They were so helpful, to make sure that I got onto the right bus and explained the hotels to me. Yes, it just seemed that when things happen the way they should, they come out right.

The night air was still very hot for me, but as I found out in Cuba, the local people were more sensitive to coldness. The bus had no air-conditioning, which didn't bother me at all; but people just wouldn't open up the windows and there was a stifling, stagnant air. There were probably over fifty people perspiring on this bus, and some of them even had colorful

110

blankets covering them. They're definitely well equipped. I find that the midnight raiders' marks on my legs are itching extremely, making me extremely uncomfortable.

To make matters more irritating, I was perspiring as if I was in a sauna. It was a long night and I didn't get a chance to sleep. The young man beside me did a much better job, and the little infant in front of me seemed to endure life's struggles a lot better than I did. I must have dozed off periodically between bumps and swerves, and as it was going past midnight I was still on the bus.

Robert F. Edwards

February 19th, Monday
Rio de Janeiro, Brazil

It didn't matter what time it was because I was still on the bus. Dawn seemed to break about 6:30; and the scenery hadn't altered that much. The one thing I had noticed about the farms was the lack of heavy machinery on them. Lunch started around ten o'clock when the bus pulled in to a station for a twenty-minute stop. I had a cup of coffee and was at least able to stretch my legs.

One thing I did notice was that Brazilian people and South Americans, as far as that goes, smoked not excessively but it seemed to be a higher number than North Americans. Also, the heritage of Brazilians was quite a bit different than their neighbors. Both the Argentines and Chileans have a very European complexion and features. The Brazilians can trace more of their population's origin to the native Indians. At one time, the Indian population was estimated at in excess of seven or eight million and today, they're around about a hundred and fifty thousand. The native Indians didn't have much resistance to the communicable diseases of the times that the Portuguese brought over, so a lot of them died of European diseases. Also, they weren't quite as physically fit for the heavy manual jobs that were demanded in the sugar cane plantations and the other hard laborious jobs. So, the Portuguese brought over boatloads of African Negroes. With the blend of Portuguese, Negro, and Indian, the general population of Brazil has this mixture. They have a much darker complexion than people in other South American countries that I had been in.

The Brazilian language, being Portuguese, was very difficult for me to understand, and I was at a loss. But the people were very happy and quite contented, even on this bus. They

112

seemed a little more outgoing than people in the other countries that I had been in, but equally as well mannered and enjoyable to be around. What I had seen at that point, my impression was that Brazil was economically better than some of its counterparts in S.A., and has a higher population density.

We were running late and twelve o'clock was the bewitching hour that we were supposed to arrive in Rio de Janeiro; and it was still close to three and a half hours before we would get to our final destination. This meant we would be on the bus some twenty-six hours and it would be closer to 3:00 p.m. before we arrived. It was unfortunate; but by the same token, I was glad that I had been able to get on that bus, and would still be arriving in daylight in Rio. Evelyn confirmed that there was a high crime rate and it could be dangerous.

Over and above that, my luck did seem to hold unbelievably. That weekend, Friday or Saturday, would be the start of the carnival. Not just in Rio; it was all of South America that has these carnivals. However, Rio was the biggest or most renowned. It would be highly difficult to get a hotel anywhere, but by arriving on Monday, at least I had a pretty good chance of getting a room.

We arrived in São Paulo, both the state and the city. I was planning, after I left Rio de Janeiro, to return to São Paulo for several reasons. Number one, it had over twenty million people and it was South America's biggest city. It was growing at a pace that was unprecedented anywhere; and as I arrived in the city, the first thing I noticed was huge high rises popping up in a helter skelter direction, with seemingly no conformity. If I had still been with John, we could have compared them to his cacti on the hillsides. These twenty to thirty stories high rises reminded me of some of the cactus plants in some of the hills in Argentina, growing where nature planted them. These manmade structures seemed to have sprouted out wherever concrete was poured.

The city was massive and did not impress me as a very pretty city, just a working city. I was glad that our destination pulled us through this direction because now I decided

Robert F. Edwards

not to bother returning back here. Just the congestion alone would be detrimental enough to seeing anything, as the bus struggled its way from one end of the city to the other. I recognized some of the retail outlets and dealerships, such as Mercedes Benz, and a big Coca-Cola distribution center.

The bus left the rolling hill terrain behind as it climbed up another range of mountains, a very picturesque country. I took a picture of an obelisk, marking the border between one province and another. By now, everyone on the bus was exhausted, and as each person found his or her way off, there were only a handful of us left to endure the ride right into Rio de Janeiro. Everybody was tired and fed up of traveling by the time we started coming in to Rio.

It was a large city and the route that we were coming in was detrimental to its blazing glory, as somewhat of a shantytown. The first real slum that I had seen was in São Paulo and much larger than this one. But both of these cities did have them and it was disturbing to me, to think of people living in this kind of squalor. Evelyn told me that the government did try to help these people but they seemed to always return to this lifestyle, and the crime level was very high.

Once we had worked our way further into the core of Rio de Janeiro, we got our first glimpse of one of the most famous of Rio's landmarks, Corcovado, the statue of Christ high up on the hill. This happened to be just above the hospital that Evelyn would be working in. Soon we got a view of the famous Sugar Loaf Mountain, and then crossed the Rio Niteroi, claimed to be the longest span bridge in the world without any towers above the deck. Towers were out of the question for this bridge, as it was located in the flight path of the city's airport, and would have obstructed it. The Santo Dumont Airport had been rebuilt recently, due to a tragic fire and was now an ultra modern, state-of-the-art facility, and artistically designed. The bus continued to wind its way through these passageways and before long, up popped the terminal.

Evelyn, my special little guardian angel was ready to help get me to the hotel. I had chosen one out of the "Lonely

114

SOUTH AMERICA EXPLORATION

Planet" book, the "Martinique" and it was only a block away from Copacabana, the famous beach. She made sure that the cab driver understood that if it was full, she suggested an alternative one. We agreed on the price to get there (ten dollars) and it was one heck of a long way from the terminal to the beach.

The beach area was very modern, with high rises, and resembled the West End in Vancouver, British Columbia with its beach lined with huge high rises and hotels to accommodate permanent residents as well as transients like myself. I got to the hotel and to my good fortune, yes, they would put me up. The room was adequate, not as nice as some of the previous ones, but it was in Rio, and one block away from the beach. It did have air conditioning, which I was breathing harder than it was pouring out cold air. However, they did have some hot water and the staff were extremely helpful and kind. Once I checked in, one added bonus point was that they had a safety deposit box. This made my day since I didn't have to worry about leaving the valuables in the room, or carrying them in my body belt and worrying about that.

Robert F. Edwards

With that out of the way, I quickly established where an Internet was within walking distance of the hotel. I sent an e-mail off, and came back with my shirt looking like I had taken another dip at the Falls. My clothes were weighing a ton by my own perspiration and of course, with the help of dirt.

I finally took that long awaited shave and shower and to my delight, there was hot water. The time was five o'clock, and I decided to rest for the better part of an hour. My next priority was nourishment, so I got myself some water, pop, a few buns, and some cheese, since my room was equipped with a little refrigerator. Yes, the peasant was alive and well, and I enjoyed this little snack immensely. I then decided that it was probably prudent to rest for the balance of the evening and book in for a tour tomorrow, which is going to be for nine hours.

I treated myself to a chocolate milkshake. Wow, how some things really do hit the spot! It was cold, wet and delicious. I walked around a bit on the beach before deciding to head on home and get a good night's rest. I asked the lady for a wake up call and to get my laundry cleaned. Boy, oh boy! A lot of work when you are the Lone Mohican, but everything was going well. I had a telephone message from Evelyn, and being such a conscientious person, I knew she would make a great doctor. Evelyn and her good friend were just checking if I was okay. Nothing like the next generation in the medical profession already looking after this old traveler. They were a wonderful couple and I do hope that both of them are able to come to Canada sometime, so I could return their hospitality and friendship.

It was not the most exciting or eventful day, but thinking of the vast distances that I had traveled in the last twenty-six hours, and then managed to secure a residence in Rio (the largest carnival city in the world) all in all it hadn't been a bad day.

Goodnight one and all. I love you dearly, Mrs. Edwards, my little treasure.

116

SOUTH AMERICA
EXPLORATION

February 20th, Tuesday
Rio de Janeiro, Brazil

I had a very restful sleep, even though the air-conditioning was only modest, at best. I seemed to have been perspiring heavily since I've started this journey. It was probably the humidity rather than the heat, or a combination of them, as I was perspiring a lot more than when I traveled through the great Sahara. Still, everything was very lush, and the heat was not preventing me from enjoying myself immensely. Rio de Janeiro, of the little bit that I had seen to date, was no-where near as threatening to me as my imagination was, as far as the crime wave or risk of being a "tourista."

Breakfast, which was included in the bill, was a great way to start the day. Pineapple, papaya, watermelon, cheeses, ham, a variety of buns, fresh orange juice and other beverages; but yes, real Brazilian coffee and not instant, add water and stir. It was the real ground, full-body coffee. For some inexplicable reason, instant coffee was the popular choice in South America. I was going to bring back some coffee beans, as it was a special treat that my wife looked forward to so much, if I could locate a store that sold the real thing.

By being here earlier than I anticipated, thank goodness, I had secured a really nice location. The room was quite large; it could accommodate three single beds in there. It was funny, the bathrooms were extremely small in these places, and the bidet was very important since every bathroom had one. Another difference in bathrooms, similar to Cuba and some of the other Caribbean countries I had visited, these regions' sanitary system was purely a sewage system. They don't break down their toilet papers, so they preferred it thrown in a waste paper basket rather than down the toilet.

Robert F. Edwards

I was glad that I had arranged to get my laundry done, since my new clothes had started to take on the wet look from my own perspiration. I suppose if I was really concerned about that, which I wasn't, I could have taken some salt pills.

I set off to explore the area around the Copacabana, which provided a lot of open-air cafés and the weather was inducive to that kind of lifestyle. I had been told by my little guide Evelyn, that it had been raining in Rio for the last week and graciously, the big guy upstairs had now blessed me with blue skies, warm weather, and gentle breezes. I had mixed feelings about staying here longer than I had planned, and taking part in the carnival, recognized as the "uno" or number one carnival in the world. On the other side of the coin, I could continue my accelerated expedition and work my way through the coast line and spend more time in Chile and the lake area, but I would have to abort the carnival. Ah, decisions, decisions, decisions. Always something to think about.

Our tour bus set off, and took us by some of the main sights, not to be missed in Rio. We passed by a colossal stadium, which I learnt was home to Brazil's soccer fans, and the World Cup Game in 1950 and where Pelé had played his last game to 200,000 crazed fans. The Maracanã stadium normally accommodates 100,000 and can be an exciting place at game time.

The city of Rio is built on some rugged terrain, with a lot of hills and tunnels. The natural barriers often reflect the separation of districts. As we went through Rio de Janeiro's Copacabana, the beach is approximately four or five kilometers long, of absolutely white sand. Besides being one of the world's most famous beaches, it was also one of the world's most densely populated residential areas. By going through a tunnel, we then passed just below the statue of the Redeemer, Cristo Redentor, which is situated on the mountain of Corcovado (Hunchback). These welcoming arms of Christ stand over 30 meters high, and this is on top of the mountain rising another 700 meters directly above the city. The residential area just below the statue of the Redeemer seems to have a lower

SOUTH AMERICA
EXPLORATION

standard of living, not a shantytown but the buildings were smaller and tiered down the mountain. Some of these 'favelas' were quite notorious in their own right, with drug trafficking, and not recommended to be on your own.

A small point of interest to me was posters I had seen throughout the streets of Che Guevara. I was first made aware of this revolutionary figure when I was in Cuba and his work with Fidel Castro. This man I learnt was originally an Argentinean doctor, and he left Cuba in 1965 for Bolivia. His claims that the Northern Hemisphere, in particular the U.S. and the Soviet, were exploiting the Southern Hemisphere have made him a popular cult figure throughout South America.

Rio has to be one of the more expensive areas to survive in, just like Vancouver, New York, London, or Paris. Of the three countries that I had visited up to date, Brazil was the most economical for a foreigner or a "tourista", provided you got down to where the locals shopped. I had just noticed a barbershop, and a haircut cost six Brazilian "quesentas" or about three dollars U.S., which was more than reasonable. One of the sad things that didn't enhance the beauty of this city was the graffiti. It was prevalent throughout the downtown areas, and these vandals had managed to excel my imagination on how they reached up into higher areas or underpasses.

We were entering the cathedral area and I took a few pictures for myself, even though this is often a feature of postcards. The Catedral Metropolitana was ultra-modern, a technology-aged pyramid, and I knew that inside I wouldn't find any frescoes of the Renaissance or the Baroque period. It appeared sparse compared to the conventional Roman Catholic Churches; perhaps it was a new wave of Catholicism's approach to a modern desire. It didn't reflect my views of a sanctuary, except for the stained glass windows that rise to the peak and at the very top was a skylight in the shape of a cross. Far below, some of the rays from Ra, the god of sun, pierced through upon the temple of the Roman Catholic altar sacrifice. Impressive in size, if not in architectural value.

Robert F. Edwards

Another building of interest was literally across the street. The Petrobras Building was an earthquake type structure where the base is a pedestal, and the higher floors extended out in a mushroom fashion. It had a sleek appearance with glossy black windows, and reminded me of one in Vancouver, very similar. I had taken a couple of pictures of this for no other reason than to compare apples to apples. The opera house, Teatro Municipal, was built in 1905 and ranked among the classics of those I had seen in Moscow and St. Petersburg.

The beaches of Ipanema were equally as nice in my eyes as Copacabana. I enjoyed looking at the inner harbor, with the dominant Sugar Loaf Hill as a backdrop, and lots of activity from small sailboats and powerboats. On top of Sugar Loaf, it was just beautiful. I got a panoramic view of the city, and the rock formations. These rock mountains divided the city and this explained the large tunnels that penetrated from one district to another. Any city that is faced with inlets or an irregular land mass has these problems to overcome. At home in Vancouver, we have a lot of inlets and the only way to get from one part to the other is on bridges; here it was tunnels, but the same congestion of traffic from one zone to another.

Remarkable, but the weather was awesome. Everybody in Hawaii would be envious of the temperature here. To my surprise, the beaches were sparsely occupied, but I was not sure when the tourist season was. Still, if you couldn't get foreigners to come during the greatest carnival on earth, then I don't know when you would attract them. It might be just too hot.

Just below Sugar Loaf Mountain was a military base and it looked well done housing-wise. Further past the high rises, I was attracted to the red tile roofs of the residential areas. At first glance, I felt I was somewhere in the Mediterranean rather than on the other side of the Atlantic. Sugar Loaf itself, by its shape, and the fact I had just met up with an Australian girl, reminded me of Ayers Rock in the Outback of Australia. They were both smooth inclines and you would need to be a good rock climber to scale these areas. I did manage to make it up Ayers Rock many years ago, but that was not going to be possible here due to my schedule. The area was heavily congested with traffic. Private cars and buses were allowed to stop at the base only momentarily, discharging passengers for the cable cars, which were the sole transportation up the mountain.

As I came off the Sugar Loaf, there was a young man at the bottom that was making videos and asked me if I wanted one, for twenty dollars U.S. I didn't think many people were giving him the thumbs up, so I said sure and I am glad I did since now I have my own private video. He spent a lot of time on it, and recorded some of my conversation also as there is always something that I have to say. Friends and foe alike know that I'm not short on words. We came across some cute little animals on the street, like a monkey or tamarin, begging for food from the many tourists. My private photographer told me that these 'coati' can be dangerous, although these ones seemed quite tame, and a few people were petting them. I understood that some Brazilians do train them to become little household pets.

Robert F. Edwards

I was impressed with this tour and I would strongly recommend to anybody on his or her first visit to Rio that they take a tour of this nature to get the overall perspective of the city. Once you see it from different altitudes, you get a good working idea of how the city is laid out and the best approach to see the specific things that you're interested in. I had asked around about the opera and so far, I hadn't any positive response on what was playing. Everybody was focused on the carnival. Carnival means "flesh feast" and this special event, in religious terms, was the feast of the flesh before Lent. Even when I was a boy, the Roman Catholic Church followers did fasting and abstinence forty days before Easter or the Resurrection of Christ. So, this particular celebration is to get all badness in before you have to sacrifice and abstain from the things that you enjoy the most. This carnival has a reputation for a lot of abuses including alcohol, drugs, and sex, just to mention a few of the ones that attach the most interest to even the pious that would condemn it but still would want to know what transpired.

I was now heading towards another part of Rio where I would be having lunch. In countries that have hot climates, they often use corrugated or metal folding shutters that cover the windows. To keep the interiors cool, they roll them down, just the reverse of Canada, where we want to reduce heat consumption rather than retain it. I have always felt this more amiable and far more economical than air-conditioning.

As I was cruising around the streets of Rio, I noticed the cabs are yellow with a blue stripe down them; not the famous yellow checkered cabs of New York, but this color must be something associated with taxis because more times than not, I have seen cabs as yellow and here is no exception. As with the Big Apple. I think that Rio de Janeiro locals have another thing in common with New Yorkers. Not only is their population quite large, but also I found them always referring to how dangerous it was. I am sure both cities have records and statistics to prove that the advice they were giving was both true and accurate, but I've been to New York and it's one of the

SOUTH AMERICA
EXPLORATION

great cities of the world and I never miss an opportunity to go there or I never get less of a high when I'm there. Rio was giving me a similar feeling. It was a very vibrant city and diversified enough with a collage of events taking place.

I noticed that even the apartment block frontages had gates and iron walls; the stories that go without saying at night, these metal corrugated doors lock down. There could be an infinite amount of reasons that the protection is required. I know in my own city, Vancouver that we have to use a lot more security systems than in previous decades. It's the times we live in. The police here are said to accept bribes and have some methods that have been so affiliated with Mexican security. I had not been here long enough to judge, and I had nothing but admiration for the people and the forces that control their lives as well as foreigners.

By midday I was back at the Copacabana beach area, which was now dotted with all forms of little umbrellas. Palm trees are gracing the boulevard as well as the beach. Oh, just the tropical paradise with vice and danger lurking at every corner. Locals said that the "tourista" would be accosted or maybe victimized, but this traveler was just enjoying himself. The Great Redeemer's hands were extended and I felt very welcome and was enjoying this opportunity to be in this city.

We stopped for lunch at a very nice restaurant with a buffet style. I have always been amazed in a lot of cities, these exquisite places are just behind a door and unless you were familiar with them, you would never guess what was inside. This was no exception to that rule. The smorgasbord was just amazing. It was such a wide range of food, anything from the conventional potato salad, and everything that you would find in a North American smorgasbord or salad bar; but also sushi with ginger and wasabi mustard. They had a lot of their own local dishes, including the artichoke, which was very popular down here. Just a real large quantity and variety of dishes to choose from. There was no conceivable way that even with a spoonful of each variety available I could have gotten it all on one plate.

Robert F. Edwards

I was sitting with some Norwegian military personnel serving duty in one of the other South American countries. The oldest gentleman in the group was more of a soldier of fortune rather than a regular, but the young lady and two other young men were in the regular Norwegian army and involved in a peacekeeping duty.

There is quite a difference between a barbecue Brazilian style versus American. After being served some of their barbecued meat, I have to agree whole-heartedly that the barbecue as we know is both primitive and barbaric. They put their meat on rotisseries and with a very sharp knife; they trim it off just like a donair, Greek style. I had a variety of ham, pork, beef, chicken, some kind of sausage, and was so full that there was no conceivable way that I could possibly accept any more of the endless servings. So, I had to start waving my hand and saying "no." The desert was ice cream, exceptionally creamy and more like what I had when I was a boy. You can't get this real ice cream in North America, no matter what the price you're willing to pay.

Once our meal was concluded, the guide asked us if we were all ready to participate in going to the statue of the Redeemer. For this portion of the trip, we took a train up through the rainforest, now a national park, the Parque Nacional da Tijuca. An early governor of Brazil saw the destruction of the jungle for wood products and was concerned enough about it to get his patriots and supporters to start a very ambitious program of reforestation. This may have been the first reforestation effort in the Americas; and was a first class job.

Once we got off the train, we then took a mini bus up to one of the falls. I have to commend these forefathers for their tremendous amount of foresight to preserve this exquisite portion of nature centered in the heart of a major metropolis, and the commitment and effort of the many laborers that put this forest back into its pristine condition. There were many beautiful falls here, including the 35-meter Cascatinha Taunay. There was a map done in marble chips showing all the treks or roads that you could take for hiking throughout this area. I asked the guide and she said the total amount of trails amount to eighty kilometers; more than a day's hike through these beautiful woods.

We returned back to the train to complete our second phase of the journey up to the Redeemer. I was told that two weeks ago, the train was attacked by a "bandito", who shot at the train and some tourists, so they had closed it down temporarily. It was a very steep climb up the mountain called "Corcovado," meaning hunchback. The mountain itself is seven hundred meters and "Cristo Redentor," meaning Christ the Redeemer is the statue at the peak. This well-known landmark is a statue of Jesus Christ with his arms stretched out. This monument was originally meant to celebrate Brazil's independence from Portugal. It's thirty meters high and the statue itself weighs over a hundred tons. The French sculptor Paul Landowski completed it in 1931, after the Vatican assisted with the financing.

This was a popular spot for tourists, and I met some people from Detroit, and finally one Canadian from Windsor. These fellows were all traveling in a pack and enjoying the Brazilian lifestyle. I also met a group of Scandinavian people and one charming young lady who was actually a Brazilian. They were only too willing to talk to me and gave me the best possible information. I spent some time talking to them about the Carnival to get a bit more insight. Many Brazilians were very dedicated to this event, and spent much of the year creating the most elaborate costumes. There is tremendous competi-

Robert F. Edwards

tion in the parades, and it was more than just a one-day event. Outside of Rio de Janeiro, the next big parade was in Los Salvador, more of the traditional style where everything was free with lots of dancing in the streets. However, a lot of Brazilians headed up for this parade in Rio and a long weekend of activities, one big blow out before they started repenting. I was still wavering back and forth whether to stay or go.

My young photographer was still following me around videotaping, but not as actively in the afternoon, so I was not getting the commentary on the back half of this trip as I did in the first half. I was not too distraught by it, and the tour guide we had now was a local resident and a better guide than the first one. She was more informative and I guess more interested in her job would be the bottom line.

On the way up on the train, a girl came and took snapshots of all of us. Now as we were coming down waiting for the train, sure enough, my face and everybody else's on the train, was featured individually on a plaque, if you want to purchase. I had enough people taking pictures of yours truly with his own camera and with the video, so didn't think that I needed to overexpose myself on a plate.

We made our way down the mountain, and into an area that was probably the most expensive area of Rio de Janeiro. "Ipanema" is an Indian word meaning dangerous or bad waters; the waves could be large with strong undertows. However, where I was standing it was not a problem, just wall-to-wall high rises. The tour guide said a two-bedroom apartment could range anywhere from about two hundred and fifty thousand right up to a million dollars U.S. There are some pretty deep pockets in this area; but like so many large cities, you walk a few blocks away and all of a sudden, you're into a very low area. The contrast is very significant.

The structure and the construction are similar to other places that use extensive amounts of cement and bricks as their main building material. Posts are built with rebar and then these support forms are enclosed stone or, in this case, it was a red corrugated brick. If the money still holds out, they would coat it with some kind of masonry stucco on the outside and paint it mostly white, with these red roofs. The entire appearance looked very Mediterranean. However, this particular one looked like it was in great need of repair, but ironically I think the poor had a better view of the inlet.

I took a few pictures of the hang gliders, swooping down from a very high altitude and if they've done it right, landing on the beach where I was standing. Also popular here were the coconuts. They were green; not like the ones that you get in Canada, old and brown with just the outer shell and a bit of meat in there. These were mostly liquid and there was very little meat in the husk part of the coconut. They chopped the tops off, a refreshing drink of coconut milk, for about a dollar fifty U.S.

The tour was now concluded, and for seventy dollars, a little overpriced but as one of the military said, it's only money and meant to be spent. So, I spent my money and was now start-ing to head back towards the hotel. Putting things in perspec-tive, with the meal and being taken to the most strategic places, I wouldn't do it twice, but it satisfied my needs and wants. Rio was just one of those places where some things were very expensive and others were very economical. Like every city, if you dance to the music of a tourist, you pay the price that is expected of you. If you start to dance to the mu-sic of a local, you can be there forever.

By the time I was dropped off at the hotel, I was feeling the heat. Like this morning, my shirt felt like I had put it in the shower. I decided that it was about time to yield to the ele-ments and save my clothes from rotting to death with my own perspiration. I also thought of trying to find a place where I could get a couple of cheap tank tops. With that in mind, I was back on the streets again. I found that I was able to get around easily; and somewhat spoiled that these people didn't speak a great deal of English but on the other hand, between the two of us, we were getting a common denominator to communicate relatively well.

Robert F. Edwards

The first place I found was more like a souvenir shop and yes, they had one type of tank. It was four dollars and fifty cents U.S. I went to another shop that had, oh yes, good old Calvin Klein. It was sixteen dollars U.S. Then, I went to a discount store and lo and behold, I managed to get two of them for four-fifty. It just went to show, if I shopped around a bit, I would find what I was seeking.

With the glow of success, I returned to my room for either my second or third shower of that day, and put on my new tank top. It was about seven o'clock, and what a difference! The weather was so much cooler and the heat of the day's sun had finally subsided. I was also in proper attire, short pants, a new tank top and a pair of sandals. I felt not only more like a local, but a heck of a lot cooler.

I started walking down the main boulevard by the beach and it was a pleasant evening to be outside. It was starting to make a lot of sense to have mid-day breaks in this part of the world, and then in the evenings, the people could stay up extremely late since they had rested in the afternoon. I thought the evenings were the most pleasant part of the day, and could understand why people stayed up as late as they did.

Walking by my favourite fast-food place, I was trying hard not to go in for a milkshake, but they were just so good the night before, my resistance was short-lived and I succumbed to French fries and a chocolate milkshake. I asked myself "Why go to a remote place so I could have almost the same things as I got at home?" However, with all due respect, I couldn't get ice cream or a milkshake like they have here.

With that urge satisfied, I started to work my way up the opposite direction that I'd walked the previous night. What I was hoping to find were these clubs that have bands, "bandas." These clubs were said to be good photo opportunities for seeing the "samba" which was their forté. I had walked to the end of the strip, and the hotel that I ended up at was "Sofitel" where I met a charming young lady from Thailand.

We talked a bit more about the carnival and different parades. It was such a big event for the local people (and obviously us globetrotters) that rich and poor found their way to Rio during the festival. However, a lot of Brazilians also went to Salvador, where it was free with more of the traditional street dancing. The northern part of Brazil has a higher blend of ethnic population and culture with the Negroes, Indians, and Portuguese. In the south, it became more European influenced, and this event was not quite as dominant in their lives. Not to say it was pagan or decadent, but probably like some of the rituals and beliefs of the Caribbean, Brazil has these blended into their culture because of the African influence. On the northern shorelines I recognized a lot of superstitions that originated in Africa and have their own connections with voodoo. It was one continent's contribution to another one's present day beliefs; and the carnival had some of these elements blended in. The young lady gave me a bit more information but did not know what streets were going to be designated for the festivals. Nobody seemed to be too sure of where; but around five or six o'clock in the evenings they would start and then go right through the night.

Not being successful in completing my quest, I started heading back down the other way where there was more activity, with restaurants and the gathering of tourists and peddlers. A lot of the kiosks were nothing more than somebody's blanket thrown out with their wares of homemade jewelry, some masks, and leather goods. Also, I noticed some marijuana smoke pipes with uniquely shaped faces or figurines sculpted from some kind of clay. I had gone by half a dozen of these before I saw some that were standing straight up, carved with their own base. For five dollars U.S., I thought it to be a novelty piece that I couldn't neglect to purchase, so my money left my hand and this stand-up 'toke pipe' became mine. Somehow working around the language barrier, I asked the peddler what the price of marijuana was down here. It was about twenty-five dollars (I think for three days supply). Some of the people I know, they might last for three days, and for others it might last for three weeks. It really would depend on your habit.

Robert F. Edwards

In my mind, the great amount of crime said to be taking place was highly overrated, at least at that moment. I was either very fortunate or I was walking through the valley of death and feared no evil. It was just a beautiful evening to be outside and I continued looking at some of the events that were taking place. One of the things that was very predominant was the amount of dogs. A lot of people actually had two. I had even seen three dogs being walked by one person and no, they were not dog sitters, they were just dog lovers. The predominant species down here seemed to be the poodle; not my favourite dog but one that these local people enjoyed.

My attention was drawn to the young children that were panhandling or selling anything from chocolate bars to chewing gum, anything to put a few dollars between them and another night on the streets. It was not so much begging, but actually marketing anything that you can change an item into dollars. More and more of the entrepreneurs were starting to display their wares, from the trunks of their cars, anything from long-haired wigs with baseball caps sewn on top, to masks. The mood was starting to build for the events of the weekend.

As I walked along, I happened to see an absolutely breathtaking costume. It was very exposed where you would like to see skin, and the areas that have been forbidden to the eye were just barely covered. The detail of feathers, fabric and jewelry that was worked into this costume was fantastic. The legs and the arms probably had more cloth than the genital area and the breasts, and the design was mesmerizing. I got talking to the owner of this costume that she would be wearing in the parade, and got a bit more information from her. These people put a lot of effort into it, and have to pay to be in the parade. I was not sure how the judging goes, but it was a real keen competition. They would start in the first parade around five p.m., which would last until nine-thirty in the morning, then go home and sleep. Then, they would take part in all the other parades for the next three days as a spectator to compare where they might stand.

SOUTH AMERICA
EXPLORATION

Getting back to the girl and her outfit, she was gorgeous, with long black hair and just a beautiful face. Her body would do the outfit justice. She showed me the headpiece, the grand finale of this particular costume. It was half a meter high and it had white feathers and jewelry, just breathtaking. I said to her that she would either be a princess or a goddess in this outfit. Between her God-given beauty and the creation of this particular costume, it was an inspiration to want to see at least one of these parades.

I started heading back towards the hotel to call it a day, at about eleven o'clock. An Australian woman who had been listening made a few comments to me about the outfit and we decided to go and have a beer. She was about in her mid-thirties. There seemed to be a general trend that I noticed of people about thirty who just quit their jobs, either sell all their belongings or put them in storage, and take a long extended holiday that either lasted until the money runs out or until they wear out. This particular lady was following that general description, and said that she was a doctor. She might have been. I guess she just got fed up with people and the profession in general, or the conditions in Melbourne and hit the open trail. She planned to spend the better part of the year down here. Rather a different person then I had talked to as of late; and after we had a beer and made a bit more small talk, she claimed to be all out for a party and may the good times roll. Her costume was going to consist of a g-string and a couple of discs over her nipples and a paint job. This confirmed what a lot of the costumes were; 'skin is in' for not just locals but foreigners alike. Rather than spend literally hundreds of dollars on a costume, they were quite prepared to paint their body and show as much as they could.

By now, the great big hand on my watch had managed to say "thirty" and the little one said "eleven", so I kissed her goodnight and made my way back to the hotel and my room. I had pretty well made the commitment that I was going to try to stay. The biggest single factor was if I could get accommodations to stay in this rock 'n rolling place.

131

Robert F. Edwards

Goodnight, my little treasure bee. I love you very much and miss you dearly. This is one place that I think you and Wendy and Cole man probably would enjoy. It is pretty darn nice and it's cheaper than a "Y". Goodnight, my sweetheart.

SOUTH AMERICA
EXPLORATION

February 21st, Wednesday
Rio de Janeiro, Brazil

After doing what I always did (my toiletries), I went down for breakfast, as it was included in this bed and breakfast. Pretty well the same as yesterday, except the food array was a little different. I enjoyed a good breakfast and started planning the itinerary. Some days were working days and organizing days and when I had asked the lady at the front desk to have the maid do my laundry, there was a breakdown of communication. So, today I asked and the man at the front desk told me that there is a laundry facility about two or three blocks away. With that as a priority as well as getting to an Internet, I started getting my day organized.

In Rio de Janeiro and probably throughout South America, the day started around ten o'clock before things started opening up. One of the tank tops that I bought was too small, so I was going to take it back and exchange it. With all these little things to do, off I went. First of all, I did find the laundromat and they said that they would have the laundry back or finished by six o'clock, which would be great if I had to leave tomorrow. Next, I jogged off to the Internet and fortunately, I found a barbershop. I was long overdue for a haircut, so I went in. One of those remarkable things; I actually got a much better haircut from a man that cannot speak my language; I cannot speak his, only a bit of hand gestures for an excellent haircut.

With that behind me, off to the Internet; a couple of e-mails from my loved ones and got caught up on the news events of the day. While I was away, the stock market in North America was taking it right on the chin and going down for the count were the technical stocks. I didn't want to think about my particular portfolio.

133

Robert F. Edwards

I then got my tank top exchanged. Easy. Sometimes countries that are highly developed also are highly irritating. I just went in and made a couple of gestures and showed the two garments and with a nod, it was like "fine, here's yours, here's mine, and is there anything else?" I didn't have to produce bills. I didn't have to go into a long repertoire of why I made a mistake in the first place.

With all these errands completed in record time, I found it was the witching hour of high noon. I am ashamed to say that I returned to my hangout and had a hamburger and French fries. This afternoon, I decided to start looking around the shops for anything unique that I might have missed. As I went through the downtown core of Copacabana, the shops were small and there didn't seem to be any rhyme or reason, a small shop with motor parts would be next to a pastry shop.

I have enjoyed the weather, although it was really hot. Even the local people were complaining about how hot it was. So, I didn't feel too bad that I was perspiring so much, as I had been told by more than one of them that the week before, it was raining. So, when I looked at it, I was very fortunate.

My biggest quest was to find some coffee. Brazil was supposed to be one of the world's highest producing countries and what was so baffling was that they drink instant coffee. Although I have to say that the coffee that I was getting at the hotel and that restaurant the other day was certainly ground coffee, very strong and delicious. However, when I went to the grocery stores, instant coffee was the order of the day. After checking with half a dozen of them, the response was basically the same: instant, instant, instant! Even when I had approached the clerks with a bean to compare what I wanted, they understood what I wanted but "no benito." Before my long journey through Brazil ends, I was determined to find coffee for my little honey bun.

I returned to the hotel to clean up a bit. By now it was one o'clock in the afternoon and like all beach bums, I thought I would head down to the beach and check out the sands. The beaches were really beautiful; there was lots of activity going on; and yes, some of the most skimpiest bikinis, real "teeny weeny, itsy bitsy" ones I had ever seen. The Brazilians took a lot of pride in body appearances. Even the men were sporting some pretty awesome shapes and they sure believed in "skin is beautiful."

As in many other countries, including Hawaii and Mexico, there was a constant barrage of people trying to sell things on the beach and it has become an irritant in many parts of the world. Often there are "private beaches"; just so these people cannot enter. Here, it was like a dance taking place. Most of them were men, but there were some women and children. They were polite and not obnoxious, but there was a constant flow of activity that continually weaved its way in and out. Anything from soft drinks to clothes to jewelry, and it goes on and on; each person had his own salesmanship. There were lots of the big beach umbrellas available and the vendors also were selling these long pieces of cloth (sarongs) that women wrap themselves in to cover themselves up from the sun. Suntan lotion unlimited. There were fellows walking around with sunglasses merchandised on huge Styrofoam slabs, all sticking out, in an array of styles. It was quite entertaining to watch these people, let alone be a spectator of the events like the sand sports – volleyball and other activities.

There was a real working ambience that at first I didn't realize, and everything was quite coordinated. Simply walking on the beach, and it was instantly, they would have said something and chairs were being dragged on the sand, umbrellas brought in, and you knew instructions were being given. Before long, through this maze of human beings lying in a hodge podge manner, pieces of furniture were being manoeuvered into the place they were heading for.

I went to one of the small booths for a pop. I found people friendly here, and the locals had a very carefree attitude. I started talking to a couple of North Americans and an older lady. The older lady invited me to sit down. Her English was limited, but enough for me. I assumed she was retired, as she was my age or around there. She told me a little bit more

Robert F. Edwards

about the carnivals. Also, I noticed that they had tourist police, strictly set up for us visitors, and if I had any questions, complaints, or any bad experiences, these were the boys to talk to.

Pamela and I decided to have supper together and agreed to meet around eight o'clock and I returned to my hotel at about five-thirty. I had to find out whether I could stay in the hotel or not, and I decided that I would like to try to stay for at least Saturday, to be able to take one night of the parade in. With that in mind, I went to the front desk and explained the situation. The fellow said yes, he could do it, and then added, "Well, it's carnival night on Friday, so now you gotta pay double." This was common, not only do hotels charge double; restaurants, taxis, anything that provided a service related to the event. Prices skyrocketed and no one was exempted, whether Brazilian or from another country.

I did a bit more wandering around, and it was surprising that around seven, it started to get dark. This was natural as it was so close to the equator and the days are more evenly spent. Also, the thing that I found so pleasant was the evening breeze coming off the ocean, which was a great bonus for this climate.

Pamela and I headed off to a restaurant, and we sat outside to enjoy the evening. I ordered an array of fruit, and different types of cheeses. It was such a delightful change from so many other countries that I had been in, where you had to be extremely careful about what you were eating or drinking (otherwise, "Montezuma's revenge"); this was the third country of South America that I had been in and the food was just delicious. Each one had its own special meals and dishes, but it was the absence of bad food that added a tremendous experience for me. After we finished our meal, I wished Pamela the best and said goodnight.

The night quickly drifted along. It was soon eleven-thirty so I went back to the hotel, and checked with the lady at the front desk that always seemed to be able to do things rather than just sweep them in. I explained the situation to her, because if I were to leave tomorrow, I would have to get myself organized immediately. However, she said yes, she could do it and I would have to pay double, but with that confirmed, my mind was at ease.

With that out of my way, I hoped that I would get to see the carnival and some of the parade, for one day at least. So, off to bed and another couple of nights would be spent in Rio.

Goodnight, my little treasure bee. I miss you dearly. One night in Rio and another night closer to you.

Robert F. Edwards

February 22nd, Thursday
Rio de Janeiro, Brazil

I don't know whether I got too much sun yesterday, or whether I was getting the "laid back" attitude of the locals. It was closer to nine o'clock before I made much of an attempt to think about what I would do that day. As always, my first priority was to get down to the Internet and let Marietta know that I was going to be staying here for a while.

In order to stay the extra nights, my agreement with the hotel was to change rooms. It seemed like a big job to go from the first floor to the fifth floor and my new smaller room. I seemed to have just as much trouble packing to go five floors up, than I did to pack to go to another country. Boy, was I ever getting laid back, to say the least.

I managed to get everything into my smaller room, which wasn't that bad. The beds were all the same size, sort of glorified cots. The only thing that this room didn't have that I really had grown to like was the little fridge for keeping my drinks cold.

It was almost eleven-thirty before I started to think, "What am I going to do today?" There was some déjà vu of when Marietta and I were on holidays in Hawaii many years ago, and the days seemed to consist of doing very little. Off to the beach!

I got a chair and an umbrella for ten quesentas and became a beach bum like the rest of them. I was actually sporting a new shade of red, which, in my case, would eventually change itself into brown, I hoped, without peeling. It was just another beautiful day in paradise in Rio. I was watching the little cable cars go back and forth up Sugar Loaf Mountain, and thinking, "Yes, I was on those the day before." I was enjoying this lazy attitude when a young lady put her chair down

138

within range of mine. Her name was Denise, and she spoke English and did property management in Rio. She also tried to get me motivated in some multi-level marketing of health products. I told her that I was definitely not interested in that, in any shape or form, in any country, but she was still a very pleasant person to talk to.

As I was turning from different shades of white to pink and then red, I commented that I would like to go to the theater, or a play or an opera, and she asked, "Where are you staying? I'll check it out and phone you; and if you're not at the hotel, I'll leave a message, then I'll phone back and make sure you got the message." So I said, "That sounds like a great idea," and left it at that.

Back at the hotel, it was quite nice to get into my room where the air-conditioning had brought it down to a very pleasant temperature; not cold, but pleasant. I could understand why these people had an afternoon "siesta" and I was quickly falling into their lifestyle. Stay up late, get up relatively early, and then take the afternoon and rest. Not a bad way to live, actually.

I had spent considerable time reading my "The Lonely Planet" and deciding on my next port of call, which was going to be Porto Alegre. It was the capital of Rio Grande do Sul, and the sixth biggest city in Brazil. For this journey, I would be passing the first really big lake going towards Uruguay and it would be about thirty hours on the bus just to get to that particular leg of my journey.

I tried to express what I wanted to someone at the front desk, and to my good fortune, the lady that was the most proficient that I had encountered at this hotel was on duty. She tried to phone three or four different places for the bus terminal. The main reason I didn't want to make the trip down there was it would cost me twenty U.S. dollars, so if I didn't have to pay that (forty quesentas), it was something I'd rather not do if a phone call could suffice. With the bus or the metro, I was not quite confident that I would know how to do that.

Robert F. Edwards

Under the most ideal conditions, I had taken a taxi to a museum and I never did get there, it cost nearly thirty quesentas; and the distance didn't seem to be as great. I didn't have my little friend Evelyn, the doctor, to negotiate the price for me. My helpful desk clerk kept on trying and even though she spoke Portuguese, she was having a terrible time with getting the run-around and being put on hold.

As I was waiting I got into conversation with a woman, Grace, a legal secretary. She was also waiting for a gentleman coming off the beach. His name was Dave, an American from New York. Grace's English was very good and she was telling me about her twelve-year-old son. Four years ago, her husband passed away. He was Polish, and at the age of fifty-six had lung cancer. She also told me that David's wife passed away. She was Brazilian, and that was what brought him down here, to spread her ashes. Here were two people from different parts of the world who had lost their loved ones. It made me realize what a wonderful and rewarding life I was having; and my wife, my daughter, and my grandson, whom I am always grateful for.

I guess it was the lack of pressure down here, but the day moved very quickly onward. To my surprise, it was seven o'clock and the poor lady at the front desk still hadn't any success with my bus ticket or information. No closer to success, I decided to go for dinner with Dave and Grace, at the other end of the strip. We had a delightful meal, I ordered some form of fried fish cut into little cubes and then deep-fried. I did notice one thing about this country, boy, do these people like fried food! They also had tartar sauce, and oil flavoured with hot peppers. The meal was delicious and the quantity very remarkable. Across from us, I noticed some of the other dishes, a chicken with garlic for just two people and it looked like they had about six chicken pieces. We finished off with a German black forest cake, again, exceptionally good.

We then took a leisurely stroll. Grace said that on this particular boulevard between the traffic, every Thursday, Friday and Saturday, they would have little kiosks to show their

140

goods. It seemed a lot of work to me, as these people would start at four o'clock in the afternoon to build their tents, put up their displays of novelties and jewelry and then have to tear it all down by one o'clock in the morning.

I enjoyed listening to the interchange of conversation between Dave who was been here more than once, and Grace, who has lived here all her life. Dave was a typical American and even more, a typical New Yorker with the hustle and bustle. He saw it one way and of course Grace saw it the Brazilian way. As an example – he was supposed to stay one day at her place and then three or four days with another friend. Anyway, that friend, for want of a better word, reneged on it and he just asked Grace if he could spend five days at her house. She replied, "Five days?" and I knew this had taken her by surprise and she thought he was joking at first. Then she asked, "You're really not joking?" he said, "No, no," and then explained the problem. She responded, "Yes, it's no problem." Just the openness of spirit that these people have and their easygoing way of taking one obstacle as it comes along; whereas Americans seem to put a lot of unnecessary pressure on themselves and don't get any further. Dave explained that Brazilians just lived for today, they didn't really have any plans for tomorrow and they don't save; they just enjoyed life at the moment, which he didn't favour.

Grace was saying, "Oh someday, I hope to come to Canada and work," and they have a lot of dreams, but I think it was just the giving spirit that puts them sometimes in adversity. For instance, on Friday, when the holiday starts, she had a few things to do for about half a day's work. Her boss said, "Well, you don't have to"; but she said, "No, I want to get it finished"; and the first thing Dave said was, "Well, you gonna get double time". She said, "No, no, I'm not even getting paid for it." That was exactly the opposite to our way of thinking in North America.

We spent some time wandering through the kiosks, and I had gone through half a dozen before I realized I had lost them, so I returned to the hotel but still no word on the bus situation. Just as I got to my room the phone rang, and it was Denise. She said, "Look, I'm really sorry I didn't phone you sooner. Sorry if I disturbed you." And I said, "Well, I'm just getting ready to go to bed." She said, "Well, I've found out that now because of the carnival, the two big theaters here don't have any performances until after the carnival." We talked a bit more and she said, "Well, I'm gonna be meeting one of my friends and then go look at some of these kiosks. Would you like to come?" So I said, "Sure, I'll come. Why not?" So, off I go again to meet up with her.

This time I saw an interesting collection of items that fascinated me; one thing in particular was the preserved piranhas. Because of the interwoven mixture of cultures in Brazil, the local Indians, the Portuguese, and the slaves that came from Africa, and the voodooism and other religions, some of these kiosks had displays of incredible masks, either gory, or diabolical. With the help of Denise, she explained that they were to ward off evil spells, but there was an undertone of voodooism that prevailed.

There was lots of jewelry; and an abundance of different types of gems. They also did tremendous work in carving of stone. I would have liked to bring back something of this nature, but putting stones in my backpack to carry, weight was a big deterrent.

It was getting close to twelve-thirty, and I decided to have a quick drink, and Denise ordered a fish dish that was very popular in Brazil. I had been told by Grace that they usually served it more in the cold periods. When the weather was cooler, they had hot food; when the weather was hot, they had cold food. Anyway, this particular restaurant had it; a flat fish, quite big, at least a foot long and maybe six inches wide. Creamy mashed potatoes were the side dish; with a Creole sauce of shrimps on top of this fish. I think I'd move to South America just for the food alone.

The world of Rio de Janeiro was starting to close up, and it was close to two o'clock in the morning, so we said goodnight to each other and I returned back to the hotel room.   That concludes another day in my life in Rio de Janeiro.

Goodnight, my beautiful wife. I love you dearly, I miss you a lot, and I wish you were with me here. It's so different being in a place like this than being where I'm usually traveling in No Man's Land. I love you, darling.

Robert F. Edwards

Well, I did something different this morning. I got up feeling fantastic and thought, "It's fairly early. I will do a little bit of catching up with the events of the last few days before forgetting about the last couple of days." It was hard to do down here, I must admit, with the weather being in the mid-eighties and even the Rio people saying, "It's too hot." It made me feel a bit better when I saw them perspiring, I realized I was not quite the northern iceberg melting before their eyes. I got caught up on some of the events of the previous day before I did my toiletries. After completing that, I was just going down for breakfast, when the phone rang.

I was thinking, "My goodness, I am getting as many phone calls here as I do at home." I really thought it would be Evelyn again, just to make sure I was departing okay; but no, it was Denise. She said, "What are you doing today?" I said, "Well, I don't really have a lot of plans." She said, "I have to work, but if you would like to go to the beach, I have to give this presentation on this multi-marketing, and it's a very nice beach. It's a different place from Copacabana, and it's up to you." So, I said, "Yeah, if you don't mind me tagging along." And she said, "After, if you want, I'll even show you some of the other places in Rio, the museum and things like that." So, I said, "Well, all I can say is 'Gracias, señorita'."

She showed up around nine o'clock and we had a quick breakfast. She was really into this multi-media marketing and as soon I mentioned that my daughter was working and was a single parent, I might as well have signed her on; signed, sealed and delivered. Denise hadn't stopped talking about how this whole thing answered her prayers, and would for anybody else who took part in it. She was quite the little

144

dynamo! In a lot of ways, she reminded me of my daughter Wendy, hard-working, focused, a determined money attitude, you would think they came out of the same DNA batch.

She also had an old Volkswagen, which brought back a lot of fond memories of when I had one; it was twenty years older but still ran well. She even spoke four languages, Portuguese, Spanish, English, and German (that I was aware of). Denise kindly helped me exchange my money at a better rate. Not a great rate, but with such fluctuation in the marketplace, it was an art all in itself. To exchange with the moneychangers, as an example, a hundred dollars U.S. would get a hundred and eighty real (Brazilian currency). To change at the hotels or at most restaurants, was at par or two-to-one (a hundred dollars U.S. was two hundred real.) But in the black market and some other places, I could get as much as a ten or fifteen percent bonus; so, if I traded in a hundred U.S. dollars, this meant two hundred and ten, maybe even two hundred and fifteen real. Quite a spread in my spending power with this exchange rate.

Denise just happened to be one of those people that if she didn't know it, she would find out; and with her help I got two hundred and ten real for the hundred dollars. She also told me that she had a two-bedroom apartment, and rented the room out. She said she'd rent me one of the small beds, for twenty U.S. dollars, if I wanted to stay; and she would get me black market tickets to the actual carnival. She just knew exactly what to do and how to handle herself.

Everybody, including Denise, had been talking about the carnival as the greatest event of the year, even surpassing Christmas, so I was starting to lean towards shortening my trip in other places or bypass them altogether to spend more time experiencing this event. The momentum was building, and accelerating almost hourly as more and more people arrived. At the hotel, there was a constant flow of check-ins. There were so many activities going, and she said, "If you want to, you can come to a club with me tonight that's especially dedicated to a Brazilian soccer team; and the outfit you have to wear is preferably black and red, which are their colors. It is a big party."

In the last two days, I had learnt more about Rio de Janeiro and some of their lifestyles than compared to anything that I had spent on the seventy-dollar U.S. tour. Sometimes it is best to take a bit of a chance and get away from what the tourist sees and the chances are that if you made a good judgment call, it will excel the benefits of the tour groups with their safety in numbers.

I was just going to see how the day worked out and take one step at a time. So, off we went, and the first step, yes, guess where? The multi-level marketing place where Denise bought some few supplies and introduced me to the organization and said, "Well, maybe tomorrow we can go and listen to it and if you have any questions, they will have the answers. I again told Denise that I was not interested. I would have to see how the day progressed whether I would rent the bed off her in her apartment.

With that behind us, we got back in her Volkswagen that has such fond memories of my past and headed throughout the city. I was beginning to identify some of the familiar landmarks that you've chosen to identify with; and that's no exception to myself. Tunnels connect much of the city, and as we passed through one after another, I recognized some of the places from the tour yesterday.

The favelas are often pictured on postcards; these homes tiered up the mountainside. Denise told me that the original people that built those houses didn't have to pay for the land and this made it very reasonable to build there. Now, there is a different system in place but because it was built during that period, it was more of a slum area. Ironically, not too far away is where some of the more chic and expensive places to live were. Rocinha was Brazil's largest favela with a population of up to 300,000 situated in Gávea, one of Rio's richest neighbourhoods.

As we drove throughout the city, I could well understand how the population of nine or ten million people fit in, as it was predominately high-rises, most twenty to thirty stories high. We then started to weave our way towards the coastline, and Denise pointed out an inlet where the rich had built their large homes and could pull their expensive boats up along-side. It was a beautiful spot, and the water was very calm but Denise said that you couldn't go swimming there anymore and there where no fish there. It was because of a common global problem – pollution. So, even the rich were suffering from the lack of people's concern over their environment.

We started to head out of town on a coastal route. It was very picturesque and I could see little islands that were dotted throughout this coastline of Rio de Janeiro. There were many islands, more than I could count; some of them were nothing more than big rocks. Other than birds, there was not much on them. However, the water in this part was so much cleaner and turquoise as it hit the shoreline.

We passed by many little wooden stores and these family operations provided everything from fuel, to meals, to chairs, anything these creative people could think of to provide a liv-ing for themselves. On the other side of the road, she told me was a reservation; an area the government wouldn't allow any building on or anything to obstruct the view of the ocean. There were many of these little operations in existence, and I understood it was on a cue system of who are number one, number two and so forth. We went as far as ninety-two and that wasn't the end. They were about a kilometer apart and I was not sure who collected the revenue, whether it was the government or some institution, for controlling that portion of the beach for operations and services.

Once we arrived at our destination, I was quite amazed at how organized Denise was. She lifted a bundle out of her Volkswagen and sure enough, she had her own umbrella and lounge chair, and she got me all set up. I couldn't help but compare her with my daughter, Wendy. They both seemed to be very organized and I don't know if they ever did meet, whether they would irritate each other, or whether they'd be inseparable twins.

She made sure that I had some sunscreen on, which I did have a bit but not a great deal, she said, "Are you going to be okay?" and I replied, "Look, if I can travel all over the world by myself, I can sure sit on the beach by myself." So, I was left to my own devices to enjoy the beach. It was beautiful and the sand was exceptionally fine. Even though I was not a swimmer, I did wade out to enjoy the surf.

Anybody that did come to this beach would need their own vehicle, and there were no buses that I had seen en route. There weren't many people there, and the ones that were I would expect were locals. They were obviously people that enjoyed the beach a lot, these chocolate brown bodies. Once again, I noticed the skimpiness of the bathing suits that Brazilian women wear. They didn't always have a great figure to accommodate this slight nod to decency. However, they believed that little is best and I thought of an old saying that I had heard, "that those legs continued until they made an ass out of themselves." Well, these women were a cheeky bunch and they didn't mind showing whether they were small, medium, or large in that area.

SOUTH AMERICA EXPLORATION

As I was sitting there watching the waves come in, I was feeling somewhat melancholy. Throughout my travels, probably ninety-five percent of the time, it was prudent that my wife let me do this alone, for both our sakes. I usually traveled in areas that were true adventures, with an element of risk, and always a degree of inconvenience. That which separates the traveler from the tourist, the big difference being that a tourist complains and a traveler accepts. In most cases my poor wife would suffer immensely under the conditions and lifestyle that I lead on these trips. But today, sitting on this beach, I missed her very much and I wished she were here. This, to me, was so beautiful and there was only one person I would love to share it with and that was my wife, my beautiful darling, Marietta. It reminded me of the sheer happiness we had together one time in Hawaii when the waves or "crashers" would come in, and she had such fun having them knock her down.

These waves also had some undercurrents to them and the water was exceptionally warm. It would be quite pleasant for a shower; that's how comfortable this water was. Also, both the water and the beach were in pristine condition and I felt like Robinson Crusoe, if it hadn't been for the few brown bodies on either side of me. A real "tropical paradise".

As the day moved along, up popped my genie, Denise, with a coconut. This was green and they punched a hole in it for straws. With this being cold and wet, the coconut juice inside was nectar from the gods. It was both thirst quenching, and refreshing, and if I ever rented a movie that showed people opening up a coconut on some deserted island, I knew I would be smacking my lips. In Brazil and throughout South America, they drank a tremendous amount of fruit juices, and rightfully so. The whole area produced an abundance of fruit and these people had found all the extractions of how to make exotic and refreshing drinks.

Denise checked back again and asked if I was okay, and if there was anything I needed, was I getting hungry? I told her that it was not really my style to be looked after. So, I said,

Robert F. Edwards

"It's very nice, but it's something new in my agenda." So, back she went to work and I was left alone again and caught up on my notes. As one hour saw another through, I moved over to sit in the shade due to the fact that it was very hot but also I could see my skin going from pinkish red to a deeper color.

There was an endless stream of people passing by, not as persistent as those at Copacabana beach but on the same concept, dragging coolers of cold drinks and food. One man (I wished I had my camera then), probably between forty or fifty years old, had roasted peanuts and as I was sitting there, he dropped off two or three peanuts for me and I said, "gracias," and he smiled. He was every artist's concept of what a beach person should be – a big Walrus mustache, a cap, short pants, tank top, a friendly smile and a lean brown body. Being a good marketer; he returned shortly after to see if I would buy some of his peanuts. I explained that I had no money and good-naturedly, he smiled and said, "So long" in Portuguese.

Out of curiosity, I was watching a young woman vigorously digging away with her hands in the sand and then eventually putting something into a beer can. She kept at this continuously, and then she would move to another part of the shoreline and continue. For the better part of half an hour, I kept an eye on her progress. When Denise returned, I asked her what this young lady was doing. Not being shy; she was like a bullet off to find out. She was down there talking to the young lady for some time and eventually, my curiosity got the better of me and I joined them. She was digging up some type of crustacean. They were white and burrowed themselves into the sand very quickly. They were quite small, about twice the size of my thumbnail; and little claws, a face like a crab, but a body like an armadillo.

Being the biggest kid in the world, I soon got down and started rummaging through the sand and I was doing pretty well, I was actually catching a few of them. The only reason I knew that I had got one was the sand moved in my hand and

SOUTH AMERICA
EXPLORATION

I didn't dare open it up; otherwise it was quickly back on the beach and just a memory. However, I was quick and determined, and was becoming proficient, and having lots of fun doing it. Denise told me that these little crustaceans tasted very much like shrimp but they had to be cleansed for about three days to get the sand out of them. We managed to collect quite a few, some very small but the big ones didn't move as fast as the little guys once you got a hold of them. I noticed also,  that when they had the misfortune of being upside down, they were like turtles, very vulnerable.

Denise and a friend had invited me to share a meal with them, and they had prepared a fish dish. The heads were still on and they were chopped up in quite a few pieces. Again, South Americans seem to enjoy frying their food or using oils and butter. I found the fish acceptable but quite bony as it wasn't filleted. I also had some iced tea, so much richer than what I was used to.

The sun was starting to set at six-thirty and we started to head back. Denise had hoped to show me around the city, but that was out because we had run out of time. She had to meet some people that were flying in from Paraguay, so we turned her Volkswagen into a high-speed performance vehicle as she raced back into town.

Denise invited me to join her later that evening, in a celebration for the Brazilian national soccer team. One of her clubs was supporting this regalia of entertainment with dancing, and so forth. She said that we probably wouldn't go until midnight or a bit later. I said, "That's fine. I could use some rest." I hade overdone myself by playing in the water and with the sun blazing down, I felt like a fried egg in a skillet. I was old enough to know better, and had been around long enough to have no excuses. However, my deep pink had turned into a bright red and I knew I had caught too much sun.

After Denise dropped me off, I quickly hustled over to the Internet and oh, my little sweetheart, my true little darling, had sent me two e-mails. It had been a good day; but it still had been a very melancholy day for me. I missed my wife very much and wished she was with me, or I was with her, I didn't care where.

By now, I thought that I should err on the side of caution, and proceeded to a pharmacy to pick up some cream to help subdue the glow and absorb some of the burn. The pharmacist knew exactly what I wanted, and we had a bit of a laugh about my color, he was very helpful. It was getting easier, with just body language; the communication level was good enough to get the help I needed.

When I returned back to the hotel, I wasn't really that tired. However, it was nine o'clock and if I was going to last the whole night dancing, I knew I had to get some rest. I had asked Denise to phone me when she was ready to leave, and at twelve o'clock the phone rang. She suggested taking a taxi, and it was going to cost us fifty real each to get in. When we got there, it was just mayhem. The street was clogged with people wall-to-wall. If a tourist tried to do this on his own, he would have to speak the language and without a doubt, be street-wise. Denise told me to get out on her side of the cab because she didn't feel comfortable with the people that were on my side. This woman knew what she was doing and got us into the club in record-breaking time. The place was packed wall-to-wall people; dancing, and swaying, and bouncing to the music. I was being very careful as I managed to slither through walls of flesh, that I still kept an eye on Denise. I just felt that if I did lose sight of her, I might find her tomorrow or I might never, it was that crowded. Ratio wise, it was about three guys to every girl; and the majority age group was probably twenty-five.

Earlier that evening, when I showed up at the taxi, Denise had said to me, "Yes, you really do look like a tourist." I had done my best to wear the colors of the soccer team of red, black, and white with my pants and a black turtleneck.

She gave me a wooden whistle to put around my neck, to make me look a little more "in".   Some of the costumes were very skimpy, and I saw a couple of women in harem costumes. Most of the men were in proper soccer attire – shorts and tank tops.

I met quite a few interesting people that evening, and my second Canadian. Sitting at my table were an American and his wife from Paraguay, and a Brazilian all enjoying the music. For the amount of people, it wasn't a disorderly group and the security was tight. They had a woman frisk the females coming in, and a male counterpart. With the problems that persist of violence and robberies, these people really did try to prevent any of that kind of mishap.

I didn't mingle around too much, as there wasn't any room, and felt it best to stay put, as I had found a place where I wasn't being trampled to death. They changed different bands and there was a variety of music but always a row of women dancing on the stage. More swaying to the music and more dancing to the rhythmic samba. The noise elevation made it difficult to hear anything over the music, so it gave me a chance to people-watch and see all of the different costumes. By now, most of the men had removed their tank tops, and there was a woman now on stage that was topless, with just a micro bikini on the bottom.

As the band played on and the hours moved ever onward into the wee hours of the morning, the people kept the motion moving and the beat goes on. The Paraguay woman was quite amorous and she was determined to take my top off, which I obliged her, and so I was now the two colors of the soccer club. The top of my body was red from sunburn, my turtle-neck was tied around my waist, and my pants were white. I was now one of the group, actually looking like a beach-comber with this wooden whistle around my neck and ever so often exercising what it was used for by blowing it. If you could call it dancing, bobbing up and down, then I hadn't stopped dancing for a couple of hours.

My Canadian connection came back, and he was still dancing. Denise had shown him a few steps of the samba, but he couldn't really move enough to do any body swing. This particular dance was a very suggestive dance and it was easy to interpret what the body movements were; and I should mention, that this was done in the parade also. It was just the way they dance and boy, talk about body language!

We made our way over to get some water, and people were pretty frisky here. One guy grabbed Denise's genital part, which she didn't appreciate too much. It was starting to get the feel of the flesh; but there was really no drunkenness or fighting or anything of that nature going on. We returned to our table and the Paraguay woman had now taken a real lik-ing to Denise and wanted her to take her shorts off. Without any hesitation, this Paraguay woman removed her pants and

154

SOUTH AMERICA
EXPLORATION

she just had a teeny bikini on. She was really anxious to see what Denise was wearing but of course, that was a "no no".

By now, it was about three o'clock in the morning and some of the early birds had been burnt down to the ground and were starting to call it a night. The floor space opened up, and we were able to work our way down onto the dance floor. I asked Denise to get up on the stage so that I could take a few pictures to send her and then some guys tried to get up also, but the security stopped them, "Girls only, fellows. "

Back at our table, the Paraguay connection with her husband had returned. She was swaying more than most people, but still coherent and a real firebug. She sprayed people with beer and with the amount of perspiration that I was pouring off, it was one time I didn't mind having beer on me. In fact, I was even taking water out of the ice bucket to wash my face. There was just no way of slowing it down; this was like dancing in a sauna.

She came over to me and not surprisingly spoke English quite well, since her husband was American too. She said to me, "I want you and your girlfriend to have sex with just me, not my husband." Yes, Evelyn my doctor friend was right when she said, "Carnival means feast of the flesh." This woman was certainly into the spirit of this carnival. I laughed and say, "Well, first of all, she is not my girlfriend; and second of all is, I'm married." Then she laughed and said, "I'm married, but I don't want him tonight. I want you and your woman." So, I guess the beat goes on and she was swaying to it.

In celebration of the soccer team, they had filled the place with a massive amount of balloons, obviously in red and black. We managed to get a hold of some and were playing up and down. The manager noticed how much fun we were having and brought us down a huge bunch, about thirty of them. There were so many people leaving that we now had room to play catch with these balloons back and forth. It was surprising how children and adults, when they do become children, have fun with the simplest things.

155

Robert F. Edwards

About five o'clock in the morning, the balloon fun was tiring, and I was ready to call it a night (or morning.) I didn't want to waste the entire day, plus I had to leave the hotel that day as well. So, with all that in mind, I asked Denise if she wanted to go also and with a "yes," we grabbed a balloon as a souvenir and hailed a taxi. I was dropped off at the hotel first, and Denise said that she would be there to pick me up at noon.

I pranced up to my room, which was fairly cool compared to what I had endured. With that, it was another day.

I can't say goodnight because it's closer to six o'clock in the morning. However, I'm going to rest, my little loved one and I miss you very much; and let the experiences continue. Another day behind us and then closer to you, my love.

SOUTH AMERICA
EXPLORATION

February 24th, Saturday
Rio de Janeiro, Brazil

Considering all the perspiration and physical exercise from noon until six, I was in relatively good fighting form by nine-thirty in the morning. I didn't see much reason to continue lying there in bed, so I did my regular toiletries and went down for breakfast. I had a fairly large one, papaya, pineapple and cinnamon rolls; and of course, juice and coffee. I returned to my room to catch up on of some of the events that had taken place in the days gone by, and just tried to get reorganized. Ever so often, I just had to take time out and catch up on some of the things that were getting behind; otherwise, I would lose control over the whole situation. After packing, I checked out of the hotel and just enjoyed sitting around watching the traffic move back. Reflecting back, I had made a very good choice of staying in this hotel as it was so centralized to the tourist aspect of Rio de Janeiro.

The other day when I was driving through the city, I could believe that there were probably a million people living here. For my first stay here, Copacabana was the best choice to participate in shows and discos and clubs, plus a lot of eating facilities. If I return here, I would probably go to the other beach areas mentioned and maybe even try hang-gliding, who knows?

Denise showed up punctually, and we loaded my stuff into her car and set off to her apartment. I was quite taken aback by the miniature size of this apartment, an under-exaggerated studio suite. It was on the second floor and as I walked through the door, there were two bunk beds. First, I thought I had a private room. Then, I got the gist that I was going to share the room with a girl that was attending school, and sometimes stayed there and sometimes didn't. The two bunk beds were in what might be considered a kitchen; as there was a sink, and a miniature stove. It was a two-burner stove with a little oven to it; just right for a grown-up Barbie to play with. As I made my way in, I had to dismantle my luggage because I couldn't fit through the corridor. I couldn't help but be amazed at the dollhouse conditions in which these people lived.

When I went into the bathroom, there was no door but some absolutely beautiful tile work. The walls were brick of some sort and then concrete with rebar. I was reminded of my trip to Russia, and the impregnable buildings of the Stalin period in the Soviet Union, which were indestructible with concrete and brick. However, those I saw in the Soviet Union had much better layouts than this, though it's not fair to compare just a few apartments.

The outside of this building looked relatively new and in good condition. The garage entrance had a beautiful wooden door that opened electronically into a mini courtyard that housed the cars. Each suite did not have a stall by any stretch of the imagination, but most of the people living here, as Denise mentioned, were elderly and probably didn't use a car because everything was within walking distance.

Continuing my tour of the apartment, down a narrow hall-way, was the best room in the house and rightfully so, her bedroom with a double bed. Off to the side was a cubbyhole that she called her office, with a window in it. I have to say I was taken aback by the condition; the apartment was clean, but very overstocked with trivia. I sure wouldn't want to own it. The walls were pink and blue, probably reflecting her eth-nic background, which has a blend of Indian, Portuguese, and Negro. I fully comprehended why she wanted a house rather than an apartment. But more power to her, being a single woman and owning an apartment in Copacabana. I have to give her full points, and it probably explained her focus on making money.

I put my gear in a closet and always my concern from day one, I asked her about safety. I did trust her personally and I also met the young girl staying with her. She was a nice twenty-five year old blonde; bubbly, cheerful and outgoing but her studious behavior for English was waning, she told me. She was happy to practice her English and showed me the costumes that she had bought for the carnival.

We decided that we would all go out for dinner and I asked Denise if she would take me to a place where they sold the food by the kilo. It was an experience that was well worth doing; I had never quite seen anything like it. It was somewhat of a smorgasbord. The amount of food was unlimited as far as variety and choice, and then the desserts would make any sweet tooth have an orgasm just looking at them, let alone trying them. The salads and the different ways that they were presented; three that I remember distinctly: potato salads in all different colors; and the beans brought back a bit of déjà vu of Cuba. They had both the black beans (which was the number one preference in Cuba), and brown beans, and red beans. The meats were two-fold: obviously the cold cuts; and then at a counter were men waiting to serve us with new, freshly cooked meats that were sliced off a rotisserie skewer.

The system for paying was neat too. They handed us a little piece of paper as we collected our plates, and this allowed us to go up as many times as we wanted. Each time, the plates are weighed in. Waitresses came around punctually and asked what we would like to drink and when served, that went on the little piece of paper as well. My eyes were bigger than my stomach as usual.

Not being able to finish my meal, which always bothered me (wasting food) I paid the bill and it got stamped "paid" on it and I thought that was the end of that, but no. Before I could get out the door, they check the bill again and rip off the stub that says it's paid. The more I was getting to learn about South America and their security procedures, they were efficient. With cheaper labor costs in Brazil, they could intensify the security by personnel rather than by electronics or mechanical devices.

Robert F. Edwards

The people, especially in Rio de Janeiro, were very conscious of theft, but you can't have this many people, without putting security in a high priority. Denise had a remarkable club for her car, which not only hooked up to her steering wheel but it connected to her brake as well. So, there was no way that you could move her car. Also, the stores, as in many other countries, had corrugated garage doors that slid down over the openings of the stores. At night, the major centers looked like a warehouse district, totally deserted.

The day had really taken a bite and by now it was well over two o'clock; so we headed back to the apartment. I was a bit apprehensive about exactly what I was doing. Once I got in, what greeted me was a large cockroach, which really mortified this woman and her response was kill it, which I was capable of doing and did. She went into quite a bit of length about it and then showed me a corrugated door that was supposed to go on the bathroom.

With a gesture of confidence I said, "Yes, I could put up the bi-fold door," you would think that I was Superman that had jumped out of the sky. With that, "Can you really?" So I said, "Well, let me look at the instructions," Then I said, "Well, you know, you'll have to cut it, and so forth, and so on." Well, to my total amazement, out came a power drill, hacksaw, and three boxes of tools. I always like to be put on the spot. With not wanting to lose face and in the spirit of generosity, I set about hanging the door. After perspiring in great depths and finally taking my shirt off, I cut, measured and assembled under the most difficult conditions. It was taking me much longer to hang the door than I expected, but I got it up, it worked and to my amazement, didn't look too bad. I had to cut the door of the frame casing and everything else with a worn out hack saw, not a job that I would want to do again.

Once finished, I wanted to sit down and discuss what we were doing. We were going around in circles and finally, I said, "Look, Denise, all I really want to do and the only reason I am staying on in Rio is to see the carnival." I had a pretty good idea now that the first, second, third, fourth day and each day had a significant difference; and today was all that was left of it. She started phoning around and asked me how much I was prepared to pay for it; and I said, "Well, I wouldn't want to pay more than fifty dollars U.S. each." I felt that I was being generous by paying her way to these events as my guide. And I said, "Well, I'm really into theaters or operas," and she reminded me that those were closed because of the carnival. "Yes, I remember, but I'd like to go to the art museums or the special historical areas," Then, she said, "Fine." and started phoning around, but we only had about an hour and a half left to go. So, finally, she said, "Well, the only one that is worth going to 'cause it will be open till six-thirty tonight is the art museum." I replied, "Fine, let's get off to the art museum. Well, then, what about the carnival?" After more phone calls, she said, "I can get the carnival tickets tonight for maybe twenty real (which was about ten dollars each) so we can get in to see part of the carnival. Then she got a gleam in her eye and said, "Oh, good, then I can keep the difference on the hundred dollars."

I realized some people gave their soul to God; others gave their soul to whatever currency the day's market was; and in this particular case, this lady rendered unto Caesar. I could see that it was better to go on a high note than a bad note; and sometimes, you have to say goodbye to the party. With that, I said, "No, I'm sorry, I just don't have the money for you, and me, and overhead expenses as well so I'll just have to leave, and I'd like you to call me a taxi to take me down to the bus terminal." Then she started to mellow a bit and said, "Well, you don't have to rush out and you know, you didn't expect me to spend all my time just going around with you." I could see that we were on two different levels. I felt that yesterday, I went along on the ride. Today, she started going full tilt into multi-level marketing and I said, "I'm really sorry, but you know, I told you I wasn't interested."

I paid her for guiding me around yesterday as well as a portion of today, and she took me down to the bus terminal. Both of us felt that the other person made a little overzealous move,

Robert F. Edwards

her on the money and me on leaving. Rio had been a very expensive part of my trip, but I still enjoyed it. Recapping some of the moments of what I saw, I kept thinking of a young girl and her boyfriend that I wished I had taken a picture of. She would always be the girl with 'the' costume for me, just a perfect figure and a very beautiful face. Her outfit looked more Polynesian in my estimation than Brazilian, feathers on her ankles and her wrists and small feathers to cover her breasts; and a micro-mini feathered skirt. The headpiece was the largest part of the costume, the better part of a foot high covered with feathers. A lot of the other costumes were efforts that deserved recognition, but this one stayed in my mind's eye.

Denise drove me down to the terminal and said, "I would come in, but I can't find a parking space. Well, if you change your mind or you can't get out, phone me and I will come back and get you," which I felt was a nice gesture even though it would probably have cost me a lot more. Who knows? Maybe the ante would have even gone up more. Now, I surged ahead to find a bus going out of town. The bus terminal was one of the largest I had been in and could accommodate a tremendous amount of traffic. Tonight, it looked like all twelve million people were at the bus station hoping to evacuate the city.

The place that I was trying to shoot for was Porto Alegre. I was starting to get proficient enough to know which bus lines traveled where and finally, I saw one that was going to that city. After considerable effort the young lady behind the counter told me that there were no more buses tonight. It was now about eight-thirty and this was the nightmare that I was anticipating, not being able to get out. With that, I asked what was the next bus leaving, and she said it was for Curitiba, and would be leaving at eleven forty-five. I, without hesitation, said, "I'll take it." I felt that, under the circumstances, I would be at least safer on the bus than sitting all night in the bus station, even if I was fortunate to find a chair for the long wait.

SOUTH AMERICA
EXPLORATION

I struggled with my luggage, which seemed to be gaining weight with each effort that I made and the horrible situation persisted as the platform that the bus should arrive on was anywhere from forty-two to forty-eight. It doesn't sound like much, but with wall-to-wall people, not knowing the language and definitely not knowing which bus was going to be there, it became an insurmountable problem. I had one hour to contemplate on this, and find a way to adjust to the flow of traffic that moved in and out. It looked like a beehive that had been kicked over and every drone was trying to save the queen bee.

Standing on the ramp, the long night continued and I was grateful to see the hands on the watch finally move from one hour to the next. Finally, with a sense of relief but also apprehension, it was now my turn to go down to the pit, to at least get in a position. Once I managed to get through the gate and security systems, I was in the midst of chaos as people scrambled to get on the buses. They had one advantage that I didn't and that was the language. I asked an older gentleman in English and his good wife tried to explain to me that yes, the woman at the desk had given me the right information. It would be between forty-six and forty-eight, but nobody except the bus driver, and of course God, knew which platform he would arrive on. The other thing that was concerning me was two-fold. One was, the buses do not run on time. It wasn't like everybody standing in a queue at an airport and then board. It was a free for all and the bus could come in on any platform that was open. Also, he might be anywhere from five minutes late to five hours late and nobody, but nobody, knows. So, trying to move back and forth in this as well became a nightmare that only one who has experienced it can comprehend.

I met up with a young man, by now my magic hour had arrived, eleven forty-five, and no bus. He said he would wait and tell me which to get on if it arrived before his. Unfortunately, his bus arrived first, and because they only stayed around for ten or fifteen minutes, off he went. So, once again, another "fly in the ointment" of this terminal. More by the grace of God and his continual benevolence of looking after this soul of adventure, I found a bus that had the right city on it. I had to make sure that it was the one that I was supposed to take, and with the help of the big fellow up in the sky, I got to the right bus, and the right seat.

It would be a long hard night and I was tired from dancing and hanging doors and perspiring. My clothes were soaking; even my socks were wet from my own perspiration. The humidity was stifling, plus the fact that there was absolutely no wind, and no fans to circulate the air. I was just soaking wet, but didn't care as I was sitting on the right bus.

In less than five minutes, maybe seven, we were on the road, so it was very easy to miss one of these long awaited events. I left Rio and the lights behind and once again realized just how large this city was. It was an exciting city and someday I hoped that at least Marietta and myself would return; if not, Wendy and Cole also. I wouldn't recommend maybe the carnival period, but it was worth the extra distance to enjoy the beautiful beaches and majestic surroundings.

SOUTH AMERICA
EXPLORATION

February 25th, Sunday
En route Brazil

Anyway, I was on the bus and no, I wasn't looking at the scenery. It was about one o'clock before I started to dry out. I had taken off my boots and was satisfied that was about as far as I could go. There was one fortunate thing that I was not sitting beside somebody, which gave me both seats. This bus, actually, was fairly comfortable and the seats reclined to a great extent; much further out than some of the buses I'd been on. The young lady in front of me had hers stretched out and like in airplanes, when you're in a reclining position, the person behind you, if they're in an upright position, is almost kissing your forehead.

However, I was just so grateful to see the outskirts of Rio dissipate and I was on my way. As the hours drifted, so did I, from a conscious state into some form of sleep. I must have slept at least for two hours, for when I checked my watch again, to my happiness, it was almost five o'clock. Within an hour, daylight would be creeping over the horizon waking us for another day. As the hours ticked away, accompanied by the kilometers, daylight appeared and we were still in very hilly country. It was lush, plentiful and there were lots of palm trees and even by Brazilian standards, this was a jungle.

In what seemed to take an eternity, I finally started to see the great lights of São Paulo. São Paulo offered little interest to my agenda and I had mixed feelings as we approached the city. The massiveness of the city, which I believe was in excess of twenty million people, made it the largest and the most rapidly growing city in Brazil.

As we entered the city, and made our way through it, I kept checking the map; the distance seemed so short for all

165

the hours that I had spent on this bus. However, "Such is life," as the Australians say; and the pleasant thing was, it didn't matter where the bus stopped; the stay was always very short; unless, of course, it was a meal break, when they gave us a chance to gulp down some food before pulling out again.

Some of the farmhouses we passed were interesting, they were made out of a wood frame construction and some of them were painted quite vivid colors, anything from wild blues to reds and other primary colors. They were all small and I didn't see any machinery. I was inclined to believe that these were small truck farming operations, and a lot of it was physical. One thing verified this, I saw a man and a woman; she had a big rope tied around her and he was pulling a two-wheel wagon up the same grade that our bus with an engine was having trouble with. I couldn't believe that they both could be overweight, in this heat and pulling that huge load up the hill. However, maybe it was just maternity spread with her, and good cooking for him.

The countryside was becoming mountainous, but not the rugged peaks of the Rockies or some of the great ranges of mountains in Europe. This area was covered with forest, and was very colorful. It must be a botanist's wonderland here, with all the different types of trees and shrubs. Even with my naïve eye, I saw many different types of flowering bushes and was even getting to recognize the century plant that grew everywhere in this region.

The highway was four-lane and then sometimes, it opened into six lanes. They had a lot of tollbooths, not just in Brazil but in all three countries that I visited, and it could be in some of the most remote areas as well. We were not exempted even riding on a dirt road; we still had to pay the toll. But, the roads in Brazil were in good shape.

It was difficult to say whether we were making good time or not. We passed through many little communities and they were all modern towns. I was grateful that I had chosen to stay in some of the more remarkable desert communities in the northern part of Chile and Argentina. They were by far my favorites. The bungalows and homes in these smaller communities were nicely done, not large homes, about fifteen hundred square feet. They used a lot of wood, for finishing their doors and shutters and accessories. Most of our homes would just cry for this type of wood to be used for our furniture. Much of the wood was a beautiful light grain, accompanied with almost black ebony, and other exotic hardwoods.

The hours continued to drift by and I was well into overtime on this bus. I would have been surprised if they ever came in on time, or even around the right time. We were going to be at least three hours late. We stopped at one of the stations to give the bus a wash and this particular chain of bus companies was large and well organized. They switched bus drivers regularly (which the other ones did also), but this was the first one that I had been on that provided a compound with huge bus washes and filling stops. After allowing us the chance to get off and grab a quick meal, then off we went.

With an hour and a half left to go before we arrived at our destination, I was amazed at my energy level and began contemplating the idea of doing another leg on this torturous trip. The place I was going to was Curitiba, the capital of Paraná, and there really wasn't much to do there. It was just a modern city and most people, when they're traveling, just give it a stop over, which I was thinking of doing. The only thing that interested me, but didn't look like that was in the cards, was a train ride to Paranaguá. It left at eight-thirty in the morning (it was past noon already) and returned at three-thirty to four-thirty, so I was out of luck on that one.

The city that I was hoping to go, and now started entertaining the idea of, was Florianópolis. This is the state capital that spreads out facing the Baía Sul. People had told me that this was where Brazilians liked to go, for the many beautiful beaches. I started to look at the map and it certainly was on the way, so I then checked my travel bible to see if I could do the next leg, which was very important. I was having a bit of trouble working on the schedule from this particular city to Uruguay.

167

Robert F. Edwards

As I was thinking it through, the city was upon us. It was a very pretty city, clean, and the one thing that Brazilians seemed to have a monopoly on, was high rises. I was glad that both my attitude and stamina were positive and was going to see if I could continue on with this adventure. A young man that I had got talking to helped me get the ticket; and yes, this place must be pretty popular. Buses left almost every hour and the one at twelve-thirty was full but the one-thirty was available. So, I bought the ticket and waited my turn outside the terminal. There was always a chance that somebody wouldn't show up. Because I had just about gone on the wrong bus once, I realized that bus drivers didn't check the ticket, and there was not much scrutiny.

Bearing this in mind, I got on the earlier bus and was feeling quite smug about it, when unfortunately they did a head count and realized that there was one too many on the bus. So, they started questioning; and I stepped up to the front and was prepared to wait my turn, but after a lot of Brazilian negotiating, he changed the ticket from one bus to the other and I was on the earlier bus. This saved me an hour. Not a great deal of time but after I had been up this long, even fifteen minutes was worth trying for.

The young man I was now sitting beside was a commercial artist and did illustrations for poets. He spoke a bit of English, and was from German descent. In the short time that I had been in the southern part, I noticed an ethnic shift. There were a lot more fair-haired people. This bus was not the best one I had been on, but I have crossed the great divide and I was now heading down the slippery side of the Atlantic. The young man beside me confirmed that this particular region was "the place" to be, and he said that if he ever could land a job and make a living, this was where he hoped to live.

Finally, after another six hours, we were within striking distance of the metropolis. Right away, I realized I had made a wise choice by enduring this extra five or six hours. It was on the coastline, and was an older city, more interesting for me. The young man offered to help me find the hotel that I was looking for since the bus that he wanted to catch was close to there. With a forced march and my luggage getting to be a lodestone, I managed to go the six, seven blocks uphill and still keep pace with him. Obviously, he was in a hurry and I said to him, "Look, you can go without me," but no, he was kindness itself, and even helped me get the ticket to Montevideo, Uruguay.

At the hotel, feeling like I had taken a shower with my clothes on, I asked to see the room. Of course, he showed me the better room for forty real, which really wasn't that much (twenty dollars U.S.), or the cheaper one for twenty, which "skin flint," decided was good enough. I would have enjoyed the double bed and the toilet within the room, but it was not essential. So, after dragging my luggage up three flights of stairs, I gratefully took off my wet clothes. I was feeling husky, maybe from the cigarettes people smoked here or the air-conditioning on the bus, but my throat was very scratchy and I just hoped I wasn't coming down with a cold.

I laid down on the bed for a long overdue siesta, and slept for about two and a half hours, but still felt quite refreshed. I was most anxious to get an e-mail off to Marietta, due to the fact that I had been sending her one on a daily basis and this would be two days now that she hadn't received one.

I opened up my window to take my wet pants and hang them out to see if they could dry a bit, when I noticed a fellow looking across at me. We got talking a little bit; a Canadian. Both he and his wife had taken a year off, and quit their jobs; I gathered. As we were talking, I happened to mention that I wanted to find the Internet. He said, "Yeah, we've used the internet. We know where it is and we even have a map which we'll give you because we're leaving tomorrow for Paraguay." This couple had lived in Toronto for about eight or nine years before they set off on their adventure and it was hard to say, but I would think they were in the mid-thirty group. We talked for a while before I started off on my quest for the Internet.

Robert F. Edwards

I enjoyed the walk, looking at the old colonial-style buildings, a déjà vu of Portugal when I was there. Small square stones made up a large amount of roadwork and sidewalks and they designed them with whites and red, where black was the dominant color in Portugal. In my continual hoarding of new things from different parts of the world, I actually brought one of these stones back. The cobblestone streets led me into the piazza with a massive tree in the center.

I found the Internet with a lot of help from the locals reading my map that my new Canadian connection had left me. He was absolutely right, but unfortunately, the place was closed so I would have to come back tomorrow. This was a disappointment, but at least I knew that there was one here. I returned to the mall area and enjoyed a juice and empanada. I discovered that there was to be a carnival here tonight and already it was nine o'clock and the music was blaring with people dancing in the streets. The parade would start it off, so with that in mind, I returned to my room and would just see how the cards were going to fall. I needed some sleep; my throat was sore, I had this nagging cough and my nose was running.

Off to bed I went; and by one o'clock, I was back with a spring in my boots to join the rest of the natives. People were really letting their hair down, and tourists and foreigners were gathered around as spectators. For the natives, the people that lived here on a day-to-day basis, it was their time, and rightfully so. I was so glad I had come here instead of staying on in Rio. The people here, in their party mode, were doing it not for commercial value, but for the sheer enjoyment of having a good time. I was able to see a lot of dancing performances of the samba, probably one of the most suggestive dances I had seen. But just the same, it has a good rhythmic beat to it and young and old were dancing. There was a party feeling in the air, a release of being conventional. There weren't the sparse costumes and topless busts of Rio in the parades; but the atmosphere was clearly a feast and celebration.

170

SOUTH AMERICA
EXPLORATION

As I walked the streets, the shish kebab was alive and well. It was skewered on wooden sticks and cooked over a charcoal fire. Such a difference in price too, at one real, about fifty cents U.S.; and the same for a beer. Rio de Janeiro was the more grandiose of the carnivals; but for local flavor this is what would be the country fair type of carnival. For me, personally, I preferred this, with fewer crowds.

The evening was more than pleasant and most of the people were more than willing to have their pictures taken on the streets. Obviously, some had better costumes than others, and had put a lot of effort into it. I was told that the actual parade was across the boulevard and down one of the main avenues. So, being adventurous and cautious at the same time, I made my way over to the park and Lady Luck was with me. At the starting area people were assembling in front of the long gray strip, just as you see on television. There were literally fifty, maybe a hundred people all dressed in the same costumes lining up. It was educational to watch something of this magnitude get organized. The costumes were multi-faceted; the ones that I was thrilled with represented little ships of the Columbus or Magellan period. Headgear was one of the deciding factors of these costumes and some of them were quite elaborate. They needed to be supported by shoulder harnesses to give them the stability as they walked. There was no way that their head alone could endure the weight that these headpieces were designed with. I had taken a lot of pictures, and one fellow in the parade was very keen to get a copy. He was persistent enough to write down his name and his address, postal code and everything else.

Many of the groups of women were dressed as ballerinas, and fairy godmother outfits. Some were dressed as flowers and the most important thing was these were fairly large groups, so they all were dressed in similar attire. These people spent all year preparing their costumes and the groups took great pride in participating in the parade. The one thing I had noticed from day one was the complete age spectrum. Some of these women were in their sixties or older, some of them

171

were in their teens and I had even seen some little children dressed up as harem girls, which seemed to be quite a popular costume for individuals.

Many costumes were very suggestive. Obviously, the ankles and the arms had more clothing than the rest of the body, but it was the headpiece that set the pace; and of course with the samba that they danced so well, it looked like a massive bunch of butterflies or birds in flight from a distance.

I asked if I could take a couple of pictures of some young girls in green flower costumes. One girl spoke English and asked where I am from; and when I told her I was from Canada; she was the first Brazilian that told me that Canadians and Brazilians were fighting. My wife had mentioned in her email a week ago, that she was apprehensive for me going to Brazil. There had been a reported outbreak of Mad Cow disease in Brazil, and beef exports were banned in Canada, resulting in some hard feelings, according to the news media. This was the first instance I had encountered, and although she didn't make me feel unwelcome, it was obvious that she knew what was going on. I told her that my wife had expressed her concern for me in Brazil and she said, "I have nothing against Canadians personally, but just against the government." This was a bit of reminder that I was not always a chosen guest in everybody's house. However, it went over well and the evening was delightful and the weather is warm.

It was about three o'clock in the morning and these people were real nighthawks. I returned back to the core of the city and had a few more beers and another shish kebab, before I made my way over to another band playing. The crowds were starting to thin; but not everybody got up at midnight. Most of them started at six o'clock in the evening, so by three in the morning, they had nine to ten hours of partying. That was a pretty good standard by anybody's stretch of the imagination.

Once again, I ordered another empanada. The woman cooked up some fresh meat, onions and there was even a bit of potato and a tomato. She cooked it on an open grill; and then stuffed a huge amount into a very large bun, all for one real, and the beers were a real also. I just couldn't get over the prices compared to Rio de Janeiro's, where the beer was five times as much, and that was on the street. I couldn't imagine if I was sitting down in a restaurant in Copacabana.

Robert F. Edwards

Almost reluctantly, I decided that it was time for me to go back to bed. It was after four o'clock in the morning and the streets were starting to thin out. I had a remarkable evening, and got to see a parade and was more than glad to have come to this city.

Goodnight, my little treasure bee and I love you very, very much and I miss you immensely. Goodnight, one and all.

SOUTH AMERICA
EXPLORATION

February 26th, Monday
Florianópolis, Brazil

Well, I got up and did the things that I normally do. My room had no fan; there was a window, but there was absolutely no air blowing in and the toilet and washing facilities were a communal thing. Not that I minded that. However, aside from the negative aspects, was the floor. People in North America would envy it, if their furniture were made out of this wood. It was gorgeous and judging by the hotel, I would think it was the original, at least a hundred years unchanged. It was hard wood, that rich black wood with soft pastel tans that I was thinking "I would just love to have furniture, let alone a floor like this."

However, I was not feeling up to the top of the mound, I had to admit; and my cold had progressively taken a step forward, my throat hurt considerably; so I was not going to beat around the bush and would start taking some penicillin. This morning I planned to spend some time catching up my notes on some of the events of the previous night. At about nine o'clock I had the breakfast; buns with some cold meats, and coffee and juice.

Once I got that down, I headed out to the mall area. It was a pleasant morning. People were getting their shops opened and everything was in full course. I was most anxious to get some e-mails off to my little honey bun and to see how things were progressing on the home front. With all these "things to do" list, off I went to the piazza. Marietta would have been fascinated with that huge tree in the centre. They had supported the tree with metal posts holding up the branches and it almost covered the entire piazza, probably hundreds of years old.

Robert F. Edwards

It was a little early before I could go to the Internet, which opened at ten. So, I found a department store to buy some new batteries for my tape recorder, but it still didn't improve the situation. I think I may have actually worn the heads out. As I was looking at my watch, it was close to ten o'clock, so I decided to head on down to the Internet; this spot had become very crowded. It seemed that every tour guide had to bring every tourist to this tree. One group must have been forty or fifty strong and all joined hands to circle this tree. Then the tour guide starts up a "Ring Around The Rosie" type of song, and everybody was in good spirits. Just when I wanted a little bit of peace and quiet, to record something, it was very difficult to even hear my own thoughts, let alone using a broken-down tape recorder to record them.

I set off to find an Internet and I saw a young lady in a doorway and asked, "The internet?" She starts laughing, moves aside, and says "Here," she was standing in the door. I had to wait for a while to get on, but it was worth it as I had two little "e's" from my treasure-bee. I felt much better after reading news from the home front. Part of the challenge of traveling was not always seeing something unique, it was being able to overcome some of the obstacles, and being able to communicate with people. I was determined to buy another tape recorder, so now I had to find a place that had one, do some price comparisons; and all without the aid of the common denominator "language." It did take me some considerable time, but I was surprised by my own ability and the cooperation that these people offered. They realized that they could communicate with me, if they had a bit of patience with themselves.

When I did find a shop, unfortunately they didn't accept credit cards, so I had to go back to the hotel for more money. Before I knew it, it was two o'clock in the afternoon and the day had been more of an adventure shopping than what I had anticipated on, since I had planned to take a bus to some of the beaches in the area. To add to my displeasure, when I had lunch in a restaurant, I managed to find an expensive one.

As I was strolling around, I went into what I thought it was a church, but it wasn't; it had four large towers. It must have been a huge marketplace at one time, and now had shops on both sides and open restaurants. These people were great for fried food. I ordered something that looked like some kind of potato and vegetables rolled into the shape of a hot dog and then deep-fried. There is a rule of thumb that I should always obey, if it doesn't taste good, don't eat it; and if you don't like it, leave it. Good rules to abide by. I didn't use them, so now I had a bit of diarrhea. Between coughing and diarrhea, the pills were coming out in abundance and I decided to have a siesta like the rest of the people and then see how the evening progressed.

With the rest of the locals, about six o'clock, I returned to the street to enjoy the coolness of the evening. I had taken a couple of cold showers and that was all that was available; but welcome due to this heat. I strolled around looking at the little shops, and tried to get myself physically motivated to do something. It was just one of those days that I had the best intentions but was derailed.

This was an easy city to get around, my type of city, a walking city. The streets were very narrow and all cobble-stoned. It was one of the nicest communities I had been in, and could see why both Brazilians and Argentineans came here for their holidays. In some ways, it was like the Mediterranean with a bit of flavor of New Orleans, or San Francisco without the hills. There were lots of little shops and I had just about been in every one of them to buy a tape recorder that ironically was now working very well.

I had planned to take on a gourmet meal tonight, but am ashamed to say that I went for a hamburger at Bob's Fast Food Restaurant. I not only had a cheeseburger, coke and some French fries, but I indulged myself in another one of their delicious chocolate milkshakes. I did a bit more strolling around, coughing and sputtering like a vehicle that swallowed

177

Robert F. Edwards

some bad gas. About ten o'clock, I decided to go back to the room, get some rest and God willing, I could get up for the carnival later that night.

So, once back in my room, if it was possible, it was even hotter than when I had left. Literally, little beads of perspiration trickled down on the sheets. I was not feeling well, lying there in the saturated heat, just as the heavy rains started outside. It was a torrential rain and although I was feeling sorry for myself, I was feeling much worse for the people in the parade. Usually, the rains didn't last too long, but for those going down the parade's strip, turned from a beautiful Cinderella into Macbeth's three witches.

I turned and tossed; I couldn't get motivated to even get dressed. Last month, my travels had been more than vigorous and my long extensions on the bus had been more than grueling. I now erred on the side of caution and decided to take the rest of the evening off and sleep.

So, with that in mind, my little treasure bee, I love you and goodnight. Goodnight, one and all.

SOUTH AMERICA EXPLORATION

February 27th, Tuesday
Florianópolis, Brazil

Between the rain outside and me perspiring inside, the sun finally came up. I was feeling extremely tired. I don't know whether it was the medication kicking in, or whether it was the cold, with the diarrhea that I experienced throughout the night, and dehydration, it could be just about anything. So, it doesn't matter what part of the world I am in, if my stomach isn't functioning properly, don't give it anything. So, today, probably along with so many other things, I would enjoy fasting. I drank a couple of glasses of orange juice and coffee, and decided to take this day in small strides. This is the day that I was going to be leaving for Vermont Hotel, Montevideo, Uruguay. The bus was supposed to leave at four o'clock and I had to be there about an hour early to process documents.

It was about noon by the time I packed and checked out of the hotel, and it seemed as if I was in slow motion, and had already gobbled up a fair amount of the day. I decided that I would like to get another e-mail off to little honey bun, but the lady had told me that tomorrow was a holiday; and believe me, it was a holiday! The large supermarket, where I was going to buy some things to eat for the bus trip was closed. This was the first major sign, and there was no business open anywhere in town that day. The Internet shop was closed; but since I was there I took a picture of it, to show just how sometimes obscure they are.

I found a small kiosk that was open and on my way back treated myself to an ice cream, which cost in real the equivalent of thirty-eight cents American. They really do give you more than your share and a little wooden stick to eat it with, value and quality that I haven't had for years.

179

Robert F. Edwards

Back at the hotel, I put my things together and slowly, slowly, slowly got ready. I was thinking I would walk down. At least, it was downhill and this was one day that I didn't have much spring in my boots. If anything, I was dragging both feet, let alone the luggage. Just as I was walking back to the hotel, all hell broke loose and the rain started pouring down. So, that eliminated any idea of strolling around. Instead, I had to decide what to do with the luggage and how I was going to protect it. I did have that last plastic bag that I had saved from the trip up the Falls and as I was thinking how to prevent wet luggage, the rains stopped just as quickly as they had started.

So, now that the rain had passed, I felt more confident and at about one o'clock I started my trek towards the bus terminal. I finally ended up taking a cab for four real. Now I had a long wait ahead of me. I had noticed, along with so many other things, that people in this part of the world smoked more than we do in North America. Also, they had access to smoking in public places. Thank goodness that the buses weren't one of them. I felt that my sore throat was directly attributable to the smoking, and this bus depot was aggravating the situation.

There was a large group of young people here. February was when a lot of people got their holidays; and this was the peak period. It was just a case of watching buses come and go, in their never-ending events. Finally, at three-thirty, I got up and checked all my documents to make sure they were in order. They wanted to take the passport but I wasn't sure what they were going to do with it and reluctantly declined, and they willingly gave it back.

I got on the bus and everything went smoothly. The bus was full and this time I wouldn't have the two seats for my own use. The lady sitting beside me, Irene, didn't speak any English but we still tried to communicate. She had been on this trip more than once and was fairly informative about stops, and meal breaks, etc. It was one of the few times that I was able to sleep extensively on the bus.

SOUTH AMERICA
EXPLORATION

As we left the city, it was still quite mountainous with some vegetation. Once we headed south, before it became too dark, I started to see pine trees and vegetation similar to the more northern regions of North America. This day ended with me still on the bus, somewhere at midnight.

So, I am going to say goodnight, one and all!

Robert F. Edwards

Once the morning had arrived, I couldn't believe the change, it was extremely flat. I felt I was back on the prairies, either Saskatchewan or Alberta. I was still in the same seat on the same bus, so nothing else had happened. This bus seemed to have its own way of attracting business, by offering little snacks and juices and pop throughout the trip, which was very nice. They even gave us breakfast or sandwiches and a form of pastry at five o'clock in the morning.

At about ten o'clock, we hit the Brazilian border and went through Immigration, which was no problem. The woman in charge motioned for me to get off the bus with her, handed over my passport to be stamped, and then back on the bus. About fifteen kilometers down the road, we came to the Uruguay border and same procedure; but this time, everything had to come off the bus as they searched the luggage, but I got through that relatively easy.

I found it a bit cooler here. Yesterday, when we were leaving the city, we had barely got outside the parameter and traffic was unbearable. At first we thought it was an accident; but for two and a half hours, the congestion just was, in fact, so slow that the smokers, including myself who didn't smoke, got off the bus and walked around. That was just how slow traffic was. So, it put our bus some three to four hours behind schedule. What was supposed to be a twenty-one hour trip was now about twenty-six hours. Now that I have traveled so much on the buses, if they ever came in on time, I would probably check to see what kind of fuel they were using. It was the Brazilians that were more provoked at the delay, surprisingly.

SOUTH AMERICA
EXPLORATION

When we left the Brazilian side, it was quite a modern building for Immigration and Customs. The Uruguay's side was old and in poor shape. As we drove along the highways, I saw a lot more cattle and sheep, all grazing together. It was big sky country, and from what I had read, between livestock and agricultural products, that was what this region was noted for. I wished I had Marietta with me to identify all the different types of trees, the ones that peel their bark, eucalyptus trees, also birch trees, but no pines now. They grew in small stands amidst the huge white plains and open skies.

For the construction of houses, they used different types of bricks and looked very colorful. A lot of the ones in Brazil and throughout South America that I had seen where usually brick, but had cement over it and then whitewashed or painted. These were just decorative bricks. In this part of the world and in Mexico, stonework, bricks, tiles and cement were the order of the day.

Traveling does sharpen my wits and this particular trip was no exception to the rule. Just when I thought I knew what I was doing, I got a curve ball. During the night, our bus pulled into a depot, and we were supposed to have half an hour to get something to eat. My bus companion, Irene, made sure that I even knew where the washrooms were. So, I got some yogurt and by the time I paid through their computerized checkout system, the bus was missing. Maybe a week ago, I would have panicked, thinking I had missed the bus. But now, I realized that in all probability, it needed gas, just as we needed food. I didn't overreact, but on the side of prudence now, I had made sure I knew which number the bus, and which company it was. This particular stop reminded me of airports, where all of a sudden, the planes were like little bees coming home with their supply line. This place was congested with about ten busloads arriving almost at the same time.

I stood waiting patiently, thinking that the bus should return to the same spot, as convenient for the people traveling on it; no, fifteen minutes went by; twenty minutes went by;

Robert F. Edwards

and finally, other buses were coming and going, but not mine. That little voice that I trusted so well said, "Maybe it would be prudent to walk down and see that the bus hasn't moved itself." Lo and behold, at the other end of the row, about twelve platforms away, where is the bus? Down there! I didn't feel too bad because when Irene came back out, she was heading to the original spot also. I let her know where it was now, and she was very grateful. So, I wasn't the only one that didn't know all the tricks that the bus drivers pulled on us travelers.

My first impressions of Uruguay were mixed. In some ways, I thought they might be a buffer zone between Argentina and Brazil and being such a small country with two huge neighbors, both in size and economic clout, I just wondered how it survived. Its currency was about twelve to thirteen pesos to the U.S. dollar, so it was quite a bit cheaper than Brazil and very much cheaper than Argentina. The buildings seemed to be in better condition in the residential areas, and the middle class was more evident here than in Brazil. As we got closer to the city, Irene found a young man that spoke English, to help translate for her. She had checked out my Lonely Planet book and knew the hotel I had chosen, and would help me get a taxi there, foreign policy at its best.

True to her word, she not only helped me to exchange some money but when she realized that the two hundred would be too hard to change; she took her money and broke it down into one hundred and two fifties, which was easier for me. She went to the hotel with me and argued with the fellow to get the price down to twenty-five dollars a night, U.S., Visa; and then left me her phone number. She said she would have one of her friend's phone that could speak English, around eight o'clock tonight. So, a very nice introduction to this country.

I found the Internet in record-breaking time, but there were no e's from my little M. This made me a little sad, however such is life. I sent her one, read some of the news, and decided that I would have a big meal. I found a restaurant, ordered a steak, French fries, and a big bottle of beer and the whole thing, including the tip, was less than eight dollars. So, with a full stomach and feeling much better than I had for the last two days, I returned to the hotel and did a bit of catch up on my journal. Also, I was able to get my laundry done, which was commendable. My room had a fan in it, which was awesome, lovely French doors, and a small balcony. My own toilet and bidet, to say nothing of television with the CNN. I caught up with all the tragedies that were going on in the rest of the world, from flooding in Africa, to foot and mouth disease in Britain, to say nothing of freak railroad tragedies, to an earthquake in Seattle. I was just hoping that we hadn't had any major ones in Vancouver.

Right on Irene's schedule, at eight o'clock, her friend that could speak English, Cristina, phoned; and we talked for a little while. She asked me what I was doing tonight and also tomorrow and I told her that I would probably do a city tour and just see how things progressed. She then asked me, "Would it be too late to go out at eleven o'clock tonight?" And I said, "No, not at all." So, she said she would pick me up with Irene at eleven o'clock.

With that in mind, I thought I would wander around until then. I walked up and down the Rio 18, which was one of the main drags in the central part of Montevideo. It was a pleasant evening, though it was threatening to rain, which also seemed to be the global forecast after listening to CNN. Everywhere was getting a bit of the tears of the sky falling down and there was no exception here. As it was getting close to the time that I was supposed to meet these ladies, I was sitting in an outdoor café by my hotel when Irene showed up.

We struggled to communicate like we had on the bus before she spotted her friend, Cristina. They were both really nice ladies, probably mid to late fifties, and just wanted to show me the city. As we drove around, Cristina described the different areas of the city. The harbor was horseshoe shaped, with many high rises. A huge boulevard separated the high rises from the beaches, and even at night the beaches looked beautiful and well maintained

Robert F. Edwards

I asked Cristina if she had an idea what the prices were and she said, "depending on the size and the building, anywhere from fifty-five thousand U.S. to maybe a hundred and fifty-five thousand." Like so many areas, the economy in Uruguay was experiencing very uncertain times and conditions. When I asked her about all the new buildings that were taking place and the prosperity of the city, and she said, "It's a mystery." I found out that Uruguay was approximately three to four million people and over half of them lived in Montevideo.

The more we drove around, I noticed it was an old and new city combined. Some of the buildings of the older period were quite unique, apartments above; and then lower down were offices; and on street level were the store facilities. We stopped at a restaurant and I asked the ladies if they'd like something to eat. They both declined, as, "No, no, if you'd like something," so I suggested some appetizers. I have no idea how many we got, probably close to twenty. Not knowing the names of them, we had ham in one group; brown bread and little cheese balls, small tarts with Roquefort cheese, others with creams; bacon-wrapped scallops, etc. We spent the better part of two hours talking, with Cristina being the translator between Irene and myself.

Irene was a professional photographer, and she and Cristina had been good friends for the better part of twenty years. They both used to work together at one time, and now Cristina was a secretary. She has two grown sons, still living at home with her. Irene was great on sports; liked dancing and Cristina did yoga and a lot of walking. Irene was adamant that I wouldn't have enough time to see the city, the beautiful beaches and all the things that it had to offer.

It was getting on to one o'clock and both these ladies had to go to work tomorrow so we headed back to the hotel. I asked about the theater and opera. Again, they showed me where it was, but it was under restoration. It just wasn't going to be an adventure of art on this particular journey. I invited them both out for dinner the next day, and Cristina said she would phone me at seven o'clock tomorrow night. Back in my little room with the double bed, and it was nice not to feel like I was in a crate; I could even bounce around. It was also not quite as hot as it had been in some of the other cities. With that, I turned off the light, goodnight to one and all.

Goodnight, my little treasure bee.
I am looking forward to seeing some e's
from thee.

Robert F. Edwards

I have to admit that no; I did not jump up that morning to do my toiletries. Instead, I lay in bed and watched CNN. I had always been addicted to news and global events, with an obsession on economics. I filled up on the latest developments, the global catastrophes, the great rains, and the continual plummeting of the U.S. Stock Exchanges. Not exactly a rosy picture to start the day, I got up for my normal routine and another bonus, hot water.

Irene and Cristina had commented that this was not a very good hotel, but it was in the core and it provided all the needs that this globetrotter required. Breakfast was rather sparse, however it was included, so one cannot be choosy; a powdered orange juice, coffee, and a few croissants. The pangs of hunger were appeased. The quest for adventure began; but first of all was my burning desire to hear from my little true love. I picked up my gear ready for the day ahead of sightseeing, and departed with camera, flash, and "The Lonely Planet" book, translation book, money (most important), and set off to the internet.

I was finding that computers at these Internet stations were like cars; they all ran about the same way, but they all felt a little different and the operating procedures were not all the same. Still, I was conversant in getting this one booted up, and in the end, no, lots of news items but there was nothing from my little true love yet. To say the least, I was somewhat surprised and have to confess that I was disappointed. I wrote an e-mail telling her of my itinerary tomorrow and there was always a danger of not being able to find an Internet. I had now decided to head down to the end of South America at the Magellan Straits. This would take anywhere from two to

188

three days, maybe longer, before I could make contact with her on the Internet.

I sent Wendy, my daughter, a short e-mail as well, as not hearing from Marietta, I was not just disappointed but somewhat anxious and concerned. The earthquake in Seattle, Washington (a few hundred kilometers south of Vancouver), was getting quite a bit of global news coverage on how severe the earthquake was and though only one person was killed, there was billions of dollars worth of damage. I would have hoped to hear from Marietta and it was preying on my mind throughout the day.

Trying to put that behind me, my next step was to see if I could book a bus ticket to Buenos Aires without going down to the bus terminal. I found a place that I could book a trip around the world with, but could not buy a bus ticket. However, very close was the turista information booth and I made my way across the piazza to talk to the young people there. Cristina, yesterday evening, had indicated that everybody spoke some form of English in Uruguay. I think she was being somewhat optimistic. The people were helpful and very accommodating but their English was like my Spanish and we were not on a conversational basis with each other.

The young people tried to be helpful and I got some brochures and information. The theater was just not in the cards as it was closed and with further discussions, I asked about some of the museums. I also had this quest to buy a gaucho's sombrero or hat, but they weren't too informative on that. Leaving the turista's office with more brochures than verbal information, I set off to enjoy my day of walking, looking and photographing whatever I feel appropriate.

I came across a tourist shop with some nice work that I might come back later to purchase, as I didn't want to carry it around all day. My other concern was no matter how well I tried to protect against the crushing effects of transport, there was always the good chance of breakage. I nearly bought one of the hats; but as far as jewelry goes, neither one of my women wear a lot of jewelry; so, no point in stocking up on that.

The thing that I observed was the beautiful leatherwork. In both men's and women's shops, there was a great deal of leather; coats, jackets, handbags, shoes; etc. On the streets, there were kiosks that had many rectangular bags, about eighteen inches high and maybe six inches in diameter. A lot of them had tooling of "Uruguay" written on them or figures of cowboys, and ranged in price from twenty-five to thirty-five U.S. dollars. They seemed bulky; and not the most practical for a backpack, and were too big and cumbersome for a purse. I didn't see many people on the streets carrying them around; so they must be just a tourist target.

I had been wavering back and forth in getting a daypack. Leather was the forte in this part of the world and with the huge cattle herds, raw material was in abundance. The Argentineans were charging about twenty-five to thirty-five dollars U.S. a bag, and a similar one here was about twenty dollars U.S. The prices were considerably better than the previous countries I had been in, with a better bang for the peso.

I passed by a church, The Church of the Immaculate Conception, not unique in any way, probably one of the more modern designs, but felt an urge to go inside. What struck me rather than the décor of the church was the confessional booth. I am a Roman Catholic, though not a strong practising one. The confessional booth had the light on, indicating that the priest was there. This particular one had a kneeling area where a woman was saying her confession. When I was a boy, and even a young man, this was a practice that one did usually Saturday night before going to Mass on Sunday morning. The confession would be heard and the priest would give absolution and penance. I remember reading in one of the great William Shakespeare's works, that confession was good for the soul.

SOUTH AMERICA
EXPLORATION

As I sat there looking around, and periodically glancing at that woman receiving absolution, forgiveness, acceptance and encouragement, I could not help but feel that the priests of this faith were far more prepared and qualified to nourish the soul, and relieve the pains of anguish and despair from the mind than the analysts, psychiatrists, and therapists of the Western world.

I personally believed, from watching this woman confess herself, both to God and to man, the sins that she felt were being relieved both spiritually and mentally. Whether it was in good taste or bad taste, I could not help but take a photograph of her, more to remind me of how ashamed I was and how reluctant I was to go to confession. Reflecting back now, I understood how it relieved me, washed me free of my sins, and absolved me of the wrongdoings I had caused to others, and against the laws of God. This short moment of reflection in a predominantly Catholic continent reminded me that some of the old ways of the faith of our forefathers were sound judgments for the soul, the body, and the mind.

Returning to the streets, I continued my enjoyable day of being a walking tourist. My next adventure outside this area was to walk over to where the theater was. It was really a shame; I was not able to even get in to see what the interior looked like. They had a metal corrugated fence around it and obviously, it was under restoration. The Teatro Solís was said to have superb acoustics, and has hosted performances of many world-class artists of the opera, ballet and classical music.

Robert F. Edwards

It seemed that every narrow street led into a different piazza, and there was always a statue, so it was relatively easy for me to know which area I was in. If I got a little disorientated, I could easily return to the piazza and get myself squared around. I continued further in this direction, into an area of the working class, where many lower income families had moved into conventillos, which were large older homes that had been converted into multifamily dwellings.

Then, I walked down to the beach area and no; it was not the same area that Irene and Cristina had taken me the night before. It was a poor area; but once again, the shoreline looked appealing and I was getting my share of exercise today. I had no complaints except for donning my Gore-Tex raincoat, between the raindrops, and drizzle. However, living in one of God's great rainforests, I was, if anything, more homesick than disturbed by the moisture falling from the sky.

Back to one of the larger piazzas, I still had an unfulfilled quest to purchase a black cowboy hat, the gaucho sombrero negro. They showed me some black hats, but no, they were not the gaucho one that I was looking for. I wished I had purchased the one in Salta, Argentina, but hindsight makes no mistakes, and I really didn't want to carry a sombrero throughout South America if I didn't have to. I was almost tempted by the ponchos, and I still might get one at some point. They were a very heavy woolen type of ponchos and the price was more than reasonable, at about thirty dollars U.S. If I lived on the prairies, I would have bought one; but I didn't want to smell like a wet sheep every time I wore it.

It had reached the hour of high noon and I decided that if I was going to have lunch, I should make a firm endeavor to find a restaurant soon due to the fact that a lot of these places have a siesta hour and I never knew whether it was two or four hours. With that in mind, I started looking around for a restaurant and down one of the little cobbled streets I saw a place on the corner that looked like a very active café and if it was good enough for the locals, it would be good enough for me. Also, to my sheer delight, they accepted Visa. I took a seat and the waiter, Roberto, asked me what I would like to drink. I replied cerveza, beer; also he asked me the size, I say grandiose, which is 6.20 ccs, the big bottle. I was actually starting to understand a lot more of the menus, and thanks to a short burst of Spanish lessons, I even knew what eggs were. I was not fooling myself that I could order in Spanish or even understand it spoken, but I would have to say that reading probably comes first. I was surprised how much more I was able to comprehend on signs and menus from what I did even a week ago.

I couldn't believe that I ordered another steak and chips, and a bit of a salad. I just wanted to see if I could eat two back to back. They also gave me pan (bread) and I really enjoyed my meal. As I looked around, I was quite amazed at the portions that people received for their money. Another thing that I became aware of, the hot dog was a very popular item and they often put mayonnaise on their hot dog, as one of the accompaniments.

Another difference here was in the serving. Of course, I had a plate in front of me, with utensils. Then the waiter brings a huge plate, mounded with big chunks of steak, heaped with French fries, and some kind of cole slaw; and he placed the one steak on my plate and left the platter also. This made so much sense. You know, sometimes you struggle with life and then somebody does something that just takes the blinders off and you can see for the first time. No matter who you are; cutting a piece of meat is a challenging feat without scattering the rest of the entrees all over the table. By having a separate plate, I could become the surgeon of the day and neatly make strategic cuts across the meat unhampered. Such a logical way to do things; and all these years, I've done it the hard way. With this newfound skill and convenient way of cutting my meat, this steak was equally as tender and delicious as the previous one. When asked if I wanted some coffee, I said yes or si, and with two espressos, two large steaks, French fries, salad, a grandiose beer, and the tip – all for ten dollars U.S.

Robert F. Edwards

With this enjoyable meal completed, I continued working my way throughout the streets and I came across an antique store with a gaucho mannequin and his attire. I thought I had hit pay dirt. Wrong again! The fellow was nice enough but says, no, he didn't have any sombreros, but thought he knew where one was and he got a map to draw me a description.

Well, sometimes things were meant to be and then other times, you just have to enjoy what you're experiencing. For the next three hours, I enjoyed the day. I saw more stores door-to-door, and again, was getting better at communicating with people; but no, after three hours of concentrated walking, and sore feet, still nobody in that area knew of such a shop. If it was there, it could have been one of the shops that were closed; with the corrugated doors down it was difficult to know whether they were out of business or closed for the day.

I had met a diverse group of people today; from young men trying to help me, to store clerks, all very delightful people. By five o'clock, I managed to find my way back to the area that I had spotted before. The fellow had a little stand of, in the politest terms, collectibles, or in the cruelest form, junk. Anyway, just bits and pieces of leftovers from bygone years.

I remembered how successful I was in Kiev when I went to one of their marketplaces and started picking through postcards and with that in mind, I spotted some postcards on his table and went through them. I picked out some that reflected the era of a bygone period. I found some interesting ones, and a small watercolor picture, and I made the purchase of these articles for about eleven dollars U.S.

My feet were telling me that they had done the best part of the day and would like a rest, so I made my way back towards the hotel, after picking up some soft drinks. I had done my very best to keep my mind off not having an e-mail from Marietta yet, but by five o'clock, my concern had mounted to the point that if I had not received any e-mails from British Columbia that I would e-mail Matt, my brother-in-law in Calgary, and ask him to phone Marietta to check that everything

194

was alright, and to e-mail me back, just in case it was our internet that was non-functioning. Off to my newfound communications center and I brought up the Internet; and my dearest daughter had replied. She advised that there had been only small damages in Vancouver, and it was Seattle that took the full brunt of the earthquake. "Everything was fine here; I'm real busy. Sorry, Dad; I didn't get back to you sooner, I love you dearly. Please stay safe, etc." I e-mailed her back asking her to contact Marietta because I still hadn't received any e-mails from her even then.

After I had a bit of relaxation for about an hour, I continued my walking, now in the opposite direction of town. It was interesting to see the amount of shops that were selling exactly the same thing. I guess it was just a numbers game.

However, I did see a place that sold cameras and binoculars and I noticed one that said "offshore". Their binoculars looked unique, and I had been told that Uruguay was one of the duty-free spots in the world; so, for a good deal, this was the place to check out. The binoculars ran anywhere from two hundred and fifty U.S. right up to five hundred U.S. The more expensive ones showed longitude and latitude readings, and the degrees as well underneath, with lights and all the bells and whistles. I wasn't prepared to make a purchase that day, but thanked the lady very much and left.

By seven o'clock, I was back again in my room, watching CNN on TV when Cristina phoned. She said that she was going to be busy that night and Irene felt that she needed her as translator; so I thanked her very much and told them both to keep in touch, and how I appreciated their kindness.

With that cancelled and an evening to myself, I started watching (I hate to admit it) television. After being thoroughly indoctrinated with the news, I switched channels. Three or four of them were American channels and they were dubbed with Spanish rather than the other way around.

So, I enjoyed a few movies before I turned the lights off and say goodnight to one and all.

Goodnight, little honey bun and I really hope that all is well. I sure miss you a great deal.

SOUTH AMERICA
EXPLORATION

March 2nd, Friday
Montevideo, Uruguay

Got up at six o'clock this morning and started to work my way towards packing, cleaning up, and getting ready to go to Buenos Aires. I paid for my laundry, which was eighty pesos; and had my Spartan breakfast; and then off to the bus station. I was able to get a bus leaving for Buenos Aires at ten o'clock and was there waiting in plenty of time. Boy, I was glad that I was early, as it was a full trip and it seemed that everybody wanted to go to Buenos Aires. The bus was air-conditioned and for the first time since I had been here, I was actually starting to feel a little chilly on this particular bus.

As I was leaving Uruguay, it was much the same as when I entered. The vast plains were dotted with some sheep, and the pampas grass was blowing in the wind, very picturesque with the white, fluffy seed heads bending and rippling. We passed some smaller rivers, quite muddy with soil erosion and run-off from further up that was taking soil out to form deltas. The homesteads were very small and not what I had expected at all. I pictured huge spreads of land with big estates on them and thousands of cattle. I am sure they did exist in the pampas area but all I saw here were smaller farms with some cornfields, alfalfa, and other crops.

There were always horses grazing, along with the cattle and some sheep. I imagine that they still did a fair amount of riding on these ranches, in contrast to Canada, the United States, and Australia where motor bikes, and trucks were the main modes of transportation. The gaucho still used the faithful horse and God love them for it.

The hours passed and so did the kilometers. The landscape was similar to the prairies in North America; great open expanses, then interrupted by brush and a few clumps of birch trees, and back to open spaces again. The journey towards

197

the Argentine border continued this way, occasionally passing a few small towns along the way. If you transplanted these towns somewhere in the mid-west of the United States or in the prairies of Canada and changed the signs from Spanish to English, it would be very difficult to distinguish any difference. Basically, Main Street with the presence of the easier, more subdued life of small town living.

We were making good time between raindrops. It was one of those days that Mother Nature would like to clear up but just hadn't got the motivation to do so and then let go another big rainfall, only to be accompanied by light rains and drizzle and then changed her mind once more to brighter days.

We approached the border and the attendant came over to get my passport. Along with all the others, he cleared us through Customs and Immigration; and this was for both sides, which I couldn't believe. This was one of the first times I could remember not having Customs jiggle or jostle my bags. I don't know whether that fellow had an 'in' with Immigration or whether there was just a unique bonding between Uruguay and Argentina.

We had passed through Customs and had gone twenty, maybe thirty kilometers into Argentina before I felt convinced that we hadn't got another border stop to go through. This was the case and we had now crossed the large bridge over the Rio Uruguay, which geographically separated the two countries. Once on the other side, the landscape remained much the same. I did notice a large sign and gate indicating a ranch of some significance with their own road. Quite far off in the distance I saw a large white house, so I imagine this was one of the more affluent ranches of the area.

We continued to pass through small villages and towns, but slightly different than the northern part of Argentina which resembled Mexican or desert-styles of construction as these were quite modern. What I had noticed in both Uruguay and Argentina was once you got off the highways, many of the roads reverted back to dirt paths. It was mainly wood constructions, some brick, some two or three-stories, but no high rises in this area.

Eventually this seven-hour-plus trip was winding up as we approached Buenos Aires. Even I noticed the city from the outskirts; so, I didn't have to worry about the bus driver not going in the right direction. Around six-thirty, we were heading into the great city of Buenos Aires; and I say "great" because it was huge, with one third of Argentina's population of 32 million living in the Gran Buenos Aires region. It appeared ultra-modern, with huge shopping malls and warehouse distribution centers, as well as familiar names like Chrysler, Toyota and IBM offices.

I had thought Rio de Janeiro's bus terminal was large, but once we pulled into Buenos Aires; this was just massive. I had never been in one, anywhere in the world, of this size. I collected my luggage and by now I was wishing that I just packed a toothbrush. My luggage was getting heavier everyday, as I lugged it through the corridors looking for the right direction. I finally asked a policeman where I could buy bus tickets; and he politely told me to go upstairs.

This bus depot had at least four floors that I was aware of and I certainly wasn't going on a reconnaissance to find more. With his help and directions, I located the booth to purchase my tickets. There were over two hundred booths with different bus lines to purchase a ticket from, and that was just on this level.

A kind woman pointed me towards the booth that I was looking for, to Rio Gallegos. This was far down, towards the bottom of Argentina and just a few of the highlights that I would be passing through were Bahia Blanca; the Rio Negro river; also the Peninsula Valdes; and a town called Trelew; and after a further seven or eight hundred kilometers would be Comodoro Rivadavia before my destination of Rio Gallegos. This next bus journey would be well over two thousand kilometers and I was optimistic that this long haul could be done with the El Expresso bus in thirty to fifty hours, I hoped. It was difficult to predict, as I had often found that when I did get to one of these buses, I was told, "Yes, you can take our line, but you're going to have a little bit of a stopover at one of these other regions to transfer on to another bus in the middle of the night or two o'clock in the morning or God knows what."

Usually, I disliked any arrival times that were at some ungodly hour. When most good people were sleeping, bad people were out. However, that was not my major concern anymore on these long haul marathons; it was connections. Almost being able to complete my thesis on bus transportation in South America, I realized that there was not one that I had been on yet, that ever arrived within an hour of its designated time. The last thing I wanted to do was be on a bus that had to go in excess of fourteen hundred kilometers and get off at some unbelievable hour, only to find that the connection that should have been an hour in waiting had vanished due to its punctuality of leaving on time.

I asked if there was another bus line that had a straight through trip and like the good competitor he was said, "Yes, they go straight through." So, off to that one and I purchased my ticket. "The Lonely Planet" book (my copy was about nine years old, and should be a bit outdated in prices) quoted about a hundred and twenty dollars for the ticket. I had paid eight-five. I hoped I wasn't going as cargo. I would have to wait until Sunday at four p.m. to find out if the bus had wheels or I had a seat.

I had a strong desire to make this quantum leap for various reasons. Number one was the glaciers and the Magellan Straits; then the trekking, the mountain climbing, the wildlife; and the Patagonian area of Argentina that was world renowned for its beauty. I had experienced the northern parts of Chile and Argentina and now I wanted to continue this quest in the southern part. I was going to give myself as much time as possible, and hoped to pick up a few extra days.

Rio Gallegos was well known for servicing the wool industry and had a population of about a hundred thousand. It was en route to Calafate and the Moreno Glaciers and the Punta

SOUTH AMERICA
EXPLORATION

Arenas or the Tierra de Fuego were are all within that range. I had a great admiration and quest to follow in some of the footsteps of Marco Polo; and with a touch of humour, I had just left the Marco Polo bus that took me into Buenos Aires.

With those arrangements behind me, I made my way to the taxi and found the hotel, which I had chosen. A little more expensive, it was thirty-eight U.S. a night or thirty-eight Argentine pesos. It was nice to have currency at par with the Americans; if only the Canadians had theirs, I would certainly be living a much higher standard, both in Canada and away. But, c'est la vie. This hotel was right downtown, centro; and was also the newest one I've been in. It was very well done, and I had a very nice room with a double bed, a television and air-conditioning. Oh, and let's not forget the bidet. North America was losing out on the fixtures that went into a proper bathroom, but the size would have to be much larger to accommodate this extra piece of porcelain. I was quite pleased with my room, and my next quest was to find an Internet. I was really developing a predictable pattern. First, the next bus ticket out of town; second, get money of the local currency; third, get a room; and fourth, the internet. I don't think a spy would have a much tighter schedule than that to make contact with the home office.

This particular hotel was one of the few lately that cash was king and credit cards and plastic people were out. I would have to try my hand at getting some more Argentine currency from my credit card. Now, with two quests in mind, I asked about the Internet and was given some general directions. On the way, I stopped into a bank and tried without success, this being Friday night.

I was experiencing the Avenida 9 de Julio, which happens to be the largest and longest boulevard in the world! Not in Buenos Aires, but in the world! This was a pedestrian's nightmare, and it was risky to even reach the centre of the intersection before the light changed, but virtually impossible to make it all the way across in one go. The next bank I tried I was successful in getting money out of Argentina's banking system and withdrew three hundred pesos. Now, with pesos in my jeans and U.S. currency, Uruguay's, Canadian too (I might add), and a little bit of Chilean, I felt like a walking bank on the road to the Internet.

I was getting a feel for the total vastness and size of this city. It was huge, but also beautiful in that the main avenues were of the conventional European design with large boulevards down the middle. They opened up into huge circles, or in the short time I had been here was learning to call piazzas. Always, conventional statues of heroes or leaders of great aspirations adorned these circles.

I quickly learned that the pedestrian did not have the right of way here. In fact, the pedestrian was the endangered species when crossing the street, even when the light was in his favor. I was extremely cautious when crossing the streets. The ones that I had a difficult time in making a judgment call on were the motorcycles. They seemed to have an obsession with either popping out of nowhere or coming close enough to give you a shave without a razor.

The streets fluctuated off the main arteries and became small, single lanes. Sidewalks were not a big thing in any of these countries, and here was no exception. Tiles prevailed; perhaps that was why North Americans had gone to concrete. These tiles seemed to break up and I had to be a little careful when walking; as it was easy to trip and fall because of a broken tile on the side streets. When I reached the Internet it was not a good time to get logged on, at about nine o'clock central time here. The place was full, which was not the main problem. Both the machines and the system were pitifully slow, and even one of the locals commented that it was very slow.

I was just about ready to give up after the better part of a half an hour's time to get into my hot mail, when there was a surge of connections and mine finally came up. My beautiful little honey bun had two great e-mails for me. I drafted her up a quick one, which I was able to send off, and read a bit of the other news items. I decided that I might as well have something to eat. All that I had today (actually it was one of the better meals provided by the bus) were sandwiches and two little pastries. I guess South Americans don't like crust, especially for sandwiches as they always cut all the crust off the bread.

I thought I would try my luck at a place called London City. This was at the end of the plaza where I was staying and I thought it would be just a little humorous if I could get a pint of Guinness and something to eat. I entered this establishment, actually a café more than a restaurant and tried to order a Guinness but only got part of it right. Cerveza is beer and I ordered a large one, I was that thirsty.

I tried to ask if they had any "sopa" (soup) but probably my accent on Spanish words was worse than if I had just said it in English. After asking a few more questions, I tried to slowly describe linguini and so on, and finally he said, "Pasta". The waiter came running back with the menu and said, "Pasta ravioli"; I said, "Si". The sauce was good, and the portions are huge; but they tasted more like gnocchi to me, as they were quite doughy. I imagine they were home-made, different anyway. One of the nice things, though, was they served olives and a bit of potato chips with the beer. With the salt and the long thirst and just the day that prevailed, I ordered another beer and with ravioli, a bit of ham, and a handful of olives, my stomach said welcome to the addition and I paid the bill and returned to my room. After flicking channels for the better part of fifteen minutes, I decided that at eleven-thirty, it was time to say "goodnight, folks."

Also, goodnight, my little love-person, I miss you very miss and thank you very much your e-mails.

Robert F. Edwards

March 3rd, Saturday
Buenos Aires, Argentina

Up and at it, checking the news and reading a little bit about what I have to do before I have to do it, and now I am going to start my day. It was raining, quite overcast and the only difference between the rain here and in Vancouver, Canada, is this was warm. I decided that I'd better start taking my Gore-Tex jacket out and get my gear ready for a day of walking in the rain. With being weighed down by books, cameras, flash apparatus, film, and you name it, I felt like a walking supply train or Commando Bob; but whether I looked funny or not, I was well-equipped to tackle anything that came my way.

I dropped the key off and had a small breakfast that consisted of a glass of juice, two little croissants, and a cup of coffee. Every country had something to offer and the Brazilians' coffee and how they made it was the way I preferred, (and I know the way that Marietta would demand), strong. Throughout South America, they heated or frothed the milk, so in the true sense, lattés which were becoming more popular in Canada and the United States as gourmet drinks; here they were considered just coffee and milk. A little more civilized, a little more economically serviceable.

With my breakfast behind me, I felt that once I started walking the streets, the day was going to be one of those rainy ones, for the first part anyway. So, I've decided that I'll go to the internet and like I promised Marietta I would write her a really good sized one. When I got there, yes, they were open and yes, I was the first one. Wow! I was able to get a long e-mail sent before checking out the news. I read of some of the disparaging facts that Mr. Greenspan had related to the world, the Federal Reserve was not going to cut rates until mid-March and the process of downsizing or recession was

SOUTH AMERICA
EXPLORATION

still on the horizon, and Europe and the rest of the world would just have to endure this correction that has been in progress. With the news I read about the foot and mouth disease and all the other terrible things that were happening throughout the world.

In my small little world of the Internet compartment, there were a group of young men chattering away. It was hard to write or even read, as far as that went. But two hours later, I had used up as much time as I wanted to spend and off I went to see the heart of Argentina, Buenos Aires. One of the places very close to where I was staying was Plaza de Mayo that dates back as far as 1580. Juan de Garay actually laid the square out and after 1810, it became known as Plaza de Mayo. Most of the buildings around here were of the nineteenth century, with a European flavor. In some ways, the buildings reminded me of some of the buildings in Paris, both inside and décor outside. Then I walked over to the Plaza del Congreso and the Avenida Santa Fe, where the fashionable shops were and huge pedestrian malls for the chic shoppers with lots of leather shops and (pardon the pun) uptown décor. It was sparsely populated at the moment due to the rain. The rain had eased off to a drizzle; but still for Saturday morning, I imagine these shopkeepers weren't too happy.

From here I went to what was known more as the theater district on the avenues of Corrientes, and Cordoba, which ran off Santa Fe. I was ashamed that I had been in quite a few of these larger cities and still hadn't gone to the theater or

Robert F. Edwards

seen any performances. However, they didn't seem to be as theater conscious as the Europeans and it was much harder to communicate down here on what was playing and maybe it was my lack of effort also. Around these great plazas, there was little traffic and they felt more like walking malls. In a lot of Canadian cities, we have tried to revive the downtown core by isolating two or three streets and making that a mall with a few benches to sit on. A poor attempt, when I saw what Buenos Aires had done by blocking off huge amount of streets.

Here, places were set aside for cafés to occupy large sections of seating in the street. The tiles and their ornate patterns gave me the feeling that it was for people, not for vehicles. South Americans had more of the European affiliate than North Americans, where "our culture or no culture" was the rule of thumb. They did a lot more walking. In all fairness to us northerners, in our affluent society, most of us have our own vehicles and don't rely on walking as a primary source of getting from one place to another, no more than we support the local transport.

I was thoroughly enjoying the day and the drizzle had become intermittent, so it was even more enjoyable. I went by a nice restaurant and in the front window they had a barbecue pit (which I took a picture of). They stretched their meat out on a rack and the whole carcass was there. It was glazed in a very slow fashion compared to our barbecuing and I remembered one woman saying that, "I really like Argentine barbecuing much better than North American" and I could see the totally different approach. I asked the chef if I could take a picture and of course, it was "go ahead". I noticed that sometimes "Monkey see, monkey do". As soon as I got my picture off, another couple was shooting theirs through the window. I also had to take a picture of McDonald's. I just couldn't believe the penetration that McDonald's had throughout the world and no wonder; Moscow was one of the last of the frontiers to be broken through.

I was standing on one of the massive avenues that go across the city, and the traffic was about four to five lanes either way. You don't have to take your life in your hands, but you sure have to be on the good side of God to get across. These drivers stopped for each other periodically and for pedestrians, never. Within that intersection, I could see at least three McDonald's probably not more than a block away from each other. McDonald's wasn't the only one. Fast food seemed to be a big part of Argentinean life in general, and in these malls, they had staff that stood outside and handed out little advertising samples to get you inside. They were everywhere and there didn't seem to be any consistency. Some of them would be five or six in a row, and then in front of an upbeat musical shop, another one would pop out there. The hot dog was very much alive and well, as with pizzas.

When I first arrived in Chile, I had been impressed with those little pasties, the empanadas and I noticed those were available as well as the conventional French fries, etc. that Argentine people enjoy. As I strolled through the mall areas, I came across a music shop and saw a big display of tango music, so I went in and spent some time listening, and purchased a couple of tapes. They use a different approach than what we do. Obviously, the tapes were sealed up but you

Robert F. Edwards

wanted to listen, the guy played them. I don't know what happened if you didn't buy them.

Some of the malls go for literally a kilometer; I started at Lima and continued on to Correntes along the great Avenue 90 Julio Bernardo de Irigoyen. By the time I finished, I had scoured the areas between Avenida de Mayo and the Avenida Santa Fe and hoped I hadn't missed anything amongst these huge complexes. Although I enjoyed this part and had bought a bit of water and soft drinks and it had even stopped raining, I wanted to return to the hotel. Yes, why not? Stay inside, have a short rest, and then tackle the late afternoon.

Feeling rested in the afternoon, I saw the Catedral Metropolitana and Casa Rosada, the president's palace. There was a long excavation corridor, which I thought was a prison or dungeons, but the two women that I talked to only spoke Spanish, so I was still none the wiser. Later research found this to be the tomb of José de San Martin, Argentina's most revered historical figure.

Each piazza seems to have a huge statue honoring someone, and of course, pigeons. They were so tame that they actually jumped on your hands and your arms; and both children and adults found this a novelty; with the reward for the pigeon as food. I felt I was in a movie set of "Three Coins in a Fountain" in Tivoli. As I continued my foot tour, I caught a glimpse of a tall ship and my sea-faring blood took on a renewed enthusiasm to get there.

I struggled to make my way across one huge boulevard after another amidst traffic that would impede the strong at heart, let alone deter the faint at heart. I did get to the other side but not to the success that I wanted. This area was unique in the fact that most of the buildings were of the same venue, of around the turn of the last century. In the backdrop, I could see some of the newer high rises, though.

I tried to work my way towards the waterfront, with little or no idea how I was going to get there, just to see the tall ship. One thing about the sailing ships with those high masts, it was hard to lose sight of the top of the mast.

I was eventually able to work my way down across the tracks, and to what I would later find out were boathouses. These were lined along the river and I now began noticing the many boats; some good sized yachts, some sail and power-boats of course, in this harbor dock. It was deceiving, at first the river seemed quite small, but when I saw the size of the boats, I realized that the river was quite wide, and obviously supplied a great amount of trade and service on it.

I continued walking past the buildings of three or four stories high; all brick; and they stretched as far as my eye could see both. This was a newly developed area, reminiscent of the older waterfront areas in the Greater Vancouver area being reclaimed also. It was on the same concept: with open cafés, even a museum here, and lots of very expensive restaurants. So, it was now the "in" thing, as my generation takes the turn of the century into its lifestyle.

By now I was fast approaching my destination, and was in a position in which to take what I hoped was going to be a nice picture of this tall ship. I noticed men were working on the catwalks and so I decided I had nothing to lose but see if there was a gangplank and who knows, "permission to come

Robert F. Edwards

aboard, Captain"? To my surprise, "Yes, you can go aboard it," and for two dollars I could even have my own tour wandering around designated areas. This ship was the flagship of the Argentine Navy and it was commissioned in 1897 and built in Liverpool, England. The Fragata Presidente Sarmiento served on thirty-seven training missions. It had three large masts with a fourth smaller one; there were two stacks which would indicate a dual purpose of both steam engine as well as sail. It was a magnificent vessel and as I wandered the deck

above and aft, I saw the huge tri-steering wheel. It was such a true ship of its period, and in excellent condition. The hull was steel and the decks were made of teak with tar to seal them. The wood in the rooms (I didn't get to see the captain's quarters, but the officers' mess) almost brought tears to my eyes to see this rich hard wood in immaculate condition on a service vessel.

This was not a fighting ship of any significance, but there were a couple of large artillery guns and a smaller cannon. The restoration and maintenance on this vessel was second to none. It had been converted into a museum with areas to display the uniforms, where originally the crew would have had their personal quarters. In this particular ship, the crew slept in hammocks, and a good friend who served in the British Navy had told me that they have advantages. "When you have hammocks, you are able to take them down and of course, the openness of your quarters is much greater for moving about than when you have bunks". In foul weather, the crew would spend more time indoors, so this particular ship had accommodated them with hammocks.

SOUTH AMERICA
EXPLORATION

Something that made me realize just how far man's technology has moved forward was the Communication Room. It was very small, and the transmitting equipment used huge bulbs that I remembered as a boy. They were similar to those used in the first televisions. They had thirty or forty of these to transmit information; and I had forgotten how cumbersome these pieces of equipment were just to fit into the appliances. Now, with so many megabytes of information stored on computer chips smaller than the size of a fingernail, it feels far greater than a hundred years ago.

When I looked up at the rigging of the ship, I took a deep breath and thought, "Would I have ever been able to do that, on high seas with those masts moving and swaying in the winds?" I couldn't help but admire the men that sailed on the tall ships, regardless of what size, and climbed up in gales to reef in huge canvas. There must have been thousands of men that lost their lives reefing sail. This was a remarkable period of men's adventure into the unknown. I gazed up at these tall masts and thought of the many stories that had never been told, of these courageous men that sailed the Seven Seas.

I was re-inspired to add to my adventure, and to sail around the cape of South America. Yes, I had sailed the Seven Seas; not with De Gama, or Magellan, or Francis Drake in their great square-rigged ships but in modern times and I could say that "the salt is with me". Standing on those decks, and in the wheelhouse, I wished that I'd been born in those times, and had felt the spray on my face. These were the kings of ships, not only for Britain, but also for all the great sea-faring nations to discover planet Earth's four corners. This had to be one of highlights and an unexpected treat to visit this ship.

With taking quite a few pictures and looking like some inspection officer checking each nook and cranny, I had thoroughly enjoyed my unescorted tour of this wonderful vessel. Of course, there were the requisite souvenirs and they were not exactly giving them away. Among the plaques, little pins and key chains, the one thing that caught my eye was a ship's

Robert F. Edwards

whistle. Originally, an officer would blow a whistle as a signal for when somebody was coming aboard. This was a unique whistle, with a sea-horse design and it required a special way of holding it to blow out the different commands required. Needless to say, Captain Edwards purchased one of these mementos to honor this occasion.

Back on shore, I found out that like the Queen Elizabeth that was docked in Los Angeles, California, to attract attention to one of the building developments, this one had been purchased for that purpose as well, along this expensive strip. There was also a Catholic university here to bring extra prestige to the area, and some art museums.

By this time, it was a little early for dinner, but too late for lunch; and I had noticed one of the steakhouses on my wanderings. I could not believe my obsession with beef, and my friends would think that I had either become Argentinean or that I had completely abandoned most of my vegetarian ways. With that, though, I looked at my watch and it was five-thirty, quarter to six. I entered the steak house and asked them politely when they would open and they just smiled and said, "Now". There was little hesitation on my behalf. The fellow showed me a table; it was a very posh-looking steak house. The waiter tried to explain their system; if I turned the card over in one way, then it was a buffet, the other way, it was for the steaks. So, I asked if I could look at the buffet. It was an elegant spread with fresh shrimp and lots of salads. The desserts were orgasmic in themselves, the variety from cheesecake, apple pie, chocolate mousse, and chocolate cake, and so forth; everything that would entice the imagination of any connoisseur. The dishes were numerous with salads and entrees, and a variety of breads or pans.

The restaurant catered to not only this part of the new inner city, but to people that still had an air of elegance about them. I had chosen the meat dishes and this was no mistake, I'll tell you. I ordered a beer, with the humidity here; I hadn't stopped perspiring since I got off the plane in Chile. I probably had the cleanest pores in the world then, but between per-

212

SOUTH AMERICA
EXPLORATION

spiration and dehydration, the first beer went down in one gulp and I quickly followed it up with another one.

Soon, the meats started to come. The first one was pork and I declined, asking for beef, and wow. I don't know whether to call it a roast or the largest filet mignon I had ever seen, absolutely indescribable. It literally cut with the precision of firm butter and when I put it in my mouth, it salivated the glands, with the seasoning they used and the sheer tenderness of the meat. Many, many years ago, in Kyoto and Tokyo I had some of the best "Kobe" beef that Japan was famous for. Whether my memory had dulled, or whether this had taken over my taste buds, I don't know; but it seemed to be far superior.

The next one that came along on these long skewers (which Brazil does also) was a sausage, equally delicious. Just as I was about to finish one, lo and behold, my attentive waiter arrived with more variety of meats, all different. I had beef ribs; a little bit fatty compared to the solid hunk of meat. Once I finished with the bones and the bit of fat that I left, out came a brand new plate before the next skewer arrived. There was also meat that was rolled with cheese inside. The Argentines have excelled in the art of cooking their meats and I would never be the same after I had tasted those succulent portions. Finally a point is reached, even with my robust appetite, and it was robust where sheer gluttony was borderline. I did order some French fries and a bit of bread, but the main course was barbarous amounts of meat. Both plates had expelled large amounts of juice, and I felt like a werewolf feasting on its prey. With another two beers to wash the succulent juices down, I was forced to say no when the chicken came.

I was now absolutely full and mellow, to say the least. This had been a remarkable eating experience and I thought that I had a good one in Rio de Janeiro, which I still commend; but now that I realized the ways of South America, and their cooking abilities with meat, I was glad that I had taken it upon myself to forget the "foot-and-mouth" disease of Britain and the plague of "mad cow" disease growing in the global community, and enjoyed beef of the pampas lands of Argentina.

Robert F. Edwards

I felt that I owed it to myself, if nothing else, to spend some time seeing the tango. Rio de Janeiro and Brazil has the samba, a very provocative and sexy-looking dance, but Argentina has the tango. It has not only made Argentina famous, but the dance itself is a work of art and very sensuous. It brought the Latin out in all of us; and passion of dancing to the forefront. The foot movements were interwoven as the two dancers changed positions on the dance floor. It was equally as aggressive for the woman as for the man; and the steps were in unison and consistency; but the actual flicking and the forward movement depended on the dancers. It had an air of the roaring twenties and with this intoxicating city of Buenos Aires, seems to fit in any period. Throughout the city, in malls and open-air places, the tango was promoted; and rightfully so. It was a music with connotations, but always the rhythm; very unique to the Argentine culture.

After watching some dancers for the better part of an hour, my day had been a very rewarding one and it was time to say goodnight to one and all.

Goodnight, my beautiful little wife. If I was going to dance, I would love to learn the tango with you and I think we'd be as Latin as any of these. I love you, my little darling. Goodnight.

SOUTH AMERICA
EXPLORATION

March 4th, Sunday
Buenos Aires, Argentina

I had woken up at around six-thirty and as I looked out the window, there was no doubt in my mind; this was going to be one hot day. There was a beautiful blue sky above and I could feel the heat starting to build at this early hour. There was no reason for me to get up quickly because this was going to be a day of tolerance and endurance long into the next day as I started my pilgrimage to the southern parts of Argentina.

However, it would be my last day in Buenos Aires and there were things that I still wanted to see and experience. With this in mind, I got up, did my toiletries and started to prepare my packing. This didn't seem to take quite as long as in some cases; but on the other hand, I was still wearing the same clothes. I knew I was going to wear these one more day; better still, probably a couple more days before I got off the bus and then did a complete change.

I got on the elevator to go down for breakfast. I had been on many elevators in my life, but this one was very unique. The elevators in this hotel were very small; maximum, maybe seven or eight people of medium build. This one had metal corrugated doors, and only went up to the third floor. I happened to be on the fourth. The first night, with all my luggage, I got out on the third floor and walked up the fourth. However, on doing an investigation, I found that this elevator had a small side door to it. I had seen large elevators in hospitals with doors opposite each other, but never an elevator with a side door.

With that out of the way, I had a spartan breakfast. I guess Sunday was a day of fasting because I only had crackers, rather than the small croissants, but it was not a big deal. I had settled up with the management and asked permission to

215

keep the luggage there until the evening when my bus started its long journey southward. I was going to miss this hotel and its refurbishing job was worth mentioning, the value here was well spent, at least in my estimation; along with being so central.

I started the day at Plaza Dorrego and on Sunday they host the Feria de San Telmo, a flea market or bazaar. Obviously, this being Sunday and the luck of the Irish was with me so I decided to check this plaza out. On my way, I had a few errands to do before that. My first priority was, of course, the Internet and I had received a beautiful e-mail from my little honey bun. I responded by sending one to her and Wendy, just to keep the channels of communication going. Also, I read a fair amount of news and it was almost high noon before I finished with the Internet.

As I was walking towards the plaza, I passed by the Catedral Metropolitana. It looked Greek in appearance; but once inside, it was one of the most beautiful churches that I had been in so far, in South America. The altar was pure silver and some of the pulpit was marble and silver. It was sheer elegance in the highest degree. There were a lot of side altars and frescoes on the dome that overlooked the altar. One of the important aspects of this cathedral, beside the sheer elegance and location was that it contained the tomb of José de San Martín, Argentina's most revered historical figure. As I went into the rotunda, there were guards dressed in period costume of San Martin, high pillbox hats, red and gold braid, with sabers, standing guard over the tomb.

To my good fortune, a Mass was just about to commence, and I not only attended but I received Holy Communion. It was something remarkable, when my roots were touched and my soul was full. I was so grateful to be given that moment of not only being in a great cathedral; not only having the honor of seeing the most revered man's tomb; but to receive holy communion to celebrate a man, a God, a way of life, Jesus Christ, that over two thousand years ago sacrificed his life for ideals that we try to obtain today as a way of life. It was an emotional moment for me as the mass ended, and I felt elevated in spirit.

The open market was not what I had expected. I hoped it to be more of a bazaar, rather than people bringing whatever they could find in their closets to exchange for something else. It was an older area of Buenos Aires and the buildings reflected this. They were much smaller in size and the maximum was about three storeys; a lot were just a single storey. However, this particular plaza was an area that the dealers were concentrated in and collectively put their goods together. The plaza itself was closed off for the Sunday event.

This was where I was first introduced to some unusual street buskers, when I noticed a man dressed up like Charlie Chaplin. These people would be in pantomime, frozen as statues and only moved when somebody threw a contribution into their little offering cups. It was well done; a woman had painted herself and her garments in a reddish-stone color and I wished I had taken a picture of her. There was also a man further up the street that was dressed in the costume of the Twenties era standing on a podium. A lot of ingenuity and thought went into it. An older woman (that should have taken heed that age does not always accelerate quality) was dressed in a tango outfit, wearing a man's hat. Another woman that was her age and maybe more had an infinite amount of bells, whistles, and flutes and jingled a tune to achieve her remuneration. Along with that, a man had tied a mannequin/dummy to his toes and danced the tango with it, this I thought being the best performance.

The rest of the piazza was closed off, with many kiosks. It reminded me so much of swap meets where the scavengers had cleaned out their attics and basements, hoping these collectibles would attract exorbitant prices. My real quest was to find some gaucho's paraphernalia and primarily the sombrero. One fellow tried to sell me a sombrero, "Get this, it's an antique; the hat is new but the rawhide is an antique, it's over fifty years old". I doubt that he really believed this himself, let alone was trying to promote it. He wanted sixty-five dollars

U.S. for it. I was still regretting that when I was in Salta, I hadn't picked up the sombrero I would have liked for fifteen dollars. I just didn't want to carry a hat around for the next two months if I didn't have to.

Anyway, after graciously saying "thanks, but no thanks," I continued on to the other booths with anything from silverware from the turn of the century; to heavy pad locks; even a blow torch; canes; and jewelry of course. Everybody forsakes their jewelry when it becomes unfashionable except for hippies and women that are searching for that new "off the beaten track" look. The prices that they were asking for these 'collectibles' were just absurd. I thought the antique dealers and flea marketers in Vancouver had lost their conscience and touch with reality, but these people had taken it over the edge.

I spent about an hour wandering through the stalls, and adding to my disappointment, I went into a restaurant and ordered pasta. Unfortunately, it was the poorest meal I had in a restaurant up to date and it was the most expensive. The pasta wasn't even cooked thoroughly, and the dry buns that were provided, this was the first restaurant that charged me for them. The diet Seven-Up that I received cost me more than the large bottles of cerveza in most restaurants. Needless to say, this was not my area of town to hang out in.

After spending some time looking at who showed up, it was tourist time and maybe a few locals were here rather than going to the beach. But the cameras were out, including mine, shooting pictures; but the business was less than brisk. Most of the pirates in the flea market were sitting fanning themselves as the spectators walked by. One of the highlights of this area for me was watching the tango dancers. An older couple that was exceptionally good were also selling CDs, but I just didn't feel up to contributing. The man would pick out some of the women from the group that were watching and danced with them. He was just one of those types of people that if you had two feet, he can make them move in the right direction and you'd look good. The next couple that I saw was younger and put a lot more body language into their steps with high kicking and interweaving of legs. A lot more erotic movements than the first couple, but both of them displayed the versatility of the tango.

It was a very moving dance to watch and I imagine it would be exuberating to participate in.

Feeling that I had exhausted everything available in this particular area of town, I started to venture back to Avenida de Mayo and my old familiar haunts. It was a very hot day, so I stopped to have a diet Pepsi and try to recapture some of the fluids that I was giving away. As I sat down, a woman started talking to me. She had just arrived from Melbourne, Australia, and we discussed some of the things I'd seen. We talked for a while before parting company.

Bingo! I managed to get what I was looking for - some blank tapes, and then headed back to the hotel. On the way, I also picked up a few postcards, as well as some beverages and a bit of yogurt for the long journey ahead. It was seven o'clock, so I started to prepare myself before I headed down to the bus station to wait for the bus. I soon got into conversation with the gentleman at the front desk, a real nice man about my age. He was telling me about his father and when trouble struck, they had to sell a huge block of their land. He was talking in hectares and I gathered his father had owned large tracts of land, somewhere in the neighborhood of three townships. He had to sell half of it to pay the bank their debt and at that particular time, it was five hundred pesos a given area and that was all his father received. He went on to tell

219

me about the horrendous problems that Argentina experienced in the 80's with hyperinflation. Now, he had a small kiosk, selling soft drinks, ice cream, novelties, and some toys. After more discussions on international affairs, this generous man not only found me a taxi but also said he would record the taxi's number just in case there was any trouble. We can never too cautious, believe me.

At the bus station, I was able to find the platform that I was supposed to be on and being the better part of an hour ahead of schedule, I was starting to get used to the procedure. Even in this huge terminal, it was nowhere near the congestion that I experienced at Rio de Janeiro. In due course and true to the handwritten ticket that I had, my bus showed up and I started to shuffle with the rest in place.

There was a woman behind me and I noticed she had a coat draped over her arm and I didn't really think too much of it at the time because there was a lot of pushing and shoving to get luggage on board. But once I got my bags stowed and started to walk away, I noticed that my security pouch was dangling from my pants rather than in its proper pocket. This was almost a successful attempt of pick pocketing, even though I had taken a lot of security measures. I had a security pouch with zippers on it, and the one pocket held my passport and tickets for the bus. The other one held my currency and credit cards. All of that was inside another pocket that was buttoned down securely and clipped to my pants with a cord that held on to the pouch. To my total amazement, not only had the pouch been taken out of my pocket, but also the zipper had been opened to where my credit card and money was. It was more the grace of God and good luck, I guess, than good management on my part that nothing had been removed. Normally, I put the pouch around my neck but my perspiration was so great that everything was soaking wet.

However, the bus was air-conditioned and I was actually cold for the first time since I had arrived. No wonder I was getting a sore throat with these extreme temperature fluctuations. Sitting on the bus, I recalled that I had only been pickpocketed twice; once in Cuba which was a successful accomplishment, and now this attempt in Buenos Aires. I realized again that security could never be too tight with my personal belongings and though I had been watching my luggage with the scrutiny of a guard, I left myself vulnerable to this slick-fingered woman.

Right on schedule, the bus took off. Through the night, it was like a torch beaming its way down the endless black tarmac into the darkness that lay ahead. I was able to sleep spasmodically throughout the night and eventually the dawn arrived.

So, I'll say goodnight, little honey bun. I couldn't say that I went to bed, but I did sleep.

Robert F. Edwards

It was surprising how many miles we traveled when all I had to do was open up the curtains on the bus and we were still in motion. To say how many kilometers would be only my estimation, but I would think this bus must have logged more than a few hundred. We were now in the pampas area of prairies. I looked out the window and if I blinked it could have been southern Saskatchewan, to say the least. It was very flat, with some herds of cattle as well as flocks of sheep, grazing on the tough prairie grass.

As in Saskatchewan and Alberta, their hay bales were very similar to what we do; as well as the rolled type that seemed to be more in vogue. They used the tree lines for windbreaks just as Canadians do to protect the erosion of the soil. I did see one large hacienda and probably the only difference from being on the Prairie Provinces was it was white, with the tile roof. The flatness was endless, dotted with sagebrush and thistles, and even a few beehives.

This land was so different from what I had seen in South America up to date, except for a bit in Uruguay. Even the soil had reverted back to clay with none of the rich terracotta prevalent in the northern parts of Argentina and Chile. This was real prairie dirt, and when the great rains did come this soil wouldn't absorb it with the same depth as some other types of soil.

Outside of the great cities in South America, it was thinly populated and this long black strip of asphalt was sparse with traffic. After the better part of an hour, I hadn't seen even a building. In some ways, it reminded me of the great outback in Australia. I did pass something that was rather unique; a pumping station of some sort. They were using two forms of

222

alternative power; one was the windmill and the other was solar power. I had often thought in places like this that have an abundance of sunlight, that solar power was more appropriate.

One of the big differences from the Outback, which had no fences, here were the strands of barbed wire and conventional wooden posts. I was also quite surprised with the lack of fowls or birds. I had seen one small prairie chicken, and other than that, only the odd sparrow; not an abundance of wildlife.

What caught my eye besides the vastness was also the cleanliness. I remembered parts of North Africa that the desert was cluttered with plastic bags and garbage. Alongside the road here I saw the odd plastic bag or bottle; but I didn't know whether it was a lack of population as the reason for it, or whether Argentines had more respect for the beauty of their country.

As we continued traveling, the grass was little tufts rather than the great pampas grass that I passed earlier that morning. The bus I was on was more of a conventional style bus that did have air-conditioning. It even had a television, and they had played a video for us last night. It was an older bus and it had worked its way through these long hauls more than once. However, it was a Mercedes and a nice riding bus.

By then, I had been in all shapes and sizes, even double-deckers that I had to go up a stairwell that would have given a fireman a nosebleed, and I had to wonder about the technical advantages of them. Sometimes the old conventional ones seemed to have the best facilities and this one had a toilet as well on it. It must be a highly competitive business in South America as there were literally hundreds of bus lines, all going in similar directions. The very first bus that I was on had been the most luxurious and I had yet to book into another with those huge, lush seats or the legroom that it provided. This coach line was not providing any food and I was beginning to wonder if they were even going to provide any stops. We had a ten-minute stop at a fairly remote terminal where I hoped to get a cup of coffee; that was three hours ago and the answer

223

was, "No, it just didn't have any, just soft drinks; so if you haven't brought it, you're not going to eat it."

We finally stopped at a seaport loading area and fuelled up. The bus took in four hundred and eighty-five dollars U.S worth of gas, so I was glad I was not paying the bill. This stop was quite typical, as once we were off the highway; it was just dirt roads and a "whistle stop." This one was a loading area for sea-faring ships taking on anything from wheat to oil products. Argentina was an exporter of oil, and this area seemed to produce almost the entire amount of petroleum products.

We passed by some residential areas so I knew we were nearing a city. It was quite large, with the usual high rises to it. I was looking for a sign that would indicate, and it couldn't have been in excess of a hundred thousand people. It was a nice layout and at least it was by the oceanside, so these people had that extra bonus. The construction was the typical brick and mortar concept. It was partly spread out, due to the fact that we were still in a very flat area of Argentina. It was a bit cooler here; maybe it was just far enough south now that the heat wave was over. Most of the windows on the homes were shuttered and had corrugated metal on the roof rather than the tiles that I had seen so much of already.

The hours kept moving along with the kilometers, and I think I had seen something like one thousand, seven hundred and sixty-eight kilometers from Buenos Aires. It would probably be the big 3-0, 0-0 kilometers before I got to Rio Gallegos. It was dusk now, and the bus just kept rolling on. Sometimes I almost forgot what day it was, let alone what time it was. The terrain had very few tufts of grass, too sparse for any amount of cattle.

The darkness crept over the daylight hours, and ever so often, we came into a hamlet or town, that to me had little meaning with no names. Some were a little more affluent than others, but they all had one thing in common; about a ten-minute stop, load human cargo off, add a few human cargo on.

SOUTH AMERICA EXPLORATION

The most remarkable thing on this particular bus was the two bus drivers. I boarded with them in Buenos Aires, and the principal driver was probably in his late forties, a pleasant, upbeat individual. He had been driving all night, and I was sure that they alternated, but I had slept one night and I was now preparing to sleep for the next night in a sardine fashion, and these men just kept on rolling. In some of the buses, the driver and the co-driver had luxurious seats. This wasn't the case here; and the driver that was resting would sit on a little bench, and I hadn't even seen them head to the back where there was the odd empty seat. Out of all the tens of thousands of kilometers I had added on the buses in this South American trip, I had never seen the tolerance and endurance that these two had demonstrated. On that first luxurious bus, there were three drivers and just about every two hours, they rotated each other. These fellows hardly took the time to go to the bathroom. If there was anything I could say detrimental to the bus or to these men, it would be that their music and I didn't have much in common. They played it fairly loud; but it was the least I could put up with considering the tolerance that these two men had.

As the night fell upon us and the music was with us, I tried to find different positions to catch some rest through the night. Nine o'clock came, ten o'clock came, and I knew that Argentineans ate late, but eleven o'clock came and we still were not stopping for a meal. Finally, at one o'clock in the morning, we stopped for about ten minutes and I grabbed some ham and cheese sandwiches and a Seven-Up just to put something in the stomach so it would quit growling.

About three o'clock in the morning, another bus was beside us, neck and neck with each other down the road until it had a flat tire. We stayed until it was repaired and again, "down the highway we go." Dawn found me looking out the window and again, the terrain was very sparse and flat. I felt that I could look to the edge of the world, but the only consolation I had was that I was heading to the end of this continent, the Cape of Good Hope.

Robert F. Edwards

Looking out the window, I had always enjoyed watching the sunrises, with those beautiful pinks and deep blues. A lot of people miss the opportunity of looking the opposite way of a sunrise, which is equally as mesmerizing. It was soon seven o'clock; and I had a sigh of relief since I did not want to arrive at four or five in the morning; very difficult to find taxis or hotels or whatever. This worry was now well behind me and feeling somewhat rejuvenated, I had decided to go on to Punta Arenas in Chile. This would be the next stop on my way to the Cape. I still had to cross over to the Chilean side, take a ferry through the Magellan Straits, and then catch another bus to Rio Grande, and then on to Ushuaia.

Looking out the window, the terrain was changing with more hills; and not much vegetation on them either. This must be an area that received little rain, but high winds. I could see the trees, the few that were visible, were leaning heavily into the winds. Also, during the brief moments of freedom from the seat on the bus, I had felt it became cooler. It was hard to believe that when I started this journey, I was soaking wet with perspiration in Buenos Aires and now, I was wearing my sweater. It just goes to show what a few thousand kilometers will do going south.

After what seemed an endless trail of asphalt, I noticed the first sign of my final destination on this leg. Rio Gallegos was only thirty kilometers away, so I was finally within striking distance of this arduous journey. With a mere half hour to endure, I started to both prepare myself mentally and physically for the next adventure to head on to Chile.

As the bus pulled into its final destination, another leg of my journey was going to commence. I managed to secure a

SOUTH AMERICA
EXPLORATION

ticket to Punta Arenas and it left at one o'clock. With it then being around nine o'clock in the morning, I really only had three and a half, four hours. With that, I made my way into town and yes, of course, my first stop, the internet; and my beautiful wife had given me a good long e-mail to savor and cherish and my loving daughter had provided me with one, also. Even Matt, my brother-in-law gave me a quick reply saying that all was well. Eric, an old traveling companion from my time in Morocco, updated me with his news, being a regular correspondent now.

After having a couple of cups of coffee, my wake-up was complete and I managed to do a complete surveillance of the town in the next two and a half hours. Rio Gallegos was around a hundred thousand population, and was supported mostly by oil and wool products. It was modern, with little historical memorabilia. I went into some of the shops that dedicated themselves to the Patagonian area and the souvenirs I found very expensive with no real local significance. What I was really looking for were some wool sweaters. I thought it would be nice to buy a real heavy wool sweater for myself and maybe a cardigan for Marietta; however, I didn't think any of them were even made here.

So, with some disappointment, I only bought some postcards and a bit of food supplies for the next leg of my journey and strolled up and down the streets. I checked with one of the travel agents about the glacier and they confirmed what I already knew; that I had to go to another city and then get an organized tour from there. With that information confirmed, I decided that it probably would be prudent to have something to eat and had an omelet, ham and cheese, with bread and coffee.

Soon I was back at my faithful location, the terminal, and preparing myself for the next leg of this adventure. When the bus arrived, it was quite modern compared to the one that transported me on the long leg of my journey. It was rather peculiar, when I traveled on the Chilean side it was a nicely paved highway and as I entered the Argentine side, it turned

Robert F. Edwards

into gravel. We continued on that until we hit the next town, which then became asphalt throughout my journey in Argentina. It was rather curious that I was heading towards the Chilean border once more and it was back to gravel. Needless to say, the bus couldn't make anywhere near the time that it would if it was on asphalt.

We had crossed over a couple of cattle grates, but I only saw sheep grazing. I didn't get a good look at it, but I thought I saw an ostrich or that size of bird, but once I checked the types of birds that persist down here, I realized it was a Rhea. I was starting to notice some large hills as we made headway into the Patagonian area. I knew that the landscape would change within the next thirty to fifty kilometers, the way the mountain ranges seemed to be progressing. At the moment, though, the vegetation was sparse with mostly thistles. These were purple in bloom, as on the prairies in Canada, and only grew about a foot to eighteen inches high. At this time of year, they looked quite pretty. I thought 'delightful to watch, not wise to touch'.

We were still on the rocky road to Chile. The bus couldn't make very good time due to the fact of the washboard conditions of the roads. The cattle grates were more precisely "sheep crossings". In Canada, we use circular tubes for cattle crossings. These ones were old railroad tracks that had been cut according to the length of the highway.

Once again, I have managed to do another border crossing. We just completed the Argentine part and to my surprise, I thought they needed a form filled out, but a stamp was given without it; and on to the Chilean side where, I don't know what happened but the lights were out in this one. This was the more conventional distance of maybe a kilometer or two between the two borders. To my delight, Customs didn't make this bus driver take our entire luggage out to search. I suppose this was partly because the border separates only their two countries of Argentina and Chile, rather than the northern parts like Peru and Bolivia that have a mix of nationali-

SOUTH AMERICA
EXPLORATION

ties. Also those borders were tighter because of the drug problems in some of the countries.

We crossed the border and conforming to the Chilean-Argentine mandate, as soon as we had reached the Chilean side, it was asphalt instead of gravel. In this part of Chile and Argentina, there were still some disputes about borders. As I wanted to get down to the far southern point of Argentina, I had no alternative by land other than to go through Chile and then cross over the Magellan Straits. Still in Chile, I had to go to San Sebastian, which was another border that crossed back into Argentina. Needless to say, the only other alternative to get to that landmass that belonged to Argentina was by boat.

I couldn't help but think what a congested mess it would be if Quebec ever separated from Canada and we had to go through this headache of crossing from one country to another to get back to our own country again. This was a prime example of congestion and inconvenience at its worst. The only saving grace down here was that it was not a traffic lane of Argentina. Mother Nature never recognizes the lines that Mankind draws on geographic maps of her terra firma.

The landscape remained consistent, and I had observed two hawks sitting on the fence watching a flock of sheep. No, I don't believe that they had their eyes on taking that back to the nest, but this would probably indicate that there were prairie gophers or small rodents that roamed the plains. I had spotted about six more rheas, and the sheep looked well fed. It was raining by then, and I expected that the parched grass might turn green by tomorrow. In remote areas of limited moisture, it was surprising what a few droplets of rain could do for the land that was thirsting for a drink.

I still had my sweater on and all through the day, with the cold winds, it was bordering on the first grips of frost. Quite a few Argentineans in Buenos Aires had told me, when I told them I was coming down this far south, they said "Be sure to dress warm". Mind you, I was in the throngs of a meltdown there, and it was natural for them to think of anything other than thirty plus Celsius as being cold.

The kilometers were quickly passing by now that we were on asphalt. Reflecting back on the incredible amount of hours that I had spent sitting looking out a bus window, I could honestly say that I did not regret it. As I approached this vast part of the world; it was far better than joining the navy and seeing the world through a porthole. Mountain ranges were starting to form in the ruggedness of this landscape as we progressed southward.

I felt that I had made the right decision even though the distances had astounded my imagination. In review, I had covered the deserts of the north, the jungles of the mid West, the vast pampas areas of the plains, and now was looking forward to the Patagonian area of mountains and glaciers. All these landscapes deserved the hours that I had spent looking through a window.

A sheep truck passed us on the road and I had thought cattle were poorly confined when they were going to market, but

sheep had it worse. This truck was about one and a half times the height of a cattle truck and it had five tiers of sheep logged into it. Standing room only! The only worse conditions I had ever seen animals go to market under were chicken trucks with their crates. If the Humane Society recorded some of the abuses for animals going to market, there would be a human outcry and it wouldn't be just about "foot-and-mouth" disease or "mad cow" disease; it would be the "mad human abuse on animals". I had seen a few guanacos; they looked like small

SOUTH AMERICA
EXPLORATION

llamas. Also, I had seen some geese, not the great Canada goose, but about that size. A lot more cattle were showing up, as the grass was getting thicker. The rheas were quite abundant; and seemed to be scattered throughout this region.

Far off in the distance, there were some buildings ahead, but I was taken by surprise when we entered the city. When I got off the bus and retrieved my luggage, I decided that the first thing I should do was secure a ticket to my next point of destination, which was Ushuaia, Argentina. This was near the cape and the furthest city in Argentina before land's end. The bus terminal was very small; more just a drive-through. This was what threw me off; that I hadn't reached my final destination of Punta Arena; but yes, I had arrived.

After I made some inquiries, there was another bus depot three or four blocks away. So, luggage in hand, I started to make the trek in the rain. After realizing that my luggage had accumulated an awful lot of weight with memorabilia and knick-knacks on each passing day, it had become more than just a burden. Struggling with it and not wanting my luggage to get wet, I gave up the quest and decided to take a taxi.

Flagging down a cab was not too difficult; but when I got to the hotel that was recommended by one of my co-travelers, it was not in business any longer. So, I asked the cab driver to take me to a boarding house, but she was full. Finally, I just said, "No, look, take me to a hotel that has a Visa." All this cruising around, in what amounted to about eight blocks, and he not only charged me a thousand pesos (while the meter only said "seven") but when he did asked the hotel if they had room, he wanted another thousand pesos for gratis.

This put a damper on my attitude; but I checked in and the young lady at the front desk spoke adequate English. The next move would be to find the other bus depot. When I asked at the station before I left, the young lady gave me the right directions but told me it was closed. From my experiences in Russia, I realized "check, then check, and then start checking again". With that in mind, I did proceed to the bus station, to find out that it was open and I was able to get the information required.

I did not have sufficient Chilean pesos (or at least I didn't think I had) so my next approach would be to a bank and try one of the instant tellers. I had found that throughout South America, MasterCard was more popular than Visa. Unfortunately, this bus terminal would only accept cash. After walking in the cold rain I finally located the right instant teller but it didn't work for foreigners. Feeling a little down in the mouth by now, I decided to find the Internet, but was unsuccessful at that, also.

With dampened spirits, I returned to the hotel considerably wetter; but at least my Gore-tex jacket was repelling the rain. The young lady informed me that it would be much cheaper if I ate at the hotel, since I wouldn't be charged the sales tax as in the restaurants. So after freshening up a bit, I ordered a beer and looked over the menu. There wasn't much on it that caught my attention, but I did remember reading that this particular area was famous for its seafood. Obviously on the Straits of Magellan, this made a lot of sense to me at least. I tried to order scallops but the waitress didn't seem to recognize this word. When she finally said "abalone", I agreed and said "certainly so". The abalone was served with tomatoes, and a salad of lettuce, more tomatoes, and slices of hard-boiled egg, with pan alongside. With another beer, added to the one that I'd already consumed, I finished my meal, had a cup of coffee, and returned to my room.

The room was adequate, certainly not the best I'd had. For twenty-five thousand pesos (around forty-five dollars U.S.) at least I was out of the rain. With the slightest bit of cold weather, everybody turned the heat on. The room was smothering with heat, so I turned off the radiator, and opened all the windows to try to cool off. I did a bit of reading and tried to think positively of what would transpire tomorrow.

Goodnight, one and all. Goodnight, my little true love; I miss you dearly.

SOUTH AMERICA EXPLORATION

March 7th, Wednesday
Punta Arenas, Chile

I woke up knowing that I didn't have to get up very early, so I rolled over in bed for an extra forty winks. The room was enjoyably cool and this helped me sleep very well indeed. It was surprising, with just the right conditions, how restful things became. Realizing that even the day had improved along with my attitude because the sun was up and the rain had subsided. A new day had begun and the adventure with it.

I did just my usual toiletries and went down to the Spartan breakfast provided, of two pieces of toast, Tang orange juice and instant coffee. However, feeling better for it and enjoying it because it was included in the price of the room, I was ready to start my adventure. With camera and "The Lonely Planet" book in hand, and determination to see this great city, I set off!

Most of the buildings were turn-of-the-last-century and in beautiful condition. Some of the architectural achievements would be a marvel in any area, let alone this remote section of the world. My first decision was to stroll down and see the Magellan Straits and the harbor. The part that I had chosen was not beach material, but the weather really wasn't beach weather either. Even though the rain had subsided, I was still wearing a jacket. It was such a contrast, compared to what I had been enduring in the northern parts of this continent. However, I thoroughly enjoyed it, took some pictures, and soon it was nine o'clock.

I discovered that I did have a lot more Chilean pesos than I had thought, which was a pleasant surprise. My next stop was to get my bus tickets, which I found would be leaving tomorrow morning at seven o'clock. With that out of my way, the next pertinent thing on my "to do" list was to find an

233

Robert F. Edwards

Internet that was open. And again, just what a difference a day makes. I found one, logged in, and had quite a few e-mails to read, but most importantly, two from my beautiful wife. Everything seemed to be holding together relatively well on the home front. As far as the news goes, whether it was from the Internet or the television, or papers, if you ever had good news, then it wouldn't be on this planet. So, from stock markets having bad days, to the vice-president having a heart attack, and a young man shooting his way through his educational program and doing away with his fellow students, the foot-and-mouth disease of England seemed to have dropped down from the top number one spot.

As I was walking through the city, I couldn't believe the number of little shops and entrepreneurs. One woman had two mannequins dressed in a sheepskin coat, and I thought I could get a wool sweater for Marietta, or myself but all hers were very expensive. I admired some leather jackets lined with wool and then saw a sea-faring captain's hat, only to find out that it was made in Germany.

I continued walking through the streets snapping pictures, and was getting the flavor of the city. To sum up, when I asked if I had arrived last night, one man said, "Yes, you've arrived at Punta Arenas, a beautiful city." It was a beautiful city and well laid-out. Even coming in last night, I noticed that the buildings were quite modern on the outskirts and a lot of duplexes. It was an easy city to get around and the river flowed through the centre, amidst large boulevards and piazzas. Many people were selling their wares and eventually, I found a woman that knitted wool sweaters and I bought one for Marietta with two penguins on it.

Mid-day was approaching, so I went into a restaurant and what a pleasant surprise! I ended up having a steak with eggs, fried onions and the ever-popular French fries, and a beer. The woman asked me when I was finished if I would like anything, coffee, and I said, "Yes, I'd like a large one; and do you have any dessert?" Wow, a lemon meringue pie. A very enjoyable lunch and if I did the conversion, would be about seven dollars U.S.

The afternoon was well under way, and my feet started to realize that I'd been walking for the better part of five hours. I went back to the hotel to unload some of the information that I accumulated from the turista kiosk that I found in the square. With my shoes off and my toes wiggling, I started to read the newly accumulated information, which was quite enlightening about the areas that I wanted to see, Puerto Natales and Torres del Paine national park. This was the real Patagonian area that was so famous for its glaciers and trekking trails and a variety of sport activities, including white water rafting, boating, fishing; a real outdoor paradise (weather permitting).

At about four o'clock in the afternoon, I felt that if I didn't get up soon, I'd waste the rest of the day. This time, I started walking in the opposite direction of town and found a very interesting, more Bohemian type of district. With good fortune I found a heavy Aran wool sweater that was just perfect for my purposes, and to top it off I bought a Chilean naval hat (black). Wearing these new pieces of adornment on my own little sailboat, I knew I'd look like an international sailor.

I happened to get talking to a young lady that was more than helpful and she spoke very good English. She seemed to have all the time in the world for me and explained about Torres del Paine Park; the infinite amount of hiking trails, which campgrounds had facilities; and which were strictly isolated and "bring your own supplies". She spent the better part of two hours providing me with maps and information. This was just the lucky break that I needed to plan the next eight to twelve days. Also, this confirmed that I had made the right choices by shortening previous trips and spending long passages of time on the buses. By having these extra days available, it allowed me the opportunity to spend time trekking through some of the most beautiful parts of the Patagonian area of both Chile and Argentina.

Robert F. Edwards

I returned to the Internet to relay this to Marietta and to give her an update of some of the progress that I had made at my end. Once I had completed that, I realized that I had just enough time to go to one of the great turn-of-the-century mansions now converted into a museum. There was much to see in Punta Arenas, located on the western shore of the Straits of Magellan. Its population was close to a hundred thousand, and attracted research and tourist ships with a custom-free zone to help encourage trade and commerce. But at one time, it was the wool boom that gave rise to the great mansions, now preserved from the turn of the century and gave the city a great atmosphere. Before the sheep arrived in the early 19th century, it was a big producer of animal hides from sealskins and guanaco. Also, there were minerals like gold and some timber in the area. But it was really the wool boom that really got things going and one of the wealthiest individuals was José Menéndes. At one time, he controlled nearly a million hectares in the Magallanes and Argentina.

Many of these mansions still dominate the downtown core; such as the museum and cultural center, Casa Braun-Menéndez. Also about three blocks from the plaza, Avenida España 959, which belonged to Charly Milward and his distant relative Bruce Chetwynd wrote about it in the his adventures, 'In Patagonia'. When I went in there, the first part was a fairly typical museum; and showcased some of the conquistador's armor and maps of Magellan's trip through the straits. I had to pay an extra two dollars to take pictures. At first, I was questioning whether my dollars were well spent as I continued into the foyer of the mansion, which, again, I wasn't overly impressed with. It was just an area displaying different hats, men's on one side and women's on the other.

It was the rooms that were roped off that enticed me, and I asked the woman who was sitting by, supervising them, if I could see inside and she said "si". First, she gave me a pair of surgical-type fabric booties to put on over my shoes, and I understood why as I entered that area. The hardwood floors were an art in themselves. I have no idea of how many differ-

236

ent types of wood were laid into those magnificent hardwood floors but the designs alone were fantastic. One of the rooms was a boudoir or the bedroom and displaying the furniture of the period. The bathroom was the size of most people's living rooms today and the bathtub could have held two large people or a small family. Obviously, people had servants in those days. The bathroom was furnished in old white porcelain with small diagonal tiles on the floor and white tiles on top.

I went into the next room, a billiards room. The pool table was a piece of art in itself, in addition to all the different wood used in the paneling, the chairs and some of the built-in furniture. Further along the same corridor was my favorite room, an office or study. The sheer elegance of the ceilings, at least twenty feet high and were highly decorated along with the walls still carrying some of the original wallpaper of the period. From here I entered a large open area with a solarium, and this brought me to the front of the mansion again. On the opposite side to the study was the parlor and just what I would expect the parlor to be - fairly feminine and could easily accommodate a gathering of thirty people to sit, leisurely talking in different groups of conversation.

Robert F. Edwards

The last room was probably one of the most elegant of all, and that was the dining room. I did not count the place settings but think it would easily hold twenty or more without adding sleeves to this huge table. Each room had its own fireplace and this one had an overpowering mantel to it.

That really concluded the part that was allowed to be seen by this mere mortal. Outside, I noticed the floor above and would assume that it would have been for servants, maybe even the odd guest that was fortunate enough to stay over. There was also a basement, probably with a vast amount of storage, and where all the cooking and preparation for the meals took place.

Back out on the streets, I felt somewhat inhibited by modern day congestion; but not being deterred, I started working my way up another street before I came upon the ever-present vendors. It was really crowded; these vendors had set up their wares on anything, from little wooden crates to makeshift tables to display goods, ranging from socks to underwear to toothpaste and toiletries. One fellow was flogging what looked like big pens; and always the artists of jewelry, travel bags and even produce was being sold. This is for the locals, not a tourist-oriented market.

I wound my way back and forth, asking a few questions, before I felt I had put in a full day. It was starting to get dark and I realized by the time I packed, and had something to eat, that it would be late enough. It was shortly after eight before I got back to the hotel to start my packing. I decided for dinner to have a pepper steak, medium rare. Well, it should have been classified as a 'cream' steak and well done. I managed to eat half of it, but thoroughly didn't like it. I called the waiter over and without any hesitation; he took the whole thing back, and gave me a brand new steak (medium rare) with the same unpleasant sauce on it. By the same token, this was much more edible; and to my satisfaction also. I ate too much, because I was only capable of eating one steak rather than one-and-a-half.

SOUTH AMERICA
EXPLORATION

After I finished my packing, I asked to settle up the bill. This was not exactly cheap, at a hundred and nine dollars U.S. for two nights, food and two dinners, (and my laundry being done as well). All in all, not a bargain but not bad either. I made sure that I would get a wake up call at six o'clock and also made arrangements to leave the bulk of my luggage here, and just take immediate traveling supplies to the next port of call.

With that, I'm going to say goodnight, one and all. I've had a very good day and an enjoyable experience in this city. Marietta, I miss you dearly and I'm anxious to be home with you, and I love you very much.

Robert F. Edwards

March 8th, Thursday
Punta Arenas, Chile

Well, I did get a wake up call but last night was just not a very good night for sleeping. I had the window open and it seemed the people were under my window all night. They weren't talking to me, but they sure were talking loud enough to keep me awake.

Plus, when I have an early commitment, I've always slept with one eye open and the other one blinking; so I was up long before the phone rang. But giving them full points, they did phone right on time. I dragged my luggage down and finally found somebody to understand that I was going to leave the bulk of it there and just carry my backpack with me.

My day had started and it was still dark. I said adios, but didn't go very far because there was an iron grate locking the front door and had to find a man to open it for me. I don't know whether people were more protective down here with their property, or whether there was a lot more crime. At this time in the morning, the streets were deserted and I was able to make my way quickly to the designated bus depot, about four blocks from the hotel.

Fortunately at the bus terminal, the doors were open and the woman greeted me, Buenos Dias, Señor. I sat patiently waiting and talked to an American couple from New York. He had retired last year at seventy and was a sea captain most of his life, until he worked the harbor in New York with his pilot's license. He looked the part of what every captain should be; bearded and fairly stocky, with an Irish background. We made some small talk and they were continuing on to where I had just come from.

The bus headed out on the long gravel road ahead. We followed the Magellan Strait most of the way up and after two

240

small sandwiches and a cup of coffee, the hours had moved forward to about eleven o'clock. We did the crossing at one of the narrowest parts of the Magellan Strait. After going up one side, we were now coming down the other. The terrain was flat and somewhat bleak. I saw large herds of sheep, a few cattle, and guanacos running wild.

At the crossing, the highlight of the whole day for me was two penguins. I got a picture of them, such cute little birds. They must have been a couple, just from the way they were standing there looking at me, and it had to be a family affair.

By about two o'clock, we hit the Chilean border, which is at San Sebastian; cleared Customs, got back in, and headed over to the Argentine Customs. It had been a long day and many miles before I arrived at Rio Grande, where I had a three-hour stopover before going to Ushuaia. I used the time wisely to find my now favorite thing, the Internet, and received an e-mail from Marietta, with a sad note to it. One of her co-workers had passed away suddenly with a heart attack at the age of fifty-two. I realized how wonderful life has been for me and for my family, and how grateful we should be that we're blessed.

Robert F. Edwards

I decided to have something to eat and walking around; I saw a place that made me think, "baker, candle-stick maker, and restaurant" all rolled into one. Unusual for me, I ordered gnocchi and a piece of meat, some bread and a Sprite for eight dollars. A very nice meal, good service, and the owner spoke very good English, for a baker. I walked the beach a bit, patiently waiting for the next phase of the bus. In the meantime, the Rio Grande lost two little mussel shells as souvenirs of Bob Edward's never-ending collection of memorabilia.

Right on time, at quarter to seven, in rolls the bus and off we went. The weather was unpredictable. At some moments, it was very pleasant; the next, it was raining; the next, the winds were blowing. It seemed like the four seasons were upon us. This bus was quite comfortable, but the bathroom door was locked and as Mother Nature came knocking on my door, I made a motion that I'd like the door opened. The fellow pointed to the front of the bus, but I was positive there wasn't a toilet there. Shortly thereafter, the bus came to an outpost and allowed us off for fifteen, twenty minutes.

The town of Puerto Porvenir seemed out of a story of Hans Christian Andersen; log cabins and very Bavarian looking. This small community really impressed me; right across the street from the bus station was a nice restaurant and a bakery. More importantly, two computers with Internet service. I never knew where the next Internet service was going to pop up so always needed to keep my eyes and ears open. If I'd known that this place existed, I probably would have spent a day here just perusing around. This was the beginning of the Andes mountain range. All the different homes (none being small) were well maintained and it was the largest amount of wooden homes I had seen up to date in any area of South America. Many of them were designed as log cabins or chalets and had a Bavarian type of décor, and this community was heavily populated by Yugoslavians.

Shortly, we got back on the bus and off we went! For me, it didn't matter whether it was in the prairies or in climates that require heating, people always had their homes far too warm and here it was no exception to the rule, even on the bus. When walking around the small town, it was just a very pleasant cool evening. But on the bus, sure enough, the heat was on and after less than an hour, I found it very uncomfortable and trying to sleep was almost an impossibility.

As the hours ticked along, at ten o'clock, we arrived in Ushuaia. There was no terminal; it was just off one of the streets in this town, known as the end of the world. I got off the bus with the rest of the passengers, all eight of us.

I found some accommodations in a residential home about six blocks away. It was only a block away from the downtown core and not completely finished, but the room for fifteen dollars a night was more than adequate for me. I was soon tucked into my bunk bed in a very pleasant room with the blue walls and blue curtains on the wooden windows. I was out of the rain and wind and prepared myself both physically and mentally for a long overdue rest.

With that, I'd like to say goodnight to one and all. Goodnight, my beautiful little wife. I miss you dearly. Bye.

Robert F. Edwards

I awoke to the light coming through the windows and almost reluctantly, I got up to see what the weather was like. To my pleasant surprise, it was blue skies with puffy white clouds. What was more remarkable, was the surroundings that my eyes gazed upon. I was in the midst of a huge mountain range with beautiful snow-capped mountains. I just gasped at the delight that my eyes feasted upon. I took on a new surge of enthusiasm.

Quickly, I went to the bathroom facilities and admired the beautiful tile work, even a bidet, but no mirror. I somehow managed to perform the task of shaving without the aid of looking at my face. I heard some rustling below and I went downstairs, by then eight-thirty in the morning. The Belgian couple I met on the bus along with a few others were there, and we had biscuits or bread, jam, cheese, and coffee. Often on these adventures, I felt I was in the midst of the United Nations with no interpreter for the many different languages being spoken.

In daylight, I could see that the house was quite large. It had a huge living room with an alcove fireplace and the kitchen was galley-style with a large eating area. The expansive staircase led up to the floors above where the bedrooms and another bathroom was. The proprietor seemed to be doing most of the work himself, what he did was very good but like so many projects, they were never quite finished. There was a bit of tile mixing in the bathroom; the cupboards had no doors yet; it was just a very unfinished masterpiece of creativity. It could have been the lack of money that did not allow them to complete the projects, or that bit of helter-

244

SOUTH AMERICA
EXPLORATION

skelter method that a lot of do-it-yourselfers have, including myself at times.

I got talking to the Belgians, and as with most Europeans spoke many different languages, English being one of them. Her last name was Mace, the same as one of my old school friend's who emigrated from Belgium, some forty years ago. We discussed what we would like to do and one of the topics that came up (that I'd been toying with) was going to Puerto Williams. If the gods had been with me, there was a boat that left for Punta Arenas from Puerto Williams. The distances were short compared to what I had done in the past weeks, but the isolation of Puerto Williams made it quite challenging.

The three of us went down to visit the shop of another friend met on the bus, Julian. With her good connections, she made some phone calls; there was a boat that would do the crossing tomorrow, probably for three hundred dollars to rent the boat. We spent some time looking around her shop, which specialized in souvenirs and tourist memorabilia of this area. There was a cruise ship in the harbor and this was really where the city made its mark now; for research vessels as well as tourist ships that docked here before sailing to the Antarctic.

Robert F. Edwards

Ushuaia was absolutely a jewel! I had found one of the most remarkable places in my travels; it accommodated everything that I had dreamed about. The mountain range cuddled around the bay, of this city of about forty thousand. This Alpine city had both the diversity of Swiss designs and architecture, as well as the Argentine day-to-day living. The city itself was very easy to get a grasp of; it worked left to right and the main streets were one-way. The houses were quite small and most of them had metal roofs, including the church on Main Street. Numerous buildings indicated that tourism was a very important commerce here.

We asked around for more information, concerning both departure to Puerto Williams and the return. For me, ideally would be to leave on Saturday morning and return no later than Tuesday by air. After checking the facilities and airlines, we found to both our disappointments that Tuesday for myself was fully booked, and Saturday for the Belgian couple was booked. The only day available was Thursday, which was not appropriate for either one of us at that point. We then decided to explore other avenues and by this time, the Belgian couple was quite discouraged and ready to abandon the whole idea. I suggested we should go down and see the boat, and talk to the captain to find out what it would cost to return. They were both pretty confident that it would be a hundred dollars each, both ways. But with good naturedness, they decided to take my advice and we worked our way down to the boats.

On our way to the wharf, we discovered another person who was just casting off to Puerto Williams. He said, "You know, you could have come with me if you had been sooner, but you're not ready and I'm casting off. It's fifty dollars and fifty dollars return." We checked that he would definitely be coming back and he said, "Oh yeah. There are other boats, sailboats that would also go back and forth. I can feel that you wouldn't have any trouble getting back. Somebody is always commuting back and forth at some point in time."

SOUTH AMERICA EXPLORATION

With this encouragement, we met Alexander, the captain of the sailboat that we had been given information on. He was of Italian descent and looked like someone right out of a storybook; flowing white beard, long hair, wearing heavy outerwear gear, plus a toque on his head, but completely bare feet. It was chilly, the wind was modest but it there was a bite in the air and the weather kept shifting. One minute, the clouds came over and then blue skies followed, there seemed to be no consistency that morning. As we were talking to the captain, a black cloud was forming and it was probably snowing on the mountains, and I expected rain down here shortly. He told us that he planned to paint his boat deck that day but didn't know if the weather would let him.

He agreed that he could go tomorrow. Of course, Edwards 'McGregor' tried to barter, and told him that the other boat only charged fifty dollars passage. The good captain looked at the boat that was just breaking out of the inner harbor and said, "That's his boat, this is mine. This is my price. You should have gone with him if you wanted his price." He said this all in good humor. And then asked, "Who speaks English?" So, we all said yes, and, "Then we all speak English", he replied. He was a straightforward fellow, and we enjoyed his company right from the beginning. After more discussion, he agreed to take me over for a hundred dollars, and he would bring me back for fifty dollars either Monday or Tuesday of next week.

With that settled, and a new adventure on the horizon, I said to my Belgian friends that I wouldn't mind having some lunch, as it was close to one o'clock. We found a restaurant on the main street, and I enjoyed a delicious meal of calamari with rice; and the squid was cooked in a sauce rather than fried. The Belgian gentleman had squid with pasta; and the lady had a salad. We shared a bottle of Argentine red wine, dry. I know why this part of the world exports wine; it was an excellent tasting vintage, and we finished it off with coffee.

I planned on doing some door-to-door sightseeing like so many touristas and looked for any souvenirs or memorabilia

Robert F. Edwards

that I might like to buy, including books. I saw one I was quite seriously thinking of buying, a book on shipwrecks of this area, printed in English. There were many books on bird watching and trekking, and so forth; but the majority was in Spanish, of course.

In the afternoon, the three of us decided to see the museum, Museo Territoial Fin del Mundo. It was well done; but there weren't a lot of artifacts. The natural history was interesting, on the early Indians called the Yahgan and Neophydes. These first natives dressed quite sparsely. Only in the winter did they wear any furs or skins, and lived in primitive little huts. To the best of my knowledge, these were the only two remaining ancestors of the people of Puerto Williams; the rest died from communicable diseases brought by the Europeans. The museum has a small replica village, and some artifacts of shipwrecks from the treacherous waters of the Beagle Channel.

The native birds of the area where displayed. One of the more significant birds was the huge condor. I had seen one in

a zoo in Australia. The bird had a massive wingspan and the head looked similar to a vulture's.

We then went into the rogues' gallery, showing memorabilia of the early penal colonies. I asked Eric to take a picture of me with the Argentine political prisoners' uniforms. They were blue and bright yellow horizontal stripes, in a heavy fabric on the outside, but also lined on the inside. There was a large incarceration of prisoners on the Isla de los Estados until 1947.

SOUTH AMERICA
EXPLORATION

I spent some time in the attached library, reading some of the English books. One of the more interesting articles that I read about Ushuaia was the temperature. It very seldom got below ten degrees Fahrenheit. The average temperature was fifty-four degrees Fahrenheit; and the high was around eighty degrees Fahrenheit. Quite a temperate climate compared to some of the extreme weather that I had experienced already in this area. They claim that Ushuaia is "the world's end" and the furthest southern city in the global community at fifty-five degrees latitude south. Of course, Puerto Williams was further south, but they disputed the fact that it was not a city; but more of a naval base and the inhabitants were supported by the naval operation of Chile. A little competition never hurt anybody, but the Argentineans still claimed they had the most southern operating city. The bases in the Antarctic were more for scientific research and really not livable communities on a sustained basis.

Because the weather was so unpredictable in this part of South America, I felt that it would be prudent if I went trekking through the national parks, especially the glacier areas that I should consider getting a poncho or tarp to cover me, even though the Gore-tax outfit probably would suffice. I did purchase a poncho for five dollars, which at least would keep my mini-backpack dry if I found myself trekking through some pretty bad downpours, which often happened here.

As I was walking through this delightful area of town, I found an ice-cream stand. So, on the way back, I planned to take advantage of this for my sweet tooth and enjoy their great ice cream. With this in mind and an added incentive, I found the internet and to my pleasure, my wife and daughter had both sent news bulletins and my family was doing well; and handling all the trials and tribulations that I had left in their capable hands.

I decided to venture out to see the further parts of the city. One of the Belgian people, a professional photographer, mentioned that some of the older buildings were exceptional. With that in mind, Shank's pony and camera in pouch, off I headed

Robert F. Edwards

ever onward in the direction of the older part of the city. Some of the houses were made of wood, but a good portion of them were metal, corrugated both on the roofs and on the sides. I continued walking in that direction and soon met up with the two Belgian companions. It seemed that we had tied an umbilical cord to each other, and once again united, we headed back towards the main core of the city.

I mentioned the ice cream and my two companions wished to experience the same enjoyment. As we strolled back, we found the ice cream store and the biggest kid of them all had a three-scooper, each different flavors; one with strawberry fruta, one had nuts in it; and the last one was a caramel. This particular ice-cream cone had three distinct pockets in the cone for each scoop. The other two were more modest with just a two-scoop, one on top of each other. Absolutely scrumptious; real ice cream versus ice milk.

We ventured back to a store that Eric wanted to see, with t-shirts. I found a sombrero that I liked, but the gentleman wanted ninety-five dollars; he said it was made out of otter skin and worth the value, but I declined to part with my money. Lillian wanted to go to another store to do a little bit of shopping, and there I found some very expensive all-weather gear for sailing. This "Musto" brand was for professional yachters in extreme offshore boating conditions, with a lifetime warranty. They advertised it where someone had jumped into the iceberg waters, of all places, to show how waterproof and thermal it was. With all this presentation and being sold for half-price, I tried it on. Some of the jackets were up to five hundred dollars and the pants well over three hundred. I saw the value in it; but managed to pull myself away. Later, I started thinking that it would be something to round off my clothing for my sailboat, and if I could get it for three to four hundred dollars, that I would be in the running. I managed to get the outfit, pants and jacket for three hundred and twenty dollars U.S. More than a bargain! A steal would be a closer thing. Sometimes, it is just meant to be. With another cold front coming on, I was glad that I had bought this warmer jacket, and was even more impressed that I was able to get it all into my small backpack.

It was at least seven o'clock when I asked my two traveling companions if they wished to go out for dinner. I had made up my mind that I was going to have king crab, much larger than the Dungeness crab of British Columbia. We were able to identify this popular restaurant by the huge King crab sign on the outside. They accommodated us traveling wanderers and found us a seat, compact as it might be. Everybody was enjoying the gastronomical delights that were being served. I did not end up having the crab. I actually ended up having the "black huka" fish of the local waters, pan-fried. It was more of a white fish, but I would recommend it to anybody traveling in this area. I also had potatoes, light bread, along with an onion and tomato salad. Along with that, I enjoyed an excellent dry Chilean wine and a large espresso coffee to round the meal off. My companions also enjoyed their meals. Lillian had cod and Eric had a casserole dish.

The night was petering into the "eleven-thirtyish" hour, and we made our way back to our "home away from home." Our landlord only spoke Spanish; but I managed to make arrangements for when I returned, so I didn't have to worry about finding a place to stay. Also, I found out that he was a lawyer and his brother was an art teacher at the university. I look at some of the art in his home; extremely large paintings had the modern style rather than the Impressionist or the Classics.

I finally realized that I was going to have to call it a night if I was going to meet all the challenges of the next day. I excused myself and went up to my room and once again made sure that I was packed and ready for the adventures tomorrow. Once in my lower bunk bed, the winds started to come up and the rain started to pour. I would just have to take one day at a time and this day had come to an end.

So, goodnight, one and all; and goodnight, my beautiful little treasure. I love you dearly.

Robert F. Edwards

March 10th, Saturday
Ushuaia, Argentina

Throughout the night, torrential rains came down with huge
bursts of wind that rattled and shook the windows. I did not
sleep well for a lot of reasons; one of them was that I was worried we would be scrubbing the trip. Alexander said that it
really depended on the weather. The weather down here was
so unpredictable and changed within hours. We'd experienced that yesterday, with the four seasons coming and going
in gusts of cold wind and then balmy, warm weather; an event
that continued throughout that day.

I looked out the window and though the winds had subsided, the rain was present and accounted for. By seven-
thirty, I had packed and put on my brand-new sailing pants
and was glad that I was not going to be soaking wet, if nothing
else. Breakfast was the usual bread and biscuits and coffee,
and my other companions joined me shortly thereafter. We
started making a bit of conversation but I reminded them that
if we were going to get there by quarter to nine, and with this
kind of weather, we'd better give ourselves as much time as
possible. We all agreed on that and said goodbye to our host
and friend, and off to the wharf we went.

As we walked, we felt the cold and all had our hoods up,
and I was wearing my mitts and so were my fellow travelers.
We looked like we were going on an Arctic expedition rather
than going to Puerto Williams. By the time we entered the
first part of the jetty, there were three or four ambulances and
police cars surrounding it; somebody had just taken out a
telephone pole, when I say taken it out, I mean they took it
out with full gusto. It was a truck and they had managed to
get the telephone pole close to the windshield, so I am sure
there were more physical injuries than just a bruise or two.

252

SOUTH AMERICA EXPLORATION

We continually trudged through this cold, wet rain, and when we got to the boat, it seemed deserted. Alexander had not docked it where he said he was going to; and my first thought was that he had aborted the idea. But no, he was there and he said, "Bring your stuff on board," so we had to haul it across three different boats to get to his and we did it like spiders trying to crawl up a newfound location. Once on board, he filled out all the documents and his wife, Dianne spoke very good English; and they knew what they were doing. They told us that we would have to wait until port authorities came down for Immigration and examine the documents, plus our passports and everything else, which was in order.

I drank matei, which is a herbal type of tea, quite popular in Argentina; and my two companions had regular tea. This matei is served in a cup; usually with a metal straw and a sieve at the bottom. I purchased a matei cup in Salta, and I rather enjoyed the drink. It was supposed to be quite good for what ails you; and I thought I probably needed all the support I could get.

By ten o'clock, the authorities had cleared us for Customs and we set sail out of the harbor. Both Alexander and Dianne said, "Oh, well, you do some sailing," as they looked at my sailing outfit. I said, "Well, I have a boat; a fair weather sailor." Today, I became an all-weather sailor. Alexander became the crew and I became captain of the tiller; and as we left the harbor, he would point to which direction to go. We had gale-force winds of over forty  to fifty knots an hour. I could honestly say I had never, in all my life, sailed in this type of weather and was surprised how well I was able to handle the sails. With all due respect it was because Alexander, the El Capitan gave me the confidence to do the job that he expected.

It was a day of sailing that probably put more salt in my veins than the last two or three years had; and sailing wing-on-wing is difficult at the best of times and I was doing that. It was a day that every person that loves sailing hopes that they will experience, to really see the stamina and the ability that they have, especially in unchartered waters. I can only think that it was El Capitan's direction; and his assurance in the way I was handling his boat and his livelihood, that gave me the confidence. I was doing a much better job than I had ever thought I was capable of doing. Also, I knew that if I got beyond my ability or knowledge; that an experienced person and true sailor was on hand to rectify the situation. I actually sailed the entire distance, which was about fifty kilometers.

It was the most bizarre weather, gust of winds and the rains, but also we had calm sections when we had to start the motor. It was the four seasons that day before we got into Puerto William at around six o'clock and docked. We were not alone and Alexander said that he was amazed at the amount of boats that were docked. Usually, he said, there are one or two, and there were at least eight that I counted. A lot of them were French people sailing these waters. We managed to clear Customs again. I had got more stamps going in and out of Argentina and Chile than a rumrunner. Everything went well and then it was a challenge to find accommodations in this small naval Chilean community.

I had been given a contact, a woman said to have a flat to hire, but nobody knew where she lived. It was starting to get dark. Dianne had said if I couldn't find any place that I could sleep on the boat; and I was actually contemplating this. I found an Internet, tucked away in a cupboard, with a telephone long distance operator. It was slow and brought back memories of about four years ago when I first had our Internet system. It worked, that was the bottom line; I got a nice e-mail from my daughter and I sent a couple off to my good wife, plus I read a few news reports.

I was making my way out of the downtown core when I ran into Dianne and Alexander. Dianne gave me another contact to try, and said, "Well, this person that operates the yacht club has accommodations". I found that one and the woman said, yes, she had one if I would bunk in with two other men from Holland. I looked at the room and said, "Yeah, that will be fine for seven thousand pesos each night." With that settled, Alexander invited me down to the yacht club later to enjoy some of the camaraderie taking place.

As I put my gear into the room with my designated bed in it, I started to reflect on what a remarkable day this was. I probably experienced more aggressive sailing and wind changes in the short seven-hour period than I had in many years. Even Alexander said that the winds changed very quickly in this channel and the number of shipwrecks proved that information was correct. I was glad I had listened to that voice inside which seemed to tell me what to do and what I need to get it done. I would have had to stay inside the cabin (even with my Gore-tex on), if I had not bought that all-

Robert F. Edwards

weather gear for yachting. I did not have it in mind, but it proved to be a wise purchase.

I dropped into a coffee shop, and sat with some teachers, one in outdoor activities, and the other more academic. It was rather funny that here we were at the end of civilization and we were watching television (and the reception was awesome). By now it was nine o'clock and that was when Alexander said the bar would be opening. The gentleman that runs the bar said that he'd give me a ride down, and as he had to open it, we were the first there.

I could not believe it – it was a sunken vessel; probably an old freighter and they used it as a dock to tie the sailboats up to. They had put decking on it to make your way to the forward and the aft. This shipwreck was a large cargo ship, and most of the compartments on the boat have sunk in the inlet. At first I thought it was a skull that they were using as a moorage facility. When we got down to what would have been the officers' quarters, it was made into a superb pub for club activities. There was a neat little bar, lots of comfortable chairs; even a real wood fireplace, and decorated with lots of pictures of the regional area and boats, as well as flags and memorabilia, and a logbook of guests that was second to none. Then, upstairs in what would have been originally the wheelhouse, were tables for billiards and card games. This is a club that I would join if I lived here; not because of the limited amount of activities in Puerto Williams, but because I finally found a club that I would enjoy going to. With the added benefit of the great scenery from the pilot house, looking at the mountains and inlet ahead, this nautical club had met all the fulfillments and imagination that I would have put into it.

By now, most of the people from the other eight vessels moored here started petering in. I met a gentleman called Simon and his friend, Andy; and the lady's name was Cecilia. They had all climbed mountains extensively together and about three years ago, Cecilia bought a boat and they started sailing in these waters. When Cecilia was at home, and Simon, they lived in England and Andy lived in the southern

256

part of France. He was a commercial artist, and Simon was a professional mountain climber. I also met a young Australian lady that Alexander knew; she cooked on one of the vessels and was from Rio de Janeiro.

As the evening progressed, I started to feel some fatigue about eleven-thirty, and decided to say goodnight. Carefully, I started to walk my way back, which wasn't much longer than a kilometer and was doing surprisingly well until I ended up in a residential area; and I knew I had taken a wrong turn. After a considerable length of time wandering around, I realized that it was completely futile. I just didn't know where the house was. I decided that it would be prudent to get back to the club and wait for the gentleman to close up and catch a ride home.

At that moment, it was back to raining again. Even though I had my jacket of world-class protection on, I didn't think I'd want to stay out all night if I didn't have to. To my delight, everybody was still at the club, but starting to get ready to leave. The commodore of the club said as soon as it got a little quieter there, he would stop and drive me home. So, we got talking; he had two sons, liked fishing and he had lived there all his life. He worked seven days a week at the club, and his wife worked equally as long at the lodging of the club. We managed to communicate with the Edwardian dialect, and he invited me to go fishing tomorrow around two o'clock in the afternoon.

When things slowed down a little bit, he asked another fellow to keep an eye on the place, and drove me back up to the house. I couldn't believe the consideration, kindness and thoughtfulness of these people. If nothing else, this trip had rejuvenated my desire to still belong to the human race. I admired and wanted to copy the way that these people had treated me and it revived my attitude towards going back and meeting the challenges that I left behind.

Once inside the house, everybody had gone to bed. The rooms had efficient Franklin fireplaces and with only a couple of pieces of wood, could heat up a whole house. Everything

257

was well done and very neat. All the beds had matching comforters on them; there was even a doily on the toilet seat. I
popped into bed and knew that tomorrow was going to be an
exciting day but one that I didn't have to meet the challenges
immediately. It was almost what I'd call a day off.

*So, goodnight, one and all; and goodnight, my beautiful little
wife.*

SOUTH AMERICA
EXPLORATION

March 11th, Sunday
Puerto Williams, Chile

I woke up in Puerto Williams, but knowing that I didn't have to get up early was the first very good step to a pleasant day. I actually got up earlier than everybody else, but that's not saying much for him or her. By eight o'clock, I had started doing some recording in my journal. It was surprising; I could easily get a couple of days behind and it never failed when this happened, I would try to remember all the things that transpired and events that were worth recording, but inevitably, after I had completed the day, I would realize that I had left out just almost as much as I had put in. So, with that in mind, I started to regress back over some of the immediate events that I had forgotten to mention yesterday.

First of all, I have to record coming into the port of Puerto Williams as an experience that I would never forget. As we entered, there was a large sand dune with a marker on it; and coming around that and into the inlet itself, the first appearances of Puerto Williams appeared. It was a small town, sitting majestically at the foot of a range of mountains. As we got closer, I saw the Chilean Navy in its full blazing glory. The two destroyers were the first time I had ever seen ships painted completely black rather than the gray attire that I was used to seeing on American and Canadian vessels.

As we got in further, I could see the naval base was the primary factor of the financial substance of this small town. Along with the residential areas, on the opposite side was the airport; and just as we are coming in to the final position of our docking, lo and behold, a little plane lands. Most of the planes that land here were small, both eight-seaters and the maximum would be twenty-seaters.

259

Robert F. Edwards

One of the most important aspects for the Belgium people was the fact of being able to get back at a reasonable time. So, their first priority was to secure some kind of confirmation to get back the following Saturday with the airlines and Lillian goes ahead with Dianne, while Eric and I stayed on board; not by choice, but because we hadn't been cleared by Immigration yet. Eventually, the officer did come down, a very pleasant fellow; and quickly stamped every piece of paper that was required, and then we were free to go.

Lillian returned with a tentative booking for Saturday. For myself, I had talked to Alexander and he said Monday or Tuesday that he would be returning. He would not be going back on Sunday, due to the fact that it costs him twice as much to get into port; whereas during the week, it was free. So, I would be staying here at least until Monday.

Much of Puerto Williams was involved in the naval operations. As I walked up from the dock, there was a big generator and above was the naval base where the military buildings for strategic purposes were. Behind that was where the quarters for the families and servicemen were located. Last night I met a couple of naval officers in the bar, one was an engineer and the other was a pilot. The engineer invited me, if I was staying on, to go to Punta Arenas on a naval vessel, but as it didn't leave until March 16th, I had to decline. It would have been an experience. First of all, going up the Magellan Strait from Puerto Williams and also being on a Chilean military vessel would have been something I could have told Cole, my grandchild about, when he appreciated the sea.

After I left the general area of the military base, and walked towards the supply depot, there was a large rectangular area set aside for the military purchases of supplies like groceries, what I would call the canteen. A small walkway on one side led to the inner village, there must have been about twenty stores and I don't think the largest would be three thousand square feet and the smallest might accommodate about two hundred square feet.

SOUTH AMERICA
EXPLORATION

The general store that Lillian, Eric, and I entered had a photocopying machine and more importantly the information required to do the trekking that they were looking for, and routes to be taken. When you enter these areas, at first glance they look like the only thing that was missing was rawhide for clothes and jerky for food; but they were on the cutting edge as well. I had been told the Internet service was not that good, and had planned to use the telephone. Tucked away in a cabinet, which I would have never spotted, was a computer and although it was using the old telephone wires for connecting, all went well and sure enough, I got an e-mail from my beautiful wife and caught up on all the dismal news of the world. With an e-mail sent home, I continued looking around the rest of the mall; it even had a casino in it, just a self-sufficient community.

The roads didn't seem to be any worse than anywhere else and it seemed like everybody owned a vehicle; a lot of trucks, some utility vehicles, and a lot of larger flat bed Toyota hauling trucks. There was a good forest line directly behind town and I noticed that most of the houses have large cords of wood stocked, so that must be the main source of fuel. I saw some propane tanks but the large generator, I had heard; supplied most of the electricity to light both the military installations as well as the local residences. The houses were small and there wasn't the pride of ownership that I had seen in some communities; but it was a fairly harsh climate here and most of them used corrugated metal for the exterior as well as the roofs. As far as yards, they were small with the odd one that had put a little bit of flowers, but most of it was just storage area.

At breakfast, I had an enjoyable time talking to the two boys from Holland that I was sharing the bedroom with. We drank coffee, ate bread and cheese for breakfast, and compared notes. The boys from Holland had just finished the trek that the Belgian people had commenced on and they said that the last day was the most difficult. They'd spent a night in the snow and their tent had ripped with the heavy snow coming down on it, they were cold and wet as they waded down the mountain in the morning. These fellows were not short to the ground; one being 6' 3", the other 6' 7"; so, if they waded, I would have been up to my waist. They were both very tired and were going to spend most of the day catching up on the sleep that had drained them in the last four days. They had a humorous story about a dog that seemed to have befriended them for the entire hike, which they nicknamed Alex; He was a local dog, but just tagged along with them and foraged for himself. They said that he would go off and catch something and come back with blood around his jaws, so he had had his meal.

As the morning quickly vanished, I had wanted to check with Alexander about tomorrow. I also wanted to go to church, and check the Internet. With those three quests in focus, I started off on my first one, to see Alexander. For whatever reason, he was nowhere to be found. I talked to the British people that I'd spent some time talking with last night as they were cleaning up their boat to leave it there for the winter. I mentioned to Simon that if he did see Alexander, just tell him that I was looking for him and that I'd check back later.

With no success at that, I left the dock and then worked my way back up to the village and I couldn't help but chuckle to myself; there was a parade. The first thing was the inspection of the servicemen, and the officer doing this inspection was in full dress, with a saber. It brought back my enthusiasm for the sport of fencing that I had taken up last year. As I walked along a little bit further, I heard the marching music of John Phillip Souza coming through a PA system.

I still couldn't find the church, and when all was said and done, it must have been in the military compound, but I was reluctant to ask the guard. I had done my best in communication, but didn't think that I needed to see how far I could push it. So, two down, no wins. I went to the Internet office and they were open; so I got another e-mail off to my beautiful wife. With one out of three, not the best batting average but still not struck out.

I returned back to the house and the good lady was there, busy. This woman worked all the time when she was there, and I'm sure she worked everywhere else that she was at. She was preparing pasta with meat, cheese, and tomatoes, yellow peppers topped with Parmesan cheese. I asked if I paid if she would be good enough to let me have some of it and of course, the answer goes without saying. So, with a big bottle of Coca-cola and this delicious meal at the table, I was another one of the participants to consume it. One of the teachers had taken some video that day, and he'd even captured on film the marching parade as well as the music, so we spent some time watching this.

By now the commodore showed up with his fishing gear, and the others asked if they could come along. Somehow, his truck was able to hold all four of us, which to me was just a pleasant surprise. We passed an area with a large statue of the Virgin Mary and then headed off on roads that led away from the port. It was not a great distance, probably ten kilometers. We passed by some smaller lakes, and for what seemed to be no apparent reason, the commodore stopped, and we all got out. I saw a round porthole plate, which was his marker to where his private lake was. We worked our way through the woods, no trails here, and after walking no more than a quarter of a kilometer was this beautiful lake with a beaver dam in it. They had imported beavers from Canada and although not quite as prolific as the rabbits in Australia, (the beavers couldn't believe that they'd hit such a payload with all this wood around) they had produced some rather annoying situations with their population growth. It was a perfect beaver dam. I don't think I had ever seen one in Canada quite as well built with its little waterfalls. Within what seemed to be minutes, the commodore caught a two to three-pound salmon. For the rest of the hours that we spent there, I lost a hook but that was the only fish that was going to give way to our desires.

Robert F. Edwards

It was a very pleasant afternoon and all three men were nice fellows to be around. They showed me some of the different local berries. There was one berry with a legend; they told me that if you eat it, that you would always return to Puerto Williams; so, of course I had one to make sure that I would return. The woods and shrubs were lush in growth and I hoped that my pictures would turn out to do it justice.

We returned back to the truck (the four sardines and one real fish) and the commodore wanted to show us another area that had been turned into an Archaeology-Biology site. Both Argentines and Chileans were very pro-Science and involved in exploring natural phenomena. This particular area was no exception to their quest for knowledge. Natural wood plaques with identification of the different plants were placed throughout the trail. In bog areas, wooden flats were laid down to build a boardwalk. For the next hour and three-quarters, we wandered through this botanical heaven, but only saw a few birds. The environmental teacher had lots of information, and was taking videos also. I asked if he would send me a copy, and I would pay him whatever was required, so we exchanged e-mails. I sure hoped that it would materialize; not only because he had a picture of me and the fish, but he was very good from what I had seen already of the music and the guards on parade, and I hoped to have some of these memories he had been able to capture.

By the time we made our way back to the house, it was just about getting dark. I had some suggestions to make on what we could do with the fish. The commodore says, "No, it's my fish", but agreed with my ideas; so I went and bought (I imagined) a pretty good wine because he was quite impressed with it. We had the bottle of wine, sitting around enjoying it, and then I excused myself to go down to check with Alexander how things were progressing.

I got down there, only to find that he still wasn't around. To my dismay, most of the boats had already departed; so, where there had been eight, there were now three. The thing that always plagued me in remote areas was my lack of options of getting out, or changing directions on my itinerary. With this nagging at me somewhat, (not that I felt that Alexander wouldn't honor his word); I just wasn't sure what was happening and just wanted to confirm that when he cast off, I was on board. If that option wasn't available or there had been a change that I wasn't aware of, I wanted a back-up system.

So, I started to walk towards the airport, and it was deceiving. When I first saw the airport from the harbor, it looked that I could walk there in half an hour at most. However, I found out this was not the case as I walked (and walked, and walked). I had to get to the neck of this inlet to cross over. These people really did like shipwrecks; there was no two-ways about it. The bridge to cross over was another ship-wrecked vessel, (much smaller than the one that the club was on); and then I worked my way through another small bridge. After the better part of three-quarters of an hour, I got to the airport. I took for granted that the place would probably be closed. Two reasons: One, no planes were flying; and number two it was Sunday. And on both observations, I was right;

but I probably walked the better part of six to eight kilometers.

With this behind me, I now had to go exactly the opposite way to return. Needless to say, by the time I got back to the house (and this time I knew where I was, even in the dark), it was about nine-thirty, quarter to ten. The good lady asked me (after I'd had some cheese, cold meat and buns which I'd bought the previous day) if I wanted her to cook the fish and I said, "mañana", but before noon if possible, because I was leaving then. She was quite concerned because she said she was going to be busy in the morning, but she would do her best. I said not to worry about it. If she didn't have time, I would leave the fish for everybody else to enjoy, and I gathered it was rather important to the commodore and his wife that I get to taste the fish because I was the person they really wanted to enjoy the fish.

Luckily, on my way back, I met El Capitan and his good wife Dianne. They were going to have the engine checked; they'd put some new rings and valves in and wanted the mechanic to check it all before casting off some time around noon on Monday, which suited me just fine. Now that I knew what was going on, I returned back to the house, confident in knowing what was going to happen tomorrow.

After a bit of discussion on computers and general conversation, one more night had fast approached the bewitching hour of eleven-thirty and I excused myself for another enjoyable sleep. The weather was so much cooler down here and I found it so much easier to sleep when it was cold; and so I was getting some good rest.

With that, goodnight, one and all; and goodnight, my little beloved wife.

SOUTH AMERICA
EXPLORATION

March 12th, Monday
Puerto Williams, Chile

Well, got up and all is well. Had a very good sleep. Did my toiletries and yes, unlimited amount of hot water. I felt like a brand new traveler, to say the least. It was about eight o'clock and the two teachers had to go to work that day, so they were up and ready very quickly, but my Dutch connection was still in bed. I have a good breakfast with the environmentalist teacher and we talked a bit before he left to start his first day of classes. Once again, I tried to explain to the landlady that if she couldn't clean and prepare the fish in time for noon that it was fine, I would leave it for everybody else, plus the wine. She seemed to understand and I paid her the bill, which was more than reasonable. It was twenty thousand pesos, Chilean, for two nights, meals, coffee, all the extras. The lodging itself was just seven thousand pesos a night; a far cry from what I had paid in Punta Arenas. I had thoroughly enjoyed the stay here with these two wonderful hosts. I went to the Internet; got another e-mail from Marietta and let her know that I was on my way to a farm en route to Ushuaia.

I went down to the dock and again, El Capitan and Dianne were somewhere else. By now, it was close to eleven-thirty. I saw the British fellows, and Simon informed me that he and Andy were returning with us. Upon hearing that news, I returned to the house, only to find that Alexander and I had passed each other once again. He had come up with Dianne and told the landlady that they would be leaving at twelve. I had fifteen minutes to get my gear and this wonderful lady had not only cleaned the fish and prepared it, but she had

267

Robert F. Edwards

stuffed it with cheese, onions and sausage and wrapped it in tin foil for me to take on board the boat for the evening meal. With all my supplies and my treasured fish, we cast off.

What a difference a day makes! The channel was just like a sheet of ice with not a ripple on it, let alone any whitecaps. Alexander told us that it was maybe four times a year that they could see the mountains as clear as they were that day. I took advantage of this by getting my share of pictures of the majestic range of mountains that surrounded Puerto Williams. With more than pleasant memories, we headed into the channel and Alexander informed us that because of the way the winds blew in this part of the channel, it would probably be best to hug the other shoreline. With such light winds, he made his way over by motor rather than under sail.

It was a pleasant cruise, with gentle winds and the skies were clear. Ever so often, we got a little gust of wind and the day stayed this way until we were in sight of the farm that we were heading to. The Harberton Ranch was the residence of Anglican missionaries and eventually in the 1970's; the Argentine government took it over for security reasons, with the Navy, and then later relinquished it back to common property.

268

SOUTH AMERICA
EXPLORATION

As we got closer to the farm, we saw a derelict ship in the harbor by the wharf. This had a big write-up in even the London newspapers, that the ship had run aground in a storm and was unsalvageable, carrying lumber; but after two days, the crew and the four passengers were rescued from the ship, so that it suffered no casualties.

Once we got into the slip at the wharf, they had to make sure that we were docked in such a way that if the winds did come up we would still be able to cast off using the motor to power out. The Beagle Channel demanded an experienced seaman; and I found out that for the last five years, Alexander had been living on his boat on a continuous basis. The captain knew his boat in such an intimate manner that I think the boat almost responded before he decided what he wanted.

Once on the shore, we visited the small museum and it explained the heritage of not only the ranch but of the shipwreck as well. Unfortunately, for me at least, all this information is compiled and illustrated in Spanish, so it didn't provide much of a knowledge base. Simon decided that he'd like to go fishing and Dianne and I chose to go for a walk around the site. There were quite a few cattle in that particular area and

Robert F. Edwards

as we walked, we finally came to another shoal or small inlet and walked along the coastline. It was not a very sandy beach, but coarse gravel and of course, very clean because of no humans to mess it up. We did notice a lot of small fish or large sardines had washed ashore and perished along with the seaweed. After four or five kilometers, Dianne was hesitant to forge any further ahead and we retreated back the way we came.

As we got closer to the ranch, there was an Indian (which I originally mistook for a gaucho) and I asked Dianne to ask him if I could take his picture. His reply was, "Do you want to take the soul of an old Indian?" I thought (she translated), "Do you want to take a picture of an old Indian?" And I replied, "Yes". With his good nature, he allowed me to take some pictures of us together. An interesting man, I wished I were an artist so I could have painted him. He wore a beret, and an old leather jacket that had given way to age and deterioration. After many years of service, it was like a tired old sweater that you hate to give up because it wears so well and keeps in warmth that you've grown used to. This jacket must have given him the same comfort. His pants were brown and

270

SOUTH AMERICA
EXPLORATION

bulky, tucked into black boots; not the cowboy boots by our standards, but the traditional style boots of Argentina. His face was well worn with many years of outdoor living, and would always be the image of a real Argentine gaucho in my mind. I listened to him and Alexander converse back and forth for a while, and he sent his boy out to make sure that Simon was okay on horseback to his fishing spot. It was a much more relaxed atmosphere than the hustle and bustle of town. The pastures and the hillsides, though not snow-capped, were lush and green, and the grass provided rich nourishment for the cattle.

With the afternoon well in hand and evening almost knocking, I was returning to the boat, only to spot some replicated huts of the original Indians now extinct in this area. There were two types: one that was igloo-shaped made out of tree branches and hides; and the other was more the North American teepee type. They were much smaller and wouldn't have housed a whole family, only one or two people. Dianne said that these people that lived on shellfish or seafood always threw the remains in the same spot. Archaeologists were fascinated by this, and could tell a great deal of the period these people lived in, how they cooked the food and prepared it, and so forth, from these time capsules in a pile.

Further along the trail, Alexander pointed out a woodpecker. I had never seen as large a woodpecker as this one, pecking away on a tree. I did manage to take a picture before he vanished into the forest. The trails were well laid out with botanical information, describing the abundance of different types of vegetation available in this area, from small flowers to large full-sized trees. There were toadstools, and many types of fungi present and Spanish moss, or "old man's beard". I came across the original settlers' gravesite, a small one with the typical white picket fence around it and half a dozen crosses inside.

We started getting ready for the evening meal. I was anticipating a feast. It began with chicken soup (home made) and then squid; followed by a baked salmon that was caught in

271

the lake. We started the meal with hors d'ouvres of cheese and breads, four different kinds of bread that each one of us had contributed to this unique meal; and El Capitan provided a white Chilean wine, which was pleasant to drink. I had enjoyed the chicken soup for lunch and another bowl now, which was delicious with real chicken and Dianne also used barley as one of the main ingredients. I did not take too much this time because I wanted to have room for the rest of the meal. The squid had been simmering all afternoon, with potatoes in a rich broth; again very filling. The squid was very tender prepared this way, and this was El Capitan's contribution. And then, my fish was served, almost a red-fleshed fish; and with the sausage, changed the flavor of the fish. If I ever want to eliminate fish flavor, definitely a piece of sausage would do it. It was very nice; however, if I'd had my first choice, I probably wouldn't have put the sausage in, so as to get a truer flavor of the fish itself. Dianne had done a great job by cooking in the stove on board.

After all the food was consumed and the conversation exhausted, it was time for one and all to prepare for the night and El Capitan pointed out our accommodations. In the aft was a double bed, where he and Dianne slept. I got a regular bunk and Simon was assigned the salon couch. Poor Andy got the forward, which didn't have much for accommodations, especially with the insurmountable amount of luggage that they brought from their climbing expedition. However, one and all quickly say goodnight, and that concluded the day's events.

Goodnight, my little treasure bee.

SOUTH AMERICA
EXPLORATION

March 13th, Tuesday
Beagle Channel, Chile

I had a relatively good sleep; but around midnight I heard the winds building on the channel and my first thoughts were if we were going to be able to continue the voyage in the morning. The winds eased off by six o'clock, and El Capitan was up and ready for the day ahead. By the time I got dressed and went topside, he had already started to prepare the boat for casting off. He started up the motor and the winds were still strong, but in this part of the world, they continually blow about twenty-four hours a day, seven days a week, three hundred and sixty-five days a year. It didn't seem to bother Alexander and by this time, Simon and Andy were up and so was Dianne and we had the kettle going; cups of tea, toast, and some jam.

Robert F. Edwards

We cast off with the skill that El Capitan had known most of his life; breaking into a headwind and clearing the port with no difficulty. Just as we were about to get underway, the sunrise started and absolutely took my breath away. Both Simon and I scrambled for our cameras. I have seen some fantastic sunrises and sunsets in my travels. I remember getting up in the wee hours of the morning to climb Tiger Mountain to see the sunrise over the Himalayas. I had also done it in Nepal. Some of the greatest sunsets I had witnessed were in the sea sands of the Sahara, and I recalled the moment of sheer exuberance when I witnessed the sunrise on the top of Kilimanjaro. Those were just a few of the ones that I had experienced, to say nothing of some of the breath-taking ones in my own country, Canada. I had to honestly say to myself that never had I seen such a breath-taking sunrise as this.

It was a burst of reds and oranges and changing, continually opening and contracting, amidst the cloud formation swirling about like bellowing smoke. The whole sky was on fire with this cascade of colors erupting before the sun broke to the surface. This was all happening above the majestic backdrop of the Andes Mountains. It took my breath away, Mother Na-

SOUTH AMERICA EXPLORATION

ture's surprises and sheer elegance. Pictures just couldn't do justice to this magnificent sunrise. It was ever-changing; patches of blue exploded from bellowing reds and yellows, confused with oranges that the clouds highlighted. If I ever traveled into an outer space galaxy, that would have to be a moment that I would expect to see. It was absolutely astounding!

In the opposite direction, the mountains had taken on a pinkish glow, and even Alexander commented that this was a very nice sunrise. With this as the starting point to our day, I could not possibly think of how it could get better. Alexander said that we would be in to Ushuaia somewhere around nine: true to his word, we arrived about nine-thirty. This channel, as he had pointed out on more than one occasion, had great diversity in weather conditions and winds. Passing by a mountain range into an opening, the winds would often rip into the channel with tremendous gusts. As we came into Ushuaia it began to overcast, and the mountain peaks had gathered some clouds.

We docked uneventfully, and I exchanged cards with Andy and Simon. We discussed the possibility of me joining one of their climbing expeditions in the future and would keep in touch. El Capitan was going to let me know when his new boat was launched, as I hoped to be one of the crewmembers on its maiden voyage to the Antarctic. It would take a month or so and who knows, the future was yet to be written and that day had yet to be completed.

My first stop was to return to my lodgings, as the plane to Punta Arenas only flew on Wednesday, so I was obligated to spend the night there. The landlord wasn't in but I left a note saying I'd like to stay and not quite sure which room I would be in, but wasn't too concerned about it. Once I had accomplished that, off to the Internet and checked my e-mail from Marietta.

At the travel agents, I learnt one positive thing and one negative thing. The positive was; yes, the plane was leaving, and I could get on the one seat left. The negative was, when I talked to Dianne, she thought the fare would be maybe a hundred and twenty dollars U.S. With the airport tax, etc., by the time I got finished, it would be two hundred dollars. I felt this overpriced for an hour-and-a-half flight, regardless where it was going. So, I made the choice; I would go by bus and purchased my ticket for tomorrow morning; seven o'clock, all lights go.

The immediate transactions were out of the way, so I went to see Julia at her little store and boy, what a welcome! She was very happy to see me and asked how I enjoyed the trip, and so forth. She had a luncheon engagement so at one o'clock, we said goodbye to each other and I told her I'd probably be seeing her later. I realized now that I was famished, so I went to a good restaurant and thought that it didn't matter how much I spent for lunch because of what I was saving on the airplane ticket. My special treat was (I am ashamed to recall) a cheese hamburger, French fries, two beers, ice cream, and apple pie.

My stomach was well fed, and I started to feel the "siesta syndrome". I was planning to take a walk to one of the smaller glaciers in this area, but fatigue and exhaustion demanded I return to the house. Still nobody was there; so I tried to find a room that didn't have anything in it, but the beds were made. By then I felt like Goldilocks, and who cares? I lay down. I fell asleep almost immediately, for the better part of three hours. Even after this nap, I was still tired, and had to force myself to get up.

I walked down to the Internet to send another e-mail to Marietta, but the computers were down for some reason, and I was faced with waiting around. By now I became aware that, "I'm in the groove". It was surprising how many people recognized me. I must be one of those "bad pennies" that once you've touched it, you remember what it looks like.

I felt drawn to look around again in the shop with the outer gear for sailing. The girl recognized me and we got talking about the adventures I had experienced and how much I thoroughly enjoyed them. After looking through more of the Musto "three layer system" articles, I spotted the inner wear jacket, at a hundred and seventy-eight dollars, regularly three hundred dollars. I was thinking how much I would really like it; and finally, at a hundred sixty, my plastic came out. I had spent about four hundred and eighty dollars U.S. on those three pieces, but if I were to pay the full price it would have been close to nine hundred eighty U.S. Like the man said, "You have the finest jacket in the world," and I thoroughly believed this.

So now with all the savings of my plane ticket spent, but on a much more long-term reward, I was off to try once more with the Internet; and still unsuccessful in three shops. I returned back to my lodgings by ten o'clock. I started to go to bed (without any sheets) and to my surprise, there was a knock on the door, it was Julia. I wasn't sure whether she was in a joint venture with the landlord, or just a strong "mother syndrome", but she was soon making up the beds. She went down and talked to the landlord, came back up, and said, "You have the bigger bed, and you can have your own room for the same price, of fifteen dollars." I was grateful to have met her and hoped to keep in touch, e-mail wise. A wonderful young lady and very knowledgeable of the whole area and everybody in it; and the advice she gave was second to none.

I said my goodnights to her, returned to my bed exhausted, and I guess this strenuous living was finally catching up with me.

Goodnight, my little precious. I'm one day closer to you.

SOUTH AMERICA
EXPLORATION

March 14th, Wednesday
Ushuaia, Argentina

Well, I got up, did my toiletries and packed my small back-pack and off to the bus. Once again, I took the long arduous journey from Ushuaia to Punta Arenas. But before I left Ushuaia, I had a going-away present and it was another sun-rise. No, it was not as spectacular or as memorable as the one yesterday, but was equally impressive and I took some more pictures as it pushed its way up the mountain range in the harbor. I think there will always be certain places that in moments of reminiscing will take me back, and Ushuaia was going to be one of those places in my life. It could be a numer-ous amount of things, but people and cities have so much in common. They leave an impression the first time and some are very lasting impressions.

Ushuaia was just a pearl in this remarkable part of the world and as I looked back over the harbors as the bus left, I hoped

279

Robert F. Edwards

that destiny brought me back here someday. For me, it would always have wonderful memories. Goodbye, Ushuaia!

The bus lumbered along the mountains and this part of the trip was an improvement over the last time I went this route, due to the fact that it rained and was the darkness of night. Today, it was bright and I saw the full splendor of the mountain ranges for the first time. The ever-changing weather down here soon gave way to rain, and then stopped, back and forth as we made our journey ever onward.

When we got to the Customs offices, I was half expecting them to recognize me and just stamp me through as part of the convoy. With a little chuckle, I was soon back on the Argentine side and we were on our way without event. The bus decided to give us a meal-stop and I ordered something like a hamburger. It was some form of meat between two very unique pieces of bread. They looked almost like biscuits with little holes in them, and there was meat inside with cheese, very filling.

We pulled into Rio Grande and for once I didn't have to wait. The bus was there, I quickly transferred, and on we went on this seemingly endless ride. It was a fourteen-hour plus ride, providing everything went well. There were so many "ifs" and "buts" that added to the uncertainty; the lines at the borders, the slowness of the Customs officers, etc. This particular time, Chile seemed very concerned with the produce and beef. They inspected us very thoroughly, made us walk through a disinfecting foam substance, and even hosed the bus down. I felt I had just come from a toxic waste area; but I guess with all the mad cow disease, the Chileans were making sure that nothing came in from Argentina.

We got to the crossing and it was really rough. I couldn't call them ferries; they were more like barges. They were sturdily constructed with powerful engines to make this crossing, and the whitecaps were so heavy that they sprayed over the bus and landed on the cars below.

Eventually the hours finally made their way to the end and we got to the terminal in Punta Arenas. I could hardly wait to get off the bus. I booked my ticket to Puerto Natales, my next port of call that left at eight-thirty tomorrow. With that behind me, I returned to the Savoy Hotel and the girl that first checked me in was on duty. She was most interested in how my time had progressed and was glad to see me. She had registered me in their computer system for the next two years, making me feel rather important.

My next project was to get an e-mail off to Marietta and to buy some batteries, which seemed to be the sole aggravation of my trip this time. Besides batteries fading, I had also left both my flashlights in Puerto Williams. I hoped that they did someone else more service than they had for me and the reason I had left them behind was I was trying to salvage batteries in my never-ending frustration. I was successful, even at the late hour of ten-thirty, to be able to get batteries; so that mission was accomplished.

The one thing that I was really counting on was to get an e-mail off to Marietta to let her know that I was in Puerto Arenas and then heading on to Puerto Natales tomorrow. Unfortunately, the one Internet was closed and the other one, no matter what they did, just could not get it to operate. So, without that success, I returned to the hotel, had a few beers and some French fries, and off to bed I went.

Goodnight, my beautiful wife, I miss you very much tonight and I wish you were with me, or probably I was at home with you. I love you very much. I miss you very very much.

Robert F. Edwards

March 15th, Thursday
Punta Arenas, Chile

I left a wake-up call, but needless to say, I didn't sleep well. I was up at what I thought was six o'clock and did all my rearranging and packing for the next part of my adventure into the park. I planned to leave my big bag and most of my contents in Punta Arenas and only take my small backpack into the park. With that in mind, I rearranged clothing, food, and just the essential for my needs in the park.

I was ready to go, but couldn't find the fellow to open the front door, which was locked. After banging on the desk for some time, I finally got a response and left. I had to lug my heavy bag, which was now becoming a lodestone, to the bus station only to find out that there was a time change and it was one hour earlier.

I was actually there at quarter to six, and the desk clerk seemed quite surprised to see me. The same bus drivers that I had gone to Rio Grande with were back, and ready to take another load of (victims) passengers with them. I don't know when these guys slept. They didn't get in until ten o'clock last night and they were here at six o'clock this morning, the same two men.

Eventually, my bus did arrive, and a pleasant surprise, it was one of the newer buses I had been on. The trip was quite uneventful. I saw a few more small farms and ranches, until about the last hour on this four-hour journey, when I started to see the next mountain ranges. We started to disembark, and I was quite excited about getting into Puerto Natales. I had the good fortune of meeting a lady who spoke English and ran a hostel, where I planned on staying for the night. I also met some Chinese people, from Shanghai, and they were talking about having a meal together of Chinese food, which not having had any for two months; I was craving it.

I started to plan my itinerary for the park, which was quite extensive, and would encompass the next five or six days. With that organized, I proceeded down to find out more about the boat trip that I would be embarking on March 22nd. This proposed to be an interesting passage because never have I experienced such uncertainty on a voyage. Everybody was nice, but nobody seemed to know what was going on. They didn't know what day it was actually leaving, or what was transpiring. I said, "Well, what about my confirmation?" "Oh, that's no problem. We will definitely honor that." Another Canadian that I met that day (from Toronto), hadn't made any reservations and he said, "Absolutely no problem. It's a big boat and it's the off-season, and Cabin-C is a bunk dormitory that holds twenty-four people." So, I wouldn't be alone for three or four days.

My next step would be to try and find the internet, which was no problem, as there was more than one internet in that small hamlet and fortunately, working. I could tell that it was backpackers' paradise and just about every second house was a hostel, and the Internet was popular. By waiting my turn, I did get on; and two great little e-mails from Marietta plus a lot more discouraging news of the stock market plummeting to new lows, and all the gloom and doom the world can muster. I wrote her that I was going to be away for two or three days in Tierra del Fuego National Park and, no Internet there.

I returned to the hostel, where I did have a private room, a shared bath, and it held twenty-five or thirty people. I got into conversation with some of my fellow travelers staying here, the Canadian fellow from Toronto and we were planning on traveling to similar parts of the park but not together. Also, four Chinese people and we all seemed to be hitting it off well. Unfortunately, the Chinese people only had a few days, the Canadian had five or six, and with myself, I was running about five.

Robert F. Edwards

I did a fairly extensive amount of information gathering ("research" would be incorrect with the limited amount of time I had put into this); there was the "W trekking"; I would start at one end, take a bus to the park, get off and take a mini-bus further in, and then start the trek up towards the Torres del Paine peaks; and then the next day the French one; and then the "gray glacier". After talking to several people, I realized the reverse was the easiest, even though it was the longest trek, but probably more appropriate in my case.

Tomorrow, I would have to get up at around seven for the bus at seven-thirty, get off at the second stop, take a ferry across, and then start the long trek up to the glacier, to sleep at a midway station. The next morning I planned to get the equipment and guide, and go on the glacier itself; sleep that night; and then the following day, work back down to another base camp and sleep there and start another trek up another part of the "W"; come back and sleep; and just see how both my money and my body were holding together; before making a decision whether I would do the last wing of the trek or not. With this decided, I made my final arrangements and bought the tickets, the total amount for this wing of the trip was seven thousand pesos.

My Chinese friends and I had decided to prepare a meal together, so I helped them get a few groceries. There was a little bit of misunderstanding, at least on my behalf. Our land-lady had also prepared a meal for us and by eight-thirty, we were eating the first course of the meal, which was lamb, corn, potatoes, squash, and some carrots. A very good meal, and with a bottle of white wine.

The next meal started at about nine-thirty and it was the Chinese one. Yan Yan was a film-producer, but also a mar-velous cook, even with just the bare essentials of ingredients. He made chicken with soya sauce and a bit of garlic that liter-ally melted in your mouth; and of course, fried rice. He served cucumbers and put a bit of salt on them and garlic, marinated, and then drained off the juices. Then he took po-tatoes and cabbage and blended those together. What a tasty meal! It was just what this traveler had longed for. We shared a bottle of red wine and conversation and before anybody realized it, it was eleven-thirty at night.

I wanted to get to bed, to meet the challenges of another long day coming up. I was looking forward to it, but also hoping that I would be able to meet the challenges of the mountains and the ranges. With that, everybody said goodnight and I retired to my little room, and off to sleep.

Goodnight, my darling wife. I miss you dearly and I am looking forward very much to being with you back home, looking after Buttons together. Goodnight, sweetheart.

Robert F. Edwards

Well, I was surprised. It was such a little bed that I had slept in, but I still slept relatively well through the night. By the time Yan Yan had knocked on the door, I had already been up for the better part of half-an-hour, at six o'clock. I felt exuberant and ready to start this adventure. That morning, once again, a beautiful sunrise; it must be in this part of the world that "red skies in the morning" was NOT "sailor, take warning".

I finished breakfast and promptly at seven o'clock, the bus arrived at the front door. The next two-and-a-half hours were something which I had become accustomed to very well throughout these adventures, sitting on the bus. The terrain was similar to what I had seen for the last week or two, but off in the distance, were the snow-capped mountains. I had the good fortune of seeing my first fox and any animal would be very proud of that tail carried high, almost the length of its body. As it was running across the field, I couldn't help but think it would be just a unique pet. There were also a lot of geese in the fields and as the bus rumbled past, they took to flight.

My Chinese companions and the other Canadian had taken a different bus so I was with an entirely new group of people. The bus came to the first stop, which was the entrance to the park, and we all had to get out and pay a thousand pesos entrance fee. Plus we had to report to the park officials on how many were going to be in the park; and secondly, what routes we would be taking. They were very conscientious about their backpackers.

As I was waiting for the formalities to be completed, I saw one of the guanacos grazing nearby, and was able to get a close-up shot of this animal. As I returned to the bus, I

286

passed by this friendly little dog and in only a few moments had bonded with him. He reminded me of my own Buttons in many ways, the friendliness and the insistence on being pet-ted.

It was back on the bus, for a forty-five minute trip before we changed our form of transportation onto the ferry. This next leg of my trip was another eight thousand pesos. As we crossed the lake, it was extremely rough, with spray coming up and over. I joined two Australian girls, Mandy and Caro-line, up on top and admired the first class vessel we were on. It was new, and of metal construction, and could probably hold up to fifty or sixty people. At this particular time, it was about twenty and as I looked around at some of my fellow trekkers, I could not help but think that either I was under-prepared or the weight of carrying their backpacks would be beyond my capabilities. Some of them would be well over fifty kilos, and then some. I didn't know what lay ahead, but from doing other treks, I knew that I could not walk five or six hours with that kind of weight on my back. However, to each his own.

Robert F. Edwards

I tried to take some pictures of the mountains. I have learnt that no matter how much film it takes, it was always better to try and capture a picture of the mountains when they weren't overcast. The cloud formations were building and it was difficult to determine whether it was coming in or going out. However, I sure hoped it was the latter.

The three of us proceeded to the trail known as "Gray Glacier", we had a pleasant surprise that it was well marked and I was fortunate enough to find a walking stick right off the bat, which assisted me throughout the walk. The first accommodation center we walked right on by and started the climb. This trek was supposed to be about four hours and we were not the first on the trail, as the others had been staying overnight here. About twelve-thirty, we were walking along the first pass. It was quite easy going the first half hour in modest terrain and fairly open paths to the tree lines. The scenery was picturesque; a lot of small shrubs, with berries and leaves starting to show the first tinge of fall. It looked quite dry and we were experiencing a bit of wind, but nothing to impede our progress.

As we got into the second hour, the winds were much stronger and the gusts were quite overwhelming, but we did get to see our first glacier. Mandy was the one that deserved full credit for that, as she climbed up the ridge and circled down a bit to see it. We had a very majestic and picturesque view of the lake. We continued on our trek and were well into our second hour, and everything was going well until we started getting some sleet and even hail.

I felt that it would be prudent to change my jacket from the sailing jacket into the Gore-tex. While I was in the process of doing this the rain started to beat down with high winds. With no shelter to change my gear with any kind of ease, it was a struggle. I was most concerned about my small Moroccan leather bag getting wet, so I took out my rain poncho to put on as well. No sooner did I get all these on and the strap broke on my bag. Thank God for my foresight in bringing

288

some electrician's tape, my universal cure-all, and I used this to patch it up.

By now, we were experiencing a lot of rain and the wind had not let up. This was not the pleasant type of trekking that you see of people with backpacks and shorts on. The trail was very arduous, and getting muddier as each step went. We met up with two Spaniards and their experiences seemed just as difficult. By now my speed was impeded with just trying to circumnavigate the pass, which was heavily laden with mud. For the next hour, I trudged through this muck and came up to Caroline who had stopped for a break. Again we started trekking off together; crossing over some rivers and creeks the best way we could and after a while she fell back for a rest. It was about three-thirty and I was wet, but thankfully not cold, and had given up the idea of trying to avoid the water in some of these trails. It was getting very steep and I was taking extra time to struggle down these cliffs. Between the water and the mud, the last thing I wanted to do was slip and fall. Even if I didn't hurt myself, I'd sure be covered in muck. As this was only my first day rather than my last day, I was careful to try and preserve what I had.

I managed to pass the odd person coming from the opposite direction and I asked one young lady I saw, "How much further?" she said, "About ten minutes". It was the best ten-minute call I had ever heard. Within ten minutes, I saw the signs and in fifteen, I had arrived at the first lodging camp. The rooms had eight bunk beds each and I think there were about six to eight rooms. When I arrived, it was quite full and more kept coming in. Mandy was ahead of me; she had dried out and put fresh gear on. As the hours dwindled, more and more people arrived soaking wet; drenched would be a better word. One young couple was soaked right down to the skin. Another man was taking off his gear and his shorts were plastered to his skin. These poor guys with all their other gear were just drenched. I felt somewhat exonerated by my preparation. The sleeves of my Gore-tex jacket below the poncho were wet and the bottom of my leggings; but other than my own perspiration, I was dry. The items that took a beating, and I was a bit disappointed with, were my boots and socks, but this was to be expected.

As I dried out, I enjoyed some camaraderie with this group of interesting people, a diversity of life, job, and nation descriptions. I met a British couple that had been here for a couple of months, and a lady from Los Angeles, Abby, who would be living in Chile for a couple of years. There was a young British fellow who had just spent six months in the Falkland Islands on a sheep farm. One of the most remarkable people that I had the pleasure of talking to that night was a young woman who had recently graduated from university in England. Her first job was two years in the Antarctic in a weather station. I was thrilled to hear some of the things they did there to entertain themselves, in the total darkness of four months out of the year. She said that they had parties, thought up games to play, and were very creative to keep themselves mentally alert. When summer came and the daylight hours were constant, they brought people from different areas to lead them out on expeditions and explore the crevasses and glaciers of the Antarctic, and see the penguins, whales and dolphins. At these weather stations, she said that after a short time, the productivity and alertness diminished very quickly from the sheer confinement that they lived in. An interesting adventure and I thought everything else would seem somewhat boring and mundane after this first job.

I talked to some men who had just finished the glacier walk; they were astounded by it and very enthusiastic about the results. I met the gentleman who would be taking us up further; a nice fellow. Both Mandy and Caroline, I was grateful for having these two Australians as my companions. It brought back some déjà vu of Penny, an Australian I traveled with in Morocco. I liked backpacking with Australians and they just seemed to have a good feel for survival, regardless of whether it was the city or the wilderness. I enjoyed both these women's company, and Mandy was planning a future trip to Vancouver. I looked forward to Marietta meeting her, and

290

SOUTH AMERICA
EXPLORATION

sharing some of the adventures that we had experienced on the glaciers.

I was impressed with the food and facilities in this outpost. They were more elaborate than what I had expected and my landlady at Puerto Natales had said it would be very expensive. Comparatively, yes, it was highly expensive; but for what they were providing, I thought it an excellent value. The wine was two thousand pesos, beer was a thousand; coffee or tea was seven hundred; the dinner meal was five thousand five hundred; and breakfast, of porridge, toast, cheese, with hot chocolate, tea, or milk – twenty-five hundred pesos.

Even though the trail was muddy, and the weather was bleak, the scenery was breathtaking. The mountains were so majestic and pristine that it was worthy of facing the elements. As the glaciers moved forward, portions broke off and formed icebergs floating in the lake. The colors were mesmerizing, a deep navy blue, and some were reflecting back the vibrant turquoise of the lake itself. The mountain peaks above the glaciers glistened with snowcaps. As I worked my way down visually, I could see different colors in the mineral rock formations and multi-hued browns and dark grays. It was a tremendous experience looking at the stone-covered wall, only to fall gently into the tree line below.

There was some similarity to the great ranges of the Rocky Mountains in British Columbia and north through Jasper and Banff. It brought back a flash of some of the mountain terrain in New Zealand, around Cook's Mountain. The sharp relentless forms of this mountain range were probably quite old, but not as compared to the Himalayas or the Laurentians in North America.

When I first entered this shelter, got my clothes off and had something warm to drink, I thought I would probably be the first one to bed. Well, that was a misconception. Wanting to talk to all these interesting people, I was the last one, turning the lights off at eleven-thirty and the other bunks in my room were already occupied. I pole-vaulted into my upper bunk, and was impressed with the sleeping bag they gave me, which was better than the one I owned at home. I had expected something full of patches and clumps of foam; but no, this one was excellent. I listened to the rain pound its way down the windows and rooftop and was very glad that I was inside this shelter rather than a tent.

It had been a wonderful day, one that I would definitely remember. The terrain that I had seen; the majestic landscape that I had walked through; and the camaraderie and experience of meeting some very interesting people.

With that, I'm going to say goodnight to one and all; and goodnight, my beautiful wife. I hope all is well with you and I am one day closer to sharing these adventures with you.

SOUTH AMERICA
EXPLORATION

March 17th, Saturday
Torres del Paine National Park,
Chile

What a surprise! I was by far the most senior person in this group, which ranged from early twenties to late thirties. And wouldn't you know it! I was one of the first up. When I said to the Australian girls last night that I was going to be sleeping in and it would be a real treat, I fully intended that. To my surprise, I was up at quarter to seven, raring to go. Last night, our guide to take us up the glaciers had said that we wouldn't be leaving until ten-thirty, depending on the weather conditions, maybe even closer to eleven if the winds were bad. So, here I was up and at it, and ready for the day. I was amazed at my stamina, as well as my tolerance for long walks in discouraging weather conditions. I didn't feel any worse for wear, and I got up with a real spring in my boots, anxious to get started on another memorable day. Thanks to God and physical fitness, I was more than ready for that day's excitement.

I went over for breakfast and was happy to see that they had porridge here. My Scottish heritage even prevailed when climbing Kilimanjaro. My comrades then attributed my success to porridge and when they neglected to take it, they didn't get to the top. Maybe tomorrow, I would treat myself to a breakfast with porridge.

It was close to nine o'clock, and I talked to some Americans, and a French couple who had ridden horseback on this trail yesterday. It was not raining at the moment, and true to his word, the guide showed up around ten o'clock. He took us over to the Big Foot cabin, a legend in itself. It was yurt-shaped, and they had worked around a huge evergreen tree, and used the main trunk as a centerpiece, and then upon the

Robert F. Edwards

branches, layered sheets of corrugated metal to create a roof, and the bended branches became the support for the sidewall of metal. They had even cut some holes in the roof, and with glass taped on, made skylights. Talk about a salvage operation! Robinson Crusoe couldn't have done any better. Even the table was made out of wood from trees and the benches that we sat on were logs. The stove that heated the place was an old oil drum, and the guides used this as their living quarters, unique but comfortable.

Although their living conditions were not elaborate, the equipment that they used was first class. Our guide had three of us, and together with his partner, started adjusting the crampons on our boots, and provided us with safety belts as well as ice picks. After loading up his own ropes and gear, he poured hot water into thermoses for us to use during the day. Once we were signed in, the five of us started the trek at about ten o'clock in the morning.

The first part was fairly rugged going compared to the trail that I had taken the day before. It was a lot more mountainous and we had to follow the lake in a circular direction, which meant up and down ravines, and over rivers. Some of the rivers were quite large, but with his experience, he knew where the shallow parts were.

The scenery was majestic and as we got glimpses of the shoreline, there were two things that inspired us a great deal. One was the beautiful view of the lake and the smaller icebergs that were floating in it. But the other was our quest and that was the glacier itself, which was getting closer and closer.

294

SOUTH AMERICA
EXPLORATION

Some of the trail was very rugged. We had to scale down rock formations and the climb was far more brisk than the previous day. As we got rid of one hour and were well into the next, the glacier was becoming more than a view. It would soon be a reality and all five of us, including the guide, developed an enthusiastic step to our walk. When we got above the glacier itself, we had to take two ropes; one to scale down on and the other one was just a safety rope. The easiest way to do this, as the guide instructed us, was to lean far out with your back horizontal and arched almost like a bow, and then walk down. Our guide commented that I got the hang of it quickly, and it was not that difficult.

We were now on the glacier and it was impossible to walk on. He told us to strap our crampons on; and believe me, we really did need them. It was amazing how well those little spikes worked. When I didn't have them on, I was just sliding and the glacier wasn't flat, but quite rugged. Once we got them on and he tied us all in a rope, off we went.

It was one of the best experiences I'd ever had. The first part, he was showing us different cracks in the ice and how it separates. We had heard the glacier breaking away last night, but then I didn't know what I was listening to. I actually thought it was thunder, which was exactly what it sounded like when big chunks of the glacier fell into the lake.

We continued our quest across the glacier, over hills and down valleys. The guide needs to know where to do the crossings, as there are big crevasses that can't be crossed safely. Because he went out everyday, he could see how much wider it was each day. He showed us one that probably was about a foot wide; and he told us that within a week, it would be double that. We kept walking on the ice for about an hour, before we came to a very deep crevasse and the water below was a deep navy blue. The ice, he told us, was the hardest ice there is. Where we were walking, the ice was more of a crystalline type, caused by the melting and freezing in the winds, but when it's deep down, it was bluish and the very hardest ice.

Robert F. Edwards

Also, there was mud on the surface from the wind blowing dirt onto the glacier. He told us that Jacques Cousteau's crew spent months here doing research and filming for the Discovery Channel. As we moved on a route that the guide was well versed with, we saw different formations of ice and Mandy described it best when she said it looked like whipped potatoes.

The hours passed quickly. Before long, it was three o'clock and none of us were showing any fatigue or wear. Our enthusiasm not only inspired our guide, but rejuvenated him. He told us it would be his last day working here, and he was going home to El Salvador to spend time with his wife and two children. He also admitted how much he loved his job and enjoyed doing it. I understood his desire to stay out here a little longer and he asked us if we were starting to get tired. We all said no; so he took us to another crevasse with a huge hole. After checking it out, he allowed us to go in then took us way down into it; that was an experience and a half.

I thought that would be the end of what we would be able to accomplish, but no, we continued to another section about a kilometer or so up. There was a large circular hole in the ice and once again, he checked it out before saying okay. He helped us through that crevasse where we saw an enormous peak, over sixty feet high. Our guide asked me, "Well, would you like to climb it?" And my reply was, "Sure, but you have to go first." With no hesitation on his part, he checked this peak of ice, just like a sliver or a cutting edge. Then he scaled this razor of sixty feet or better, and he was up there for the longest time. Mandy and Caroline were getting cold, but what he was actually doing was putting little screws into the ice to put the ropes down. He told me later that this is a very dangerous procedure because if the wind had come out, it would have knocked him over before he got the first peg in and tied himself to it. Then if the wind came, the peg would support him.

It was the better part of twenty minutes before he was able to get the other ropes down the way he wanted. Then he scaled down just like he belonged on the ice. He asked which one of us was first, and I said to his Chilean friend, "You go first." We helped him straddle the crevasse to where the ropes were, and then he scaled up with the ice pick and crampons. The idea is to literally crawl with your toes and the ice picks; the same as if you were on the floor crawling, except this is vertical. He used the rope for support, tightening it unless he was ascending. The first man got to the top and then leaned back and just walked back down, holding the ropes.

Even with his success story behind us, both Mandy and Caroline decided not to try it. So, it was up to me, now or never, and I did have reservations about it. It looked daunting, to be climbing up a sheer block of ice. The Chilean fellow that had just accomplished it said that it was difficult, but not obviously impossible. I started to straddle down and Caroline promised to take lots of pictures. I told her, "Please take as many as you can because I'm not gonna do this twice."

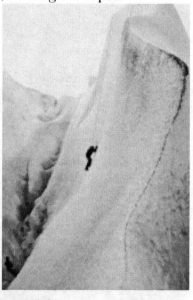

The hardest part was actually at the beginning to try to get over the little humps at the bottom. Once I started climbing straight, it was relatively easy and I found that it was not as difficult as my imagination perceived. I was about three-quarters of the way up, only to lose the crampon on my left leg. This became a real dilemma, and since I couldn't get any grip whatsoever with my left leg, I became like a pogo stick, except with no stability. The only alternative was to wedge my way back down with my ice-picks and my one foot, depending on the support of the guide and his skill with loosening the rope as I continued to hop my way down with one foot. My left foot without the crampon was absolutely useless. It took

Robert F. Edwards

twice as long as going up, but I managed to get down and the other three greeted me with loud ovation. They were thrilled with my success and nicknamed me "Billy Bob".

We all agreed that it was a wonderful day and we'd had more than our share of experiences in this unusual part of the world. I looked at my watch and it was close to five o'clock. We knew that it would be dark before we returned and with that, the guide said to us, "Well, do you want to start to head back?" The five of us gazed around, with torn emotions, wanting to spend just a little longer on these rolling hills of ice but also to err on the side of caution for our return.

Our guide felt the strongest tug, for he wouldn't be back here until next season, and would soon be heading up to Bolivia to guide people up through the mountains there.

Ahead of us lay varying ice formations. As we headed back, it was no longer a new experience; but rekindled some of the moments that were so breath taking. Unfortunately, my crampon must have been damaged. The guide kept tightening it, but even his patience was frustrated by the lack of correction and it kept slipping off and it impeded the entire group's

298

progress. His explanation was that the crampon was Chilean and my boot was German.

As often happens when I am traveling, the way back always seems a little shorter than the way forward, and especially so in trekking. This is either due to the fact that I was not sure what I was doing, or where we were going, or how I would be able to cope with it; but on the way back, I was well versed with the terrain and the obstacles that confronted me. By this time, we were all fairly seasoned to walking on the ice, which has its little tricks to it; for going down, you don't go down sideways, you go down forward and you spread your legs and walk straight down. Same with going up, whether it's a sheer ice face or a large cone, you go straight ahead. You don't place your crampon sideways, but try to get as much surface as possible on the ice to get the grip.

We passed one crevasse after another, each a special moment. I'd often say to one of the girls, "Look at it. It's so beautiful." I could not get over the different formations in the ice below; the blue crystals seemed to be dancing. Even though it was only a matter of hours before, it seemed to have changed, if not physically at least in my imagination. Also, it was interesting to see the edge of the glacier come closer and closer as we walked towards the first phase of the rock. It was surprising to all of us, but when we had to scale the mountain with the rope for going down, we were very awkward and apprehensive. Now, when going up, we were prepared and knew exactly what we had to do, and got up there like a bunch of monkeys climbing a tree.

I also learnt that my Moroccan leather backpack that I had brought with me was great for a little daypack if I was going to town, but it was completely inadequate for rugged terrain. The backpack that they had provided to put the crampons, safety harnesses and axe-pick in, plus all my camera equipment, was much more comfortable to walk with and better balanced for displacing the weight. So, another bit of knowledge that I had gathered on this particular trip.

Robert F. Edwards

After we had scaled up the ridge, we took off our safety harnesses. I'd forgotten that I even had the safety harness on, it was that comfortable. The way back was just as arduous and difficult, with a lot of rock climbing and trekking through heavy bush and muddy trails. Somehow the four of us were able to keep pace with our experienced guide. He was a tall man, with a long stride and in great physical condition from running up and down these mountains. It started to get dark and we had set a fast pace through these treacherous trails, but none of us seemed to be showing any fatigue. Mandy and Caroline were both feeling the cold.

When we started our way back through the bush, we got the crampons off, which I have to admit my feet preferred them on. After wearing them for the better part of the day, I found that when I had them off, every rock felt like I had a pair of moccasins on instead of my boots. By now we started warming up, and were putting out a fair amount of energy climbing ridges, and crossing over the flowing creeks. At eight-thirty, we arrived back at the Big Foot depot and shed all the gear off. We told Rodriguez, our guide, that we owed him some beers because we stepped on the ropes, as this was the tradition, every time you step on the rope, he gets a beer.

With that agreed upon, Mandy, Caroline and myself made it back to the bunk site that we were staying in. Like all good citizens of this alpine village, we took our boots off and went to our designated bunks and removed our damp clothes. It hadn't been too bad a day, weather-wise, all in all. We had a few touchy moments, but generally speaking, mostly overcast with a flash of blue sky periodically.

We had just gotten ourselves organized when Rodriguez showed up with our first beers. We were one of the first that day to return from the glacier and the new group was most anxious to find out what our opinion was and what had transpired that day. I spent some more time talking to the young woman that had graduated from a university in England and her very first job was a two-year stint in the Antarctic. A friend of hers had been on one of the other islands in the Antarctic and they were able to radio back and forth over their stint there. She was telling me about the supply ship for the research stations; it would take a total two years supply of everything, from food, alcohol, and toothpaste right down to toilet paper. Three months was total blackout, with no daylight and when they had to check the various stations, for readings, etc., they needed a torch, but also had ropes tied from one place to the other to hang on to, so as not to get lost. The buildings were placed on huge jacks and as the snow increased in quantity, they just jacked the buildings up to accommodate the new levels of snow.

I was finding that the people on this part of my trip were more adventurous and outgoing. I also met a girl from Sweden and we talked for quite a long time, just about life and the pursuit of adventure. She told me that her boyfriend wanted to return to Sweden and lead a more conventional life, but she wanted to work her way on to Australia. I mentioned some of my adventures down there, only to find out that she was one of the guides. She seemed amazed at my enthusiasm, not just for the day that I'd spent climbing glaciers, but also for my enthusiasm for life in general. To be very candid about it, we were enjoying conversing so much that we didn't realize that the rest of the group had departed to their rooms. Finally, the staff motioned to us that it was 'lights-out' time as it was eleven-thirty; I said goodnight and went to my bunk, only to find that all my roommates were well asleep. I quickly undressed in the dark and hopped into my upper bunk.

That concluded a remarkable day in my life and I'd like to say goodnight to one and all; and I love you very much, my little treasure bee. I hope with these notes that you'll be able to share some of the experiences that have made this day such a worthwhile one in my life. I miss you so much in this beautiful forest, as we both love camping and being together so much in the woods. Goodnight, my sweetheart.

301

Robert F. Edwards

March 18th, Sunday
Torres del Paine National Park,
Chile

I didn't have to look out the window to know that this was not going to be sun tan lotion weather. Throughout the night, the strong winds pounded the windows and shook the trees, accompanied by rain. Also, what I thought was thunder, but now knew was not the clapping of the clouds and the demanding flashes of electrical power, but actually part of the glacier breaking away into the icy waters below. I was grateful that I was sleeping inside and not in a tent flapping like a bird's broken wing in this strong blowing gale. Downstairs, I joined my fellow trekkers and looked out the window. It was one of those days that most of them were content to sit around the fire and make notes, play cards, and read books. For myself, this was the last day at this camp depot before I had to make the next trek down to where the ferry was.

I spent some time reading up on the areas in this national park. The most important feature of this particular park was the Torres del Paine. These were the famous granite pillars often photographed of the Patagonian area in Chile. If not the finest South American national park, it was one of the most picturesque, with its turquoise lakes. I would never forget the moment that I saw the first glacier floating in those icy blue waters. It was a very diverse landscape, with frothing rivers and cascading waterfalls.

The little creeks or rivers often had trails running parallel to them. On the trails, I have to give the Chileans full points. They haven't made it so easy that the average person feels it just a stroll in the park. They've kept its majestic true beauty, but also marked the trails so that you don't need a guide.

SOUTH AMERICA
EXPLORATION

There were orange spots on a tree or a rock to indicate the paths, especially necessary when crossing some of the large boulder areas. It was nice to know that I was still on the trail and the Chilean National Park had done an excellent job.

As I have noticed on a few occasions before in this section of South America, the weather had four seasons in one day. Today, I thought we were going to have only one season, and that was bleak cold insipid weather. A cliché I had often heard, "Fools rush in where angels fear to tread", applied to me for this day and I would be part of the fool expedition. I had a meager breakfast of hot tea and a few buns that I still had from the previous day and packed my small bag. I covered as much as I could with plastic bags to protect from the rain, dressed myself in a layer formation with my entire Gore-tex outfit over my regular clothes, grabbed my walking stick, bid everybody farewell, and set off in the rain.

I wasn't supposed to trek alone in the park. I didn't know that until after I started, but that's the type of person I am; I learn things at the end rather than at the beginning. However, when I did ask about getting lost, people told me that it was rather difficult, since the trail was well marked and you would often see other trekkers along it. This was a truism, as I found out on the long four-hour walk.

I had only gone a very short distance before my bag broke. The straps gave way and the soft leather of my poor little Moroccan bag was just not meant for this vigorous torture test. I now looked like a signalman with all the red tape used to bind it together. I hoped that the plastic bag would reinforce the contents of this abused little daypack, and on I went.

This was not trekking at its finest. The problem with trekking was the same thing as with camping. When the weather was beautiful, there was nothing in the world that's finer; when the weather was mean and miserable; there was nothing more discouraging and dampening to your spirits as your body continually fights the elements that are determined to win. I continued on, the only thing in my favour was that the wind was on my back rather than in my face. My bag was

303

proving to be a hindrance with the strap being on one shoulder rather than placed equally on my two shoulders. It not only cut into it, but the bag acted like a rudder as the wind flapped it from one side to the other, throwing me further off balance. If I hadn't had a good walking stick, the sudden gusts of wind from Mother Nature would have landed me face down in the mud.

I periodically looked back at the glacier and it was not with the fondness that I had of yesterday, it was just to see how much distance I had covered, hoping that it was a greater portion than I had. It was only by straddling the trail, which was running water and muck that I could avoid getting stuck in the mud, along with everything else. My pants were covered, but at least I hadn't fallen. I hoped it was midway, and I had managed to go through sleet, hail, rain, and huge gusts of wind, but still felt the desire to go forward. I knew that Mandy and Caroline were somewhere behind me on the trail, but I was more than confident that their spirits were pushing them forward as well.

I passed a German lady on the trail and asked her how much further it was. Her information dampened my spirits. I'd hoped that it was about an hour and she told me two; and from the way she was walking, it would be a long two hours for me. I put my head forward and using my walking stick to straddle the trail from side to side, I trudged on. I could feel the buckle cutting deeper into my shoulder but didn't have the will to stop. I feared that once I stopped, it would be a real effort to get going again.

This endless challenge dragged on, before I came to a clearing where the trail widened a bit and was drier. I took the pack off to ease my shoulder and thought "What the hell; nobody's gonna believe me that I walked through this crap", so I took a picture of it as well. I knew I was making progress, even though it seemed like every two steps forward, one was being held back. The glacier was a fair distance away now.

I moved the backpack to my other shoulder, and on I trudged. I hadn't seen anybody on the trail other than the

SOUTH AMERICA
EXPLORATION

German lady. After a short period of time, two other people passed me on the trail going in the same direction. As I kept moving forward, I could honestly say that there was nothing that I was enjoying about this, only the thought of a hot cup of tea kept me pushing through the rain. Every time I thought of taking a rest, I aborted that idea. As I turned around to look, the clouds were darkening behind me. I was walking almost as fast as it was approaching so if I couldn't outrun it, at least I wouldn't be in the thick of it if I kept this pace.

To my surprise, I made it in four hours. When I walked through the door, everybody looked up at me in amazement. I don't think I could have been greeted with that many eyes if I was an abominable snowman that fell through the door. I felt exhausted and it took a real effort to get my boots off. After checking in, I noticed a different atmosphere in this particular hostel, and not the same service level. At the campsite I left that morning, they were a fun-loving bunch. The four staff members I had gotten to know each and everyone of them. They were friendly and always ready to provide service.

This group, I was standing there somewhat baffled and very exhausted and they continued talking amongst themselves like I was invisible. Eventually, out of endurance that I wasn't going away, they obliged me by recognizing me. I checked in for two nights, and asked for a towel. The first thing was "yes, you're gonna be charged more for it." I felt like saying, "You can charge me ANYTHING, if I could have a hot bath." I was able to shower though. Then I was shown my bed, and this time I chose the lower bunk. My wet clothes felt as heavy as my spirits, but after I peeled them off, I started to feel a bit revived.

It wasn't very long before my two Australian buddies showed up. I poured them some tea and we compared notes on the trail, and soon were feeling better. Caroline jumped up and said it was Wine Time. Red Chilean wine never tasted quite as good as that one did, and really hit the spot. It warmed parts of the body that had cooled with enthusiasm, if not the weather. We drank and conversed with the other people there

305

growing gradually, one by one. Other people that had faced this rainy cold bleak day staggered through the door. As each one followed the next, their condition deteriorated, wetter and more exhausted. Fortunately, I had been the third one in from the trail that day. I will never forget one poor fellow; as he stripped down, even his t-shirt and boxer shorts were wet. This was a day that proved what being prepared was all about. The group was talking about how bad it was, and most of them spent the day looking at the weather rather than being out in it.

However, one liter of wine proved not to be enough, so I ordered another of the same vintage. The three musketeers clicked our glasses for another round and the conversation continued. The girls went into the kitchen and prepared themselves a meal, and I ate the last of my bread and cold cut ham. I expected to be one of the first to retire that night. I had no intentions, especially when on the trail, of staying up late. It was funny how a warm stove and good conversation could change my mind.

People were starting to recognize me; I guess the word got out that I was the one that climbed the glacier. It must have been my Australian companions that were promoting my achievement because people were coming up and saying, "Oh, you are the Canadian that climbed the glacier."

The third liter of wine was Mandy's contribution to our evening. The fatigue that we endured that day was dissipating and the Irish brogue started to come out in me. So, I knew that I was starting to get inebriated. It was eleven-thirty before we knew it. For one and all, it had been an interesting evening and had lifted our spirits. I do not know whether it was the spirits of the alcohol, or the camaraderie, or just the sheer warmth of the building, but once in bed, I did not need a lot of rocking to sleep. My thoughts were questioning whether I would continue trekking the next day. If it was going to be another rainy day, I had the option of staying indoors, which Mandy and Caroline had reconciled to. I was almost thinking of heading back to Puerto Natales and trying another adventure rather than sitting around watching raindrops fall on the buildings.

With that in my thoughts, I will say goodnight to one and all. Goodnight, my little loved one. I am one day closer to you and one day that I will say was quite an adventure. I love you dearly.

Robert F. Edwards

What a difference a day makes, or a night, whichever way you look at it. It was Monday; the beginning of a new week and the skies must have recognized they had pushed us as hard as they could. I could not believe what I was looking at, blue skies. It was the first time in what seemed to be weeks that I had seen this much blue sky. I was sitting, having a cup of tea, when the girls showed up and quickly pointed out the window, they were just as happy as I was. It was the kick-start that I had been looking for. With some bread in my stomach and a whole new attitude in my mind, I was ready to tackle the Francis Trail.

The three of us started off a little before nine o'clock to the next campsite, which was right on the lake. This was where I could catch the ferry to connect to the buses that ran either to Puerto Natales or further along the park area following the "W" trek. It was pleasant not to be feeling the wind, rain and bleak conditions of yesterday. I was feeling that I could be out here forever, and the scenery was breath-taking.

As I started climbing, I met up with the German lady again and we walked together for fifteen or twenty minutes. She was a great walker; there was no two ways about it. The girls were now further behind and as I kept walking, the view of the lake became more evident and the impressive mountain range ahead. The first hour of walking vanished quickly and I soon came to another smaller lake.

By this time, the girls had caught up with me. They were stopping to take pictures along the way and just enjoying the walk. There were still puddles on the trails and we had to circumnavigate around a bit, but it was a sheer pleasure this

308

day, and each curve brought another breath-taking scene. I had thought the first trail, the Glacier Trail, was beautiful and it would have even been more outstanding if the weather had been like today. This one embraced a mountain corridor and as the clouds burnt off, we saw small glaciers floating in the lake nestled inside.

The first two hours melted away and we came to the midway point with a swinging bridge. It was not as large as Vancouver's "Capilano Canyon" but it sure did swing about as much. Only two are allowed to go on it at any one given time, and there was quite a river frothing below. We had been following along this river for some time, leading into the lake area. As we got on the other side, there was a campsite. All of us agreed that if we were going to stop and camp, this would have been an ideal place. It was sheltered, but there were no toilets or facilities. As the winds in this area could be horrendous, the shelter provided by the trees was important. Even though today was a complete reversal of what I had endured yesterday, the winds were strong enough to be white capping the lakes. The smaller lakes were frothing so much that when the huge gusts of winds came, it lifted the water right up into the air as sprays. I had no idea what the wind force was, but imagined between forty and fifty knot winds. I took some pictures of the spray coming off the lake, as I had never seen that happen anywhere else in the world, just from the sheer wind force. I could appreciate this campsite was well chosen for those brave hearty souls that decided to sleep in this area.

I passed by the Americans that I had met earlier, and they seemed to be in good spirits. They were going to be camping for five or six days throughout the park; and with no hot food. The reason I knew this was Caroline wanted to have a cigarette, and they did not have any matches, lighters or anything. I knew what they were feeling. I was into my third day without a hot meal and it would have been nice to have something hot in my stomach, and tea wasn't quite the same as food.

Robert F. Edwards

The next two hours where going to be more invigorating. We had to cross over some fairly aggressive rivers, and scale more rugged rock trails. Even with the more challenging terrain, we were making good time and enjoying it. There was only a very short distance in the trail that was in fairly dense forest that didn't give much of a view. One of the things that I've always found rewarding in trekking through mountain terrain was that the view just got better and better. Today was no exception. As I turned around, there was an awesome view of both lakes set in the panoramic valley below and ahead were the beautiful majestic mountains.

I've never tired of looking at mountains, and some more rugged with sharp peaks and interesting formations than others. Older ranges of mountains, including the Himalayas, are well known throughout the world for their height and their altitude, but I have always been very grateful to live in a part of the world with the Rocky Mountains. They are to me, some of the most beautiful mountains and I am proud to be a Canadian.

This particular mountain range of the Andes held some majestic and rugged landscapes. This was an area that every artist dreamt to capture on canvas, and every photographer hoped would be his most valued landscape. I was not alone in this thinking and the two girls continually kept our cameras clicking as we gazed at the clouds lifting from the mountaintops, hoping to see more. Mandy brought up a point and it was possible, a lot of the weather conditions probably condensed in the mountains themselves and were creating some of the cloud formation. An added bonus, as we were standing there gazing at this remarkable phenomenon, one of the many glaciers broke away with a clapping of thunder. There were also a couple of condors flying overhead.

I had also noticed some interesting vegetation, which the Park had taken a great deal of pride in marking, unfortunately for me, just in Spanish. We didn't notice any animals in the Park, not even squirrels, or chipmunks. There were also no insects; at least at that time of the year, so there was always a benefit to something. The girls had noticed neat little flowers and the vegetation changed with the terrain. In some areas, it was alpine, and sparse, in other areas lower down close to the riverbeds, a lot of bushes and broad-leafed trees.

We continued the ascent, and got to a look-out point with a good view of one side of the mountains. It was snow covered with the glaciers on it, and the other side sheer rock with a sandy color and then a rich dark brown on top. I commented to the others that it looked like an ice cream cone with a chocolate topping on it. And wouldn't you know it, then everybody wanted an ice cream cone.

After four hours of vigorous walking, the girls had caught up to me. Their schedule was to continue on to the next campsite near the famous Torres del Paine. This meant they would have to get back to our camp by six, check out and make their way to the ferry and then on the bus to the next depot. I had planned to spend one more night at this campsite, but their idea seemed more appropriate than wasting part of tomorrow on the ferry, and the short bus ride, and then not having much time in the day for doing anything. With this window of weather, I was in favor of their agenda, and hoped I could get my money back or if they could give me a change of the voucher to go to the next one. It was not an insurmountable amount, only seven thousand pesos, and the other one was eleven thousand pesos.

Our trek back was just as enjoyable as going up. The valley below was breath-taking, with the view of the two lakes, one turquoise and the other dark rich blue. We could see a hotel that Mandy was told cost up to a thousand dollars a night. During the last two hours, one of Mandy's legs starting cramping up so she wanted to keep going until she got back to the base camp. Caroline and I stopped at different times to take a look as we continued our way onwards. There was a long gorge that we followed down and then back up the hill and it wasn't too much further before we arrived at the camp-site.

As we strolled in, it was such a different and vibrant day compared to the one that we endured yesterday. We all sat around with a satisfied feeling and savored a cup of tea, made our presence known as always, and then checked our directions for the ferry. With a complete of air of confidence in ourselves, we met the ferry, right on time. There was a load of people waiting, all part of a tour judging from the identical bags that they had packed their gear in. No disrespect to the rich and affluent, but I was glad that I was a true backpacker and belonged to the Lonely Planet Club. I had such a free spirit compared to the herd mentality that these people had and the quantity of luggage they were bringing in could have started up a new community. My poor little Moroccan back-pack looked like it had been dragged across the Patagonians, and was the size of a small grocery bag compared to the monolithic containers that this group was dragging on board. They had porters rushing down with wheelbarrows to haul the entire luggage.

The ferry cast off, and such a tremendous difference. It was calm and the mountains were more than visible. It was such a pleasurable boat trip from the last time when we were en-during the heavy waves and spray off the bow. This time we were seasoned troopers, and found that the coffee was free, to

SOUTH AMERICA
EXPLORATION

add even further to our pleasure. When we got off, there were three mini buses to take us to the next port of call.

Darkness was upon us before the driver took off along a small trail and then came to a bridge. He stopped at the bridge and we were thinking, "What the heck is going on?" But they were lining the bus up and without exaggerating; it was only inches to spare on either side as he precariously crossed the bridge. I said to the girls "If they ever got a new bus and God forbid that it was just a few inches wider, it would shear the sides off."

Finally, we got to the new location and there were two separate camps. One was where the rich and famous hung out, and the other was what we were more used to, where the girls had reservations for. I was thinking that I did also, but the fellow wasn't quite sure. After some conversation and phoning (while the bus driver waited which I thought was more than decent), yes, I was at the right spot, the cheaper one. It was eleven thousand pesos for the night, plus sleeping bag; and for supper, it was sixty-five hundred. By now I had only got about two hundred and fifty pesos left after I paid my bill.

We sat down for supper, and I met a fellow from New Zealand. Believe it or not, he was working with a couple of Canadians; one from Kitimat and the other one, from Penticton. I had soup, chicken, potatoes, a bun, and coffee, plus an apple strudel. This was the largest meal I'd had in about three, four days, and I thoroughly enjoyed it.

The three of us ended up bunking into one room together, and we had decided to get a fairly early start on the next day, if the weather permitted. We were hoping that tomorrow the good weather would hold for the trip to the Torres del Paine.

It was one of the first nights that we didn't close the place down, even though it was an older group. We all wanted to have a shower and there actually was some hot water. This facility was, by far, the best out of the three that we had been in. I shaved, had a shower and got completely set up for the long trek tomorrow. It was supposed to be the hardest going, four hours in, four hours out, and then on to Puerto Natales.

Robert F. Edwards

Comfortably in my little cot with my sleeping bag wrapped around and once again, I say goodnight folks.

Goodnight, my beautiful wife. I love you dearly and I can hardly wait to share all these experiences with you. I miss you, sweetheart.

SOUTH AMERICA
EXPLORATION

**March 20th, Tuesday
Torres del Paine National Park,
Chile**

We didn't have to worry about it being a great day. At seven o'clock, the sun started beaming through the glass of the window, letting us know that it was going to be one awesome day. Shortly after seven o'clock, I couldn't contain myself any longer and made my way down to the dining area. The New Zealander was ready to take off for his morning climb. The rest of the group, which were all in my age spectrum, were mustering themselves around the breakfast table.

For me, it was a moment of catch up time on my notes and thoughts of the previous days. Soon Caroline popped up and we both looked at the sky and said, "There isn't a cloud in the sky," – there was not even a whisper of white.

Shortly after, Mandy surfaced and we all decided that we'd take advantage of the day and get an early start. Before, we had been reluctant to get too early a start because of the cold mornings, but today was an exception. We were starting our adventure for the day about eight-thirty in the morning. I erred on the side of caution, but was grateful that I did not put all the garb on that I had done the previous days to protect myself against the elements. Instead, I put my Gore-Tex outer pants on over my shorts rather than over my pants and wore a turtleneck plus just a shirt rather than a shirt and a sweater and a Gore-Tex jacket. Thank goodness! We had not been more than about an hour on the climb and between the sun coming out in full blazing glory and myself perspiring, I had not only my jacket off but also my shirt, and was walking in my t-shirt and Gore-Tex pants only.

The climb, I was told, was going to be the most difficult out of the three and it started off right after the little bridge that we crossed over. A very steep climb. As we ascended up by the river, following the river in, there was little or no let up in the ascent. It was grassier, some rocks but not continual rock climbing. But all of us would stop at different intervals to catch our breath and looked down at the valley below, getting smaller as each turnabout was made.

Once we got over the first mountain, a small one, we started the descent into the valley below. It is like over hill and dale, the easiest way to describe it. Once we got to the top, we went right down to the riverbed again, and this took approximately two hours. At the bottom of the riverbed, there was a campsite and even lodging provided. For those riding horseback, to take the full brunt of the grade, this was the end of the trail for them.

We started our climb back up from this point. It wasn't a great distance before we came to the bridge crossing over the river and another pleasant campsite. We all three made the comment that though the day was just beautiful and by far the best we had up to date, the scenery was lacking compared to the previous trails that we'd been on and it was the most vigorous out of the three trails.

SOUTH AMERICA
EXPLORATION

The next hour was just up and down the terrain, which offered little to the imagination, but was challenging to the endurance of the muscles. However, the last forty-five minutes was absolutely grueling. It was a rock face of boulders, maybe from a huge glacier that rolled down and left its debris or maybe it was an avalanche at some time. Maybe once upon a time, when the earth was young, it could have even been a massive river and this was a riverbed. I had no idea, but I do know that between rocks, boulders, and stones, we were going up altitude-wise very quickly. It was difficult trying to find a trail or a way of climbing without having your knees meet your jaw. It was vigorous and I did not feel too bad when I stopped to catch my breath and both Mandy and Caroline were making the same comments.

We met a Portuguese lady that said, "Oh, go ahead, you're in better shape than I am." So, with that, we passed her by and eventually got to the top to see the Torres del Paine, and they were beautiful. There was a small lake down below them. On a day like today, we had achieved what most climbers dreamed of having as a reward. The view was very clear and visible.

Robert F. Edwards

I could not help but think of the two girls from Copenhagen that I had met last night. We had been sitting around talking and what a sad story. When they made the climb up to Torres del Paine, they had only got a little better than midway and the guides turned them back, telling them that the weather and the conditions were too bad. One girl went back to the camp only to find that her knees had given out and it took her over five hours to walk back, which was less than a two-hour walk. They were both good spirited about it though.

As I gazed upon these pillars of endurance, I thought of their trials and tribulations and our success. What a day it was! I recalled what the young man had told me about the famous "W" trek that I had now just completed. He said that going up to the Grey Glacier was probably the easiest. The next was going to the Francis Glacier, and the Torres del Paines being the most difficult. With the weather that I had experienced, I would not have seen any of the park except the first or second day if I had taken the route these ladies from Copenhagen tried. Many years ago, I used to say I was lucky and these last years, I have been saying I am blessed by the ability to achieve something, by going the opposite trend to most people. I have achieved completion.

We stopped for a photo session and spent the better part of an hour on the top before we started our descent. It was easier, as mentally, we knew that it was downhill, both the first forty-five minutes of bouncing from rocks to rocks and then the final stretch. Mandy set a rapid pace since she was getting a muscle cramp in one of her legs and did not want to stop. Caroline and I took it a bit more leisurely. But all in all, it was close to nine hours from the time that we had started until stomping into the luxury hotel, about a two-kilometer walk from our campsite.

We had all made a pact earlier during the day that once we got back; we would celebrate this walk, if not the whole adventure with a beer. Without any further ado, we walked in and I knew Caroline's eyes were looking for Mandy, and I was looking for MasterCard or Visa. We both found what we were

318

looking for. Mandy laughed and said she had been waving at us as we walked, but she could see where our concentration was, not on the window but on the trail ahead. We all had a couple of good laughs and Mandy had already got a good bite out of her beer and I ordered some more. We were all mentally and physically stretched, but I had a feeling of accomplishment. Definitely, this was something worth remembering as endurance.

Nobody seemed to know what the kilometers were versus the hours on these trails. All I know is that after accomplishing this, most people were behind us. There were a few that passed us, but for what it was worth, we were in the top ten at all times returning to the base camps, so we must have been in good shape. I was thinking of the Francis Glacier to walk for literally eight hours, standing for five-minute breaks, not sitting or dilly-dallying. Hit the park for eight hours, and especially on those vigorous trails, spoke well for what we had done.

When we were sitting around having a beer, there was a feeling of accomplishment as well as recalling the moments of splendor, the moments of endurance, the breath-taking vistas of mountain ranges, the valleys which soared up to rugged, majestic peaks covered with snow, glaciers dipping into ice-filled lakes, and trekking through snow, ice and muddy trails to the glaciers. It was going to be a difficult, if not impossible, task to surpass this beautiful area of our world. For anyone inclined to walk through the wild side of life for enjoyment of solitude and beauty; this was a must-see area to visit. No, not just visit, join it and surrender to its beauty and its majesty, pristine and untouched by commercialism. It was a jewel well placed at the end of the world because it deserves only those that wish to see, what could have been the end, of what beauty lies ahead.

We walked back the two or three kilometers to our campsite, checked out our gear and the bus would meet us there later. We took advantage of the wait and I order a hamburger, almost as big as the plate that it was served on. It was large

Robert F. Edwards

enough to share with the two girls, and still be more than adequate. And merrily, the same bus driver showed up with the same bus. At seven o'clock we were back on the same trail leading to the narrow bridge. Once again, precision was the order of the day and he made it across. Without further ado, we were on the other side and at about seven-thirty, the big bus arrived, and we were on our way back to Puerto Natales.

The trip back did not seem to be quite as arduous or long as the one going. It was at night and who knows, maybe I fell asleep. There were quite a few other people on the bus and after five or six days in the park, everyone was exhausted and thankfully the bus did not have the music going this time. As I looked ahead, it was just a steady road and the strong determination of the driver to get home. By ten-thirty, the lights of Puerto Natales came into view and with a feeling of relief, I was glad to get off the bus. It had been a long day, to say the least.

Once off the bus, I made my way back to my lodgings and knocked on the door. My landlady opened the door and welcomed me as if I were her long-lost son. She showed me up to my room and sure enough, my luggage was exactly in the same spot I had left it. So, now in a room by myself with two beds in it, all my possessions that I had traveled with accounted for, I got undressed, opened the window, and pulled the heavy woolen blankets back.

Goodnight, friends and people that are sharing this adventure with me. I miss you very much, my dear beautiful wife. I am looking forward to telling you of some of the experiences I have had in this park. Even though I wished you had been here, I knew in my heart that these climbs would have not been possible for you, either mentally or physically. They have been more than just vigorous, and with steep ravines, your comfort zone would have been stretched beyond its limits. However, it does not mean that I did not carry you in my heart and my soul all these miles. I love you, my beautiful wife, and my treasure. Goodnight.

SOUTH AMERICA
EXPLORATION

March 21st, Wednesday
Puerto Natales, Chile

Well, I slept in this morning to the tune of about eight-thirty and was still tired. I could feel the back of my legs; especially my calf muscles were tight. I guess after all that walking; it would take them a while to relax. Also, I noticed that morning across my feet, even though the crampons wouldn't stay on, they had left marks across my toes. So, they were on tight enough, they just wouldn't stay on, regardless.

It was ironic, that with all the tromping around in the wilderness with rain, soaked clothes and wind-blown face, I had felt at the "top of the mound". Back to civilization now, and last night, I developed a scratchy throat and unfortunately, my landlady was also coughing and sputtering. It was that time of year, in any country when you change from one climate to another, you get colds.

After the breakfast, which always consisted of bread, biscuits and instant coffee, I said that I was still going to try and have a good day, so started to get myself organized. This lady's daughter showed up and I asked her if I could go to the caves today. She basically said, "You know, really sorry, but there's not enough people going to the caves. You need at least three to make it worthwhile and if you want to go on a glacier sailboat up the inlet, it's about thirty thousand pesos and you have to do it in the morning, you get back at five, and that's too late for today too."

I reconciled to the idea of not getting everything done that I wanted. But, most importantly, my great thrill in life was to get to an Internet and see if my true love had a new message for me. I spent my favorite hour reading my mail, the news and business information, the entrepreneur still imbedded in

321

my genes. Then I set off to the bank to withdraw another hundred thousand pesos.

I decided to walk around the streets and find out a little bit more about the people that lived in Puerto Natales. One of the things that can be said about small towns anywhere in the world, people have a quieter, more interwoven life with each other. I noticed that the children, it did not matter what age, all wore uniforms to school, and this was prevalent throughout the countries that I had been in. I liked the neat appearance of these young people; the girls dressed in pleated skirts, and knee high woolens socks, and the boys with their blazers. Most of the colors were blues and grays, with some burgundy colored uniforms.

The policemen were dressed in a uniform with a military look to it, as they walked the beat. Our policemen seem to have given up walking for the comfort of a motorcycle or a patrol car, but these police were still interwoven with their community. As I was sitting having lunch, I watched as two policemen were talking to some citizens, just general conversation about some music cassettes they had bought. I remembered this same attitude from the sixties as experienced in Canada and was still being practiced down here. People were friendly, sincerely friendly. When I was coughing and sputtering at the Internet café, the girl there was doing the same thing, and we laughed about it. Before I was finished, she had brought me over a hot lemon drink. The thoughtfulness and a little of the kindness that I remembered as a boy.

I was still determined to check into any possibility of seeing the caves. That old mantra of mine, a hangover from my Russian travels surfaced, "check, check, check, and then check again." Everyone I asked kept giving me "Maybes" as a possibility. The guy didn't speak any English, but somehow, I paid nine thousand pesos and arranged to leave right away. He could not change the pesos, so I went to a store, picked up some bologna and buns and a pop, and was ready to go to the caves. It happened to be a taxi that was taking me, so I assumed I was paying a premium, but at least I was going.

SOUTH AMERICA
EXPLORATION

The caves, Cueva del Milodon were said to be interesting to see, and were twenty-four kilometers northwest of Puerto Natales. Captain Hermann Eberhard had discovered, in the 1890's, the remains of an enormous ground sloth, about twice the height of a normal man. It was classified as an "herbivorous milodon" that ate leaves and small trees before becoming extinct in the late Pleistocene age.

It was a pleasant day and warmer than the one I had experienced climbing the Torres del Paine. With just a jacket, my camera equipment, and of course, my two sandwiches, I started off. The taxi driver, not being able to speak a word of English and my Spanish improving but still not conversational, we took the ride out needless to say quietly. What a beautiful day for the scenic trip around the harbor as we left the city and made our way towards the site.

Once I got there, I had to spend another two thousand pesos to the park administration. I took a few pictures of the actual bones of the great sloth and read some of the information on the findings of the scientists, detailing how much manure, skin and remains of this gigantic sloth were found. The cave itself was about thirty meters high and it went back quite a distance. Part of the ceiling in the cave looked almost like cement with rocks placed in and exposed. A first I thought it was man-made, but the museum described how the glacier was able to contract and this particular cave was formed, providing shelter for this animal. I met two Greek young men and they were good enough to take some pictures of me standing beside the stone replica of the sloth itself.

323

Robert F. Edwards

If they turned out, I would have a comparison record of how much larger this creature was than me and being 5'10", I think it is almost twice the size. It was quite a large cavern, and I could easily imagine prehistoric man as they dragged their meat in, and sheltered from the elements. Once Man discovered fire, the caves were deep enough that the flame wouldn't blow out in a bad storm. Our prehistoric ancestors would have had a communal atmosphere, protecting themselves against an alien environment. Today, the view from the cave was of a picturesque range of mountains and a lake centered in between. Maybe they didn't have television in those days, but they surely had a view that was more than enjoyable.

Leaving the cave, there was a trail for hiking of approximately three to four miles. Why they changed the measurements from one denominator to another, I didn't know; but I decided to stroll up this the well-marked path. Wooden signs were engraved and varnished, explaining the plants and the vegetation of the terrain. At midway point there were even a couple of benches to sit on and enjoy the view. From this lookout point was a beautiful view of the valley and way off in the distance, Puerto Natales.

I took a leisurely stroll back down, and the taxi driver was waiting for me. One of the rangers commented to me that I had set a record on how fast I was; nobody had ever gone up and down quite as fast as I had. It was a very warm day and I had left my jacket in the car and even with my short sleeves, I was perspiring a bit. The climb was more than modest, but I guess to the average person, I had set a pace second to none.

We drove back to the city, and from here I headed down to the boat navigation center. The boat would be leaving tomorrow, and I was told to have my gear there by four o'clock. I made arrangements to bring my stuff there by noon and could leave it there while I had a leisurely lunch. It was now about three o'clock in the afternoon and I decided to have an early dinner. I ordered that old stand-by, a hamburger and French fries or papas fritas. The hamburgers were more than generous with the cheese and tomatoes, about six inches in diameter. With real meat, I could not believe it! And I also indulged myself in a couple of beers, to wash down the salts and grease that I had been depriving myself of those last days in the mountains. Now, feeling thoroughly satisfied, I decided to do what most Latin American countries pride themselves in, and have a siesta.

After a bit of relaxation, I went to a piazza, close to the church and there was an old train replica as the centerpiece. The trees were well groomed, and throughout South America, I had seen street cleaners. And yes, they really did use brooms; and yes, they really did sweep up the streets. Even in this small community, there were throughout the streets little garbage cans to put debris in. Very clean people and clean cities. On a hygiene note, in this part of the world a custom that I couldn't get used to and that was toiletry; "Don't flush the toilet paper down after you've used it. Please put in the baskets that are provided." I first experienced this in Cuba and it seemed to be prevalent throughout South America. This was the only hygienic thing that was offensive to me. I almost preferred the Eastern method of the "dung hand" than putting my used toilet paper in a basket.

I enjoyed seeing some of the older buildings in town. Similar to my own heritage home in Canada, they used wood that was tongue in groove for paneling in the same way. It was nice to see a building of this vintage in good shape and reused for administrative purposes. I went into one of the only churches that I had seen of any denomination. From the outside, it was an attractive looking church, but inside I was quite surprised. For this part of the world, it was rather plain. There was a blue ceiling and the altar and "Stations of the Cross" were not very elaborate. Some of the saints had reached better favor here than others. There was a priest that had to be canonized and must be the patron saint, either of this church or this community.

I returned back to my lodgings for a quick supper. It was potatoes, a bun, some kind of meat in batter, and a salad, lettuce only. I spent the evening talking to some of the fellow boarders, a German fellow from Bonn and an Englishman from Birmingham. The Brit had motorcycled quite extensively throughout the world. He had broken a strut on his bike, had now managed to find one and was back on the bus tomorrow at six o'clock; to not only retrieve his bike but to repair it. He was the second schoolteacher I had met that had abandoned his profession in Britain. After discussing different places, we realized that we had both seen some vast areas of this planet Earth.

I chose to say goodnight at the bewitching hour of ten-thirty. I was doing relatively well but not feeling at the "top of the mound". When I hiked down from the caves earlier, as I said in an e-mail to my good wife, "I felt twenty years younger and totally energized". Tonight, I was down a pint of energy and the cold was giving me tightness in my chest.

My beautiful wife, I am one day closer to our home and our lifestyle together. I miss you dearly and am not only looking forward to being together again, but also renewing the moments that we bring each other such happiness and contentment in our lives. I hope that we do get a chance to do a lot of camping this year. This part of the world has renewed my memory, recalling the moments of enjoyment that we've spent with our little camper. Goodnight, my beautiful wife, I love you dearly.

SOUTH AMERICA
EXPLORATION

March 22nd, Thursday
Puerto Natales, Chile

I would have to call this 'the lost day'. I got up feeling congested, but full of desire to meet the challenges of the day, which was going to be a departure on the boat, or so I thought. I had a nice hot shower and felt much better for it. A lot of the little aches and pains and discontentment that I had the previous day had vanished. I had my usual spartan breakfast and packed my bags ready for a sailing trip.

The day started off relatively well. My plan of attack was to be at the dock around twelve o'clock, drop my gear off, have a nice lunch, do a last minute check around the city, then onto the boat, and off we sail. The first part of the day was well in hand by the time I had checked my e-mails and sent one to Marietta. I explained that I was sending my last e-mail for a while, as I was moving on to the boat. I read a little bit of news and made sure I cleared off all the junk mail so that I wouldn't have the system plugged when I arrived in Puerto Montt, and felt well under control. I was still coughing and sputtering like a John Deere diesel with bad fuel, but the kind lady at the café provided me with a couple of slices of lemon and hot water, which eased the immediate congestion.

By then, it was about eleven o'clock and I leisurely wandered around. I felt that control was the better part of valor and walked over to a taxi station, made arrangements for them to bring a cab over, and settled up with my landlady. That was when she got really quite excited and made me wait, then phoned her daughter. Her daughter said, "No, no, no. It's tomorrow, it's not today." Anyway, I was adamant that it was today because the fellow had told me vigorously that it was. However, I said to her that if in the event it wasn't, I would be returning. She smiled and good naturedly settled up the bill. I even gave her a thousand-peso tip and got in the cab. Seven hundred pesos later, I was at the port for the boat.

There was no boat in the port. I went in and asked, "Well, what's transpiring?" And the fellow says, "Ah, I've got your ticket," which was nothing more than a photocopy of some illegible document. And I asked, "Will I still board at four o'clock?" He says, "Mañana." I say he said today. He smiles and says, "Well, you know, I made a mistake. It's tomorrow." So, the local people knew exactly what was going on. The guy that wrote up the ticket didn't have a clue whether the boat was even seaworthy, I suppose.

Another seven hundred pesos later and a bit red in the face, I appeared back at Nicko's and the good-natured landlady looked at me as if to say, "Well, you know, I tried to tell you, but you wouldn't listen." I put my gear back into the room and sheepishly said I'll be back later.

I went down to my favorite café with the Internet, sent my good wife another e-mail saying that the boat was somewhat delayed and I would be going tomorrow. With that, I ordered a beer, an enjoyable steak, potato salad, a couple of buns, another beer, a coffee, still feeling disappointed. It was not that I disliked Puerto Natales, but I was thinking of how many other places I'd rather have spent an extra day; or if I had known that this day was here, what I would have planned to do with it.

It was a community that offered very little architectural design. Most of the buildings were of corrugated aluminum siding. A lot of them seemed to be do-it-yourself projects and it brought to mind a conversation I overheard of the two fellows from Holland that I met in Puerto Williams. When they asked the people there why their buildings were somewhat dilapidated and they were driving nice vehicles, the reply was "It's a status symbol. Everybody knows what you're driving, but nobody knows where you live". In some ways, these neighborhoods seemed to reflect that. I felt down a pint of enthusiasm that day and was probably looking at things with a jaundiced eye rather than with my normally optimistic view.

I trudged back to a small park near the place I was staying and did some catching up on my notes. I didn't really feel like unpacking, since I was assured that tomorrow at four o'clock I would be boarding. It was now five-thirty and I was not feeling that good, the cold had finally caught up with me. I had a dry cough and my nose was running, and I felt like the weather; cold, bleak, and overcast.

In that mood I returned to my room for a "siesta". Even at nine o'clock, when they knocked on the door for dinner, I excused myself and said that I would pass, and just rolled over and continued to hack away and take the cough drops.

I am going to say goodnight to one and all. Not my best day of adventures, but definitely one that is less. My little treasure bee, this is one day I really wish I was having a "winko" with you. I would have been a happier guy. Goodnight, my beautiful wife.

Robert F. Edwards

March 23rd, Friday
Puerto Natales, Chile

Well, I had a restless night coughing and sputtering and I am sure that a lot of the residents of this place did not know which one that they would rather strangle, the dogs that were barking or the person that was coughing. However, I did feel somewhat better, got up and had my meager breakfast. A Canadian from Toronto had arrived during the night and he was also going on the boat that day.

Off to the Internet, and yes, I got another little e-mail from my true love, which was really nice to start the day off. I read the news and all the bad things that were happening in the stock market, the discouraging news of the Mir space station going to its watery grave back on Earth, and other events in the world that had taken place in my absence. Rob, the Canadian popped in, and also a girl that I had met on the trail and we talked for a while. I made arrangements with Rob, that I would meet him back at the landlady's place by two-thirty, and at three he and I could start heading down to the wharf to board the boat.

I was anxious to get on to another part of my adventure and had spent enough time in Puerto Natales; it didn't seem to have any romance left for me. I walked down to the boat and watched them unload its cargo. It was funny, that morning when I first looked, I saw all those people on board and I thought it was ready to cast off. Now I realized that it was the people coming in that had not been able to disembark yet.

At about noon, I decided I might as well have one good meal just in case the food on the boat was less than rewarding. I found a nice restaurant that accepted my magic piece of plastic, and ordered fish soup, a steak, tomatoes and onions, a custard dessert, two beers, and a large coffee. It was a very nice restaurant, with all the elegance and prestige of any large city's more elegant establishments. Probably the only thing that detracted from it was that the fellow charged me for an extra beer. Usually I didn't check the bill but this time I did for some reason. I am sure it had happened to me more than once and other people as well, but that was the only negative thing.

Back to the landlady's place, and Rob was all ready to go. We got a cab and took all our gear down, and as the people started to arrive, there seemed to be quite a few of us. At four o'clock, we all started to make the trek to the boat. The amount of cargo that this ship was taking on was immense. It consisted of trailer loads of livestock: sheep, horses and cattle. While we were walking beside one of the cattle trucks, the cows squirted out and with more luck than timing, it didn't hit anybody including myself.

The purser was a man of about forty years of age. He had a mountaineer background as a guide but he said that because he worked with people pretty well all his life that was how he got this job. He didn't know the channel or the ocean conditions as much as seafaring Chileans, but he spoke excellent English. A very organized, highly cooperative individual, with good leadership qualities. He gave us an introduction before we started our trek to the ship and said, "Look, we can all have a good time but we've got to do it my way and we've got to respect the ship, we've got to respect the crew, and we've got to respect each other. And if we do that, everybody's going to get along good. You know, if you don't and you want to do it your way, then we're going to have some trouble." He was very straightforward on what to expect.

The luggage and big rucksacks that most people were taking (including my small one that weighed twice as much as anybody else's) was on a wagon that he told us it would be delivered to the meeting room. I couldn't believe how everything was starting to become organized, because up to this point it had appeared chaotic and nobody knew when, or what was happening. Today, things were right on target and were moving in an orderly fashion. He told us once we get to the ship what we could expect and to meet in the eating area, and then he would assign bunks and register us in.

I was still apprehensive with only a photocopy of a ticket but lo and behold, I was on the passenger list and soon checked off. So, in and accounted for. He told us not to rush, that he would call out the designated area, then take us down and assign us our quarters. With Rob and myself, we had got our luggage and were more than ready but he said, "Look, if you're not in a hurry, just sit tight and I'll do you right." So, we patiently waited, and watched the others get assigned bunks in different sea quarters and eventually we were rewarded.

He got us a cabin. So, Rob and I were sharing a cabin for four, it was wonderful. The ship had been recently refurbished and was in first class condition, and our cabin has its own bathroom for four. It was outside the cabin, but it was still ours. There were even little curtains to draw around the bunks. And just the two of us, it didn't really matter. The storage compartments were more than adequate, and we had double space with two people less.

The other passengers were in an open area, without any doors on them, and the toilet areas were to accommodate people up to maybe twenty or more. As that was where I was supposed to be, this was a major upgrade. Both Rob and I were chuckling like a couple of kids that had just managed to get out of doing homework.

We were both on an emotional upbeat. First of all, the ship itself was a nice vessel; there were no two ways about it. They had replaced an older ship with this vessel and as the purser said, "You just cannot compare this with the other previous one; it's not the same ship at all". Just from some of the things that I had overheard from other people, I guess the old ship was pretty tired; its toilets were backed up and just worn out. In our cabin, we not only have blankets and sheets and even towels, while the other ones just have mattresses. So, we had really lucked out, especially myself not having a sleeping bag. I would have had to bear the additional expense, or sleep in my clothes.

It was quite remarkable when I allowed God to let things happen in an orderly fashion rather than try to make rules myself. I had originally planned for this to be the first leg of my trip, and now was grateful, reflecting back on the journey that this was the last leg. It was going to be nice to have a couple of days of relaxation, especially since I still managed to keep this cold which I was losing but not as fast as I'd like to.

We soon had our gear sorted out and tucked in to the designated areas. The ship was late leaving, as they were still loading on containers. The ship was capable of holding well over two hundred containers. They all had to be brought in on trucks because there were no cranes in this particular port.

By seven o'clock, we were all quite ready for dinner. They served a big piece of chicken and rice, a very nourishing soup, a small salad and bun, a big plum for dessert, and juice. The food was good, and I was more than full. We shared some white wine that Rob had bought and just enjoyed a lot of conversation with a woman from Australia who had joined us also.

After looking around the ship a bit, I had chosen to take a shower, now that I had a key to the room. The shower, the whole bathroom, was just a delight, in a modern cast molded plastic. The custom of not flushing paper down the toilet did not apply here, and it was back to the North American standard – 'put it all in the toilet and give it a swish'. They had automatic timers on both the taps for the sink and shower. It took a little while for the shower to produce hot water, but it was one of the best showers I had had in probably weeks, if not a month.

Once finished, I felt rejuvenated and joined the others upstairs in the dining facilities. The meal schedules were quite rigid; eight to nine for breakfast, twelve to one for lunch, and seven to eight for dinner. It seemed everybody was waiting in line to get his or her share. That evening meal they ran short.

Robert F. Edwards

I didn't know what arrangements they made, but was confident that nobody went hungry.

The conversation touched on subjects from hiking to cultural differences, primarily in the western sector. Upstairs, we shared a few beers and mine had a Patagonian label on it. I took the bottle back down to my room and I was going to try and get that label off, hell or high water.

As I was lying in the top bunk in my cabin at the bewitching hour of midnight, I heard the casting off of the lines. We were underway, so tomorrow morning, I would be at sea. It astonished me to think of how things really did work out for the better in all aspects. If I had been impatient, I would have been on a ship far inferior to this. Again, if I had been in a rush to find my quarters, I wouldn't be enjoying the private upgrade. Patience was a virtue and I should be grateful that this virtue was starting to develop in my older age, to be more in sync with the global community.

With that, I'll say goodnight to one and all, and goodnight, my beautiful beloved wife.

SOUTH AMERICA
EXPLORATION

March 24th, Saturday
At Sea, Chile

I got up at six-thirty and dressed quickly to catch the sunrise
that was going to take place to my surprise, at seven o'clock.
I thought it would be a little earlier. The winds were blowing
quite strongly and the sea showed a bit of white capping. One
of the brave souls that accompanied me up on deck had a
GPS System indicating time, speed and sun rise. Surprisingly,
my inferior watch from Argentina did keep accurate time. At
seven o'clock, the sun broke over the horizon and blessed the
clouds with a beautiful cascade of colors glowing over the barren rock shoreline.

It was a different type of scenery from what I had experienced in other parts of Chile and South America. This rocky
shore had only sparse vegetation: lichen, moss and low growing shrubs. The main reason for this was the high winds off
the sea that blew constantly, and brought no soil or sediment.
This coastline was very barren, however equally as picturesque as anything I had seen. The comparison to my home-
land and the British Columbia coastline was very similar.

It was a beautiful part of the world that we were crossing
through. The purser said that we might see whales, sea otters
and dolphins, maybe even a condor on shore. One thing that
had been null and void on this trip was the Animal Kingdom.
I just hadn't been that fortunate to see many, and was determined to make use of my photo telescopic lens before this trip
was over. I had lugged the heavy thing around from one location to the other and for the few pictures I had taken with it, I
could have left it in its bag at home.

Breakfast was very good – porridge, some fruit cocktail, a
bun with a piece of meat in it, juice, and coffee. What a tremendous difference compared to some of the sparse meals I'd
had at bed and breakfast places. It was always amazing how

my appetite soared to new levels when I was on a boat. I wasn't doing anything except as the Brits say, "chilling out", or in my case, "vegging out". It was surprising; I didn't know where everybody was. The ship wasn't that big and the facilities for us were limited to where we could go. Even in our cabins, we got the aroma of the farm from the poor cattle below on their one-way journey.

It was mostly young people on board, maybe one or two a little older than myself, but that would have been the limit of the geriatric group. Most people were quiet, very subdued, a little bit of talking, reading, playing cards, or resting in their bunks.

I refrained from going down to inspect the animals in the holding containers. When I did it yesterday, it upset me thinking that though they weren't mistreated, they were packed in there for their final journey. If I had any interest or belief in being a vegetarian, looking at those poor living creatures would have inspired me to take another view on the subject matter.

It was interesting to watch how aggressive the crew was, working on the floors and keeping the ship in pristine order. There is always so much work that goes into maintenance; whether it was a small sailing boat like mine or a large ship, the day-to-day operations were a laborious task. At eleven o'clock, it was mostly an overcast day, but with the odd patch of blue sky. It was a mesmerizing sky, as I was looking at two different shades of blue. One was a light pastel blue, and the other one was a deep navy blue, with only a large cloud separating the two shades. The sea channel was still white capping and the winds were very strong. It was not inducive, except for those hardy souls, to sit out on deck. The channel was opening up, and from my vantage point I could see more open sea.

Lunch was served and I quickly got in line. Mashed potatoes, piece of meat, bread, juice, and a plum. I wolfed it down like I was starving. I couldn't believe that when I was trekking for eight hours, and I didn't even stop for water and now all I could think of was eating. My next thought was an afternoon "siesta" or as my good wife calls them, "winkos". It seemed too early for me, so I went back on deck, looked around for a while at this scenic channel, and lo and behold, we saw a whale. Some of other people saw it before I did, and by the time I went down and got my camera lens, I could just spot it in the distance. The ship was traveling at about fourteen knots, and the whale in the opposite direction.

With that excitement out of the way, I chose to go down and have my siesta. My poor steerage passengers, the cows, now had manure on their faces and they looked a sorry lot. The barnyard smell was permeating the cabin areas, which was nobody's fault. As their final destination was much more sorrowful and regrettable than mine, I sure didn't find their excretions offensive. I just found their conditions deplorable.

After my nap, I went back up top. A lot of people were playing cards and we had a meeting on safety regulations; how to put life jackets on, and certain procedures to be followed during a drill or, God forbid, the actual event took place. I met the Navigations Officer and the Second Mate. While munching on some snacks, Rob my roommate, and I spot a small iceberg. This time, I have my telescopic lens ready for a picture. We passed a point called "Vancouver" in the channel, which I also took a picture of the marker. It was a picturesque voyage, as the ship endlessly continued its course, ever onward and forward through this beautiful corridor of mountain ranges.

We were invited to the bridge to get a full presentation of the latest

Robert F. Edwards

electronics and facilities that guide this boat and assist the captain and his crew in safe passages through these chartered waters. There was not much else to do, but just relax and vegetate in these surroundings. Of course, there was always conversation, and besides Rob, I talked to a girl from Switzerland, and also started to talk to a young man that was wearing a Canadian flag, only to find out that no, he was not Canadian, but from Switzerland as well.

It was a beautiful evening. It was just starting to show dusk and there were some low level clouds that looked like they had fallen from the sky and the mountains peaked above them. The higher clouds were pinkish brown, almost black sometimes. Heading up into this passage were the first snow-capped peaks that I had seen. There was absolutely no wind at the moment, which was rather odd, especially in this particular part of the Patagonians. The area was noted for not only its beauty and majesty, but also the unpredictable weather changes. This mild moment was not only welcomed but also thoroughly enjoyed. In this part of the world, it was not really a rule of thumb that "red skies at night, sailors' delight; red skies in morning, sailors take warning." It seemed to me that, "red at night, sailors' delight; red skies in morning, who gives a damn? It's just the same as last night."

As the sun fell below the horizon and darkness soon followed, all of us hungry beavers headed quickly into the eating area. At ten to seven again it was dining time – one of the great moments of the day on board a ship when you felt quite relaxed and nostalgic. Tonight, we were also going to have a video. With a captive audience it didn't matter what the movie was, the attendance would be good even if the production was not an Academy Award performance. I couldn't believe how much I had already eaten today. When I was sailing on my own, my appetite was robust but I had always blamed it on the strenuous activities. Here, I was "vegging" or basically doing nothing except talking to other passengers, and lounging around and my appetite had reached new levels of desire. I wasn't alone. We were all anxious to take part in the meal.

338

SOUTH AMERICA
EXPLORATION

We all lined up to have asparagus soup, a bun, juice, mixed vegetables (cabbage with carrots and peas), and salmon. Without a doubt, it was one of the very best salmon I had ever eaten in my entire life. It was served with a buttery sauce on it, just delicious and cooked perfectly. There was no dryness, and yet it was done completely through. I had to give my compliments to the chef, to be able to cook huge quantities of this fish and be consistent. We were so impressed (and somewhat hungry as well) that Rob said, "I wonder if we could get another piece". Guess who went up and made his request known. With no hesitation, he gave me two pieces of fish equally as big as the past two. Now my belt was really pushing against my stomach, or the other way around, fully satisfied.

After dinner, I met an interesting man from Wyoming. Jim had motorcycled down here and had a slight injury with his leg. He had gone all through Bolivia, Ecuador and Peru, and now he was on his way down into Chile. He was taking advantage of the voyage to rest up his twisted ankle and was a nice fellow to talk to, a man in his late forties or early fifties, and seemed to have that cowboy attitude. There was also a young girl, Sandra, from Cornwall, that caught me having seconds, because she was also having seconds in vegetables. We started to laugh and kibitz with each other a bit.

About nine o'clock, the purser came in to get the video prepared for us. It was a movie I had seen before, but watched it anyway until about ten-thirty, before I went up to the lounge area and joined Sandra. She was going to be over here for six months and had already taken a trip from Ushuaia to the Antarctic on the Canadian vessel that Rob had talked about. Her passage was sixteen hundred dollars, but she said it was very worthwhile. Everyday, they went out on a tour, saw whales and walked right up to huge walrus and penguin colonies. They had lectures on ecology everyday by professionals from scientific research institutions. It was professionally done and she had thoroughly enjoyed the eleven-day trip. I asked her about the food and she said it wasn't much better than this

Robert F. Edwards

cargo ship that we were on, so obviously not the cruise line facilities of Alaska or the Mediterranean.

Somewhere around midnight, we docked at Port Eden as there were eighteen passengers getting off. It was a beautiful night, and the stars were in full exposure, a very mild evening compared to some of the other times. I personally would have liked to have gone into town just to look around. From the lights and the information I had, it was a small population of less than four thousand. Nobody else seemed to be inspired to go ashore and we were not exactly sure when the boat would embark. There was a posting on board that the ship would not navigate the narrow neck of the channel during darkness. Under Chilean law, ships had to enter this narrow portion during daylight hours.

I almost talked the night away with Sandra and by one o'clock, Rob had gone to bed, but I soon followed suit. It has been a very leisurely day on the high seas. As I had expected, the ship didn't leave the port until around six thirty in the morning to approach the narrow channel for the sunrise at seven. So we were docked for the night. Goodnight to one and all.

My little beautiful wife, I am one day closer to you and it's coming on very quickly now. We'll be together and I love you very very much. Goodnight, my sweetheart.

SOUTH AMERICA EXPLORATION

March 25th, Sunday
Port Eden, Chile

I had a pleasant sleep and I was correct on our movement. We were now underway. It was an overcast day and yes, the channel had considerably narrowed. Traveling through the mountain terrain and beautiful fjords reminded me so much of the Georgia Strait and British Columbia coastline, but without the trees. It made me appreciate what I have back home as well as what I have akin to the people in Chile. There was a bit of snow on the mountains, but as we were now thousands of kilometers from the Puerto Williams area, it was getting milder.

Breakfast on Sunday was an omelet with ham, cream of wheat, juice, and bread. Quite filling and rewarding. Rob, my roommate, was more than concerned about the seas. At twelve o'clock or shortly after, we would be entering the open sea and the purser had said that sometimes it was very calm; other times, it was choppy. For those inclined to be seasick, they had medication, so who knew what lay ahead?

I went down to check on the poor animals. The cows were in rough shape. This was probably the second day now that they hadn't had any water. Two of them were just lying down in the muck that had been created. Of course, the smell of manure and livestock had penetrated into most of the cabin area, which was unfortunate, but nothing compared to the fate of those poor beasts.

The scenery passed blissfully by, as we traveled on at approximately fourteen knots. The ship set a smooth and continuous course and I finally decided to get cleaned up, had a shower and shave, all the things that go with sanitary conditions. Gosh, how the morning moved along!

Robert F. Edwards

By the time I went back up on deck, there was a spotting of a whale. This was our second spotting and this time, I was prepared. I had the zoom lens with me, which so far I had managed to pack throughout the trip as a weight rather than a useful piece of photo equipment. However, this time, it was in the right position and I did get a couple of pictures. It wasn't Moby Dick; and nobody could identify whether it was a sperm whale, but a whale nonetheless, splashing around, making its way in the waters. I spent a sufficient length of time hoping that a pod might be following, but he was traveling alone that day.

Soon, lunch was being served. We had a pork chop, mashed potatoes, and soup that was questionable. I was in doubt as to whether it was some kind of gravy that they added a few things to, or whether it was actually a soup. However, the meal in general was more than acceptable.

Afterwards, I went back on deck and we had now broken into the open waters. I could feel the huge swells of the ocean, but the ship was not bouncing in any way. It rolled a bit when taking the broad side waves, but the swells were maybe a foot at the very most. For me, it was a pleasant time sitting out, catching rays in the sun, and eventually I decided that this South American lifestyle warranted a siesta. So, off to have a few "winkos", as my beautiful wife says and I wished I was having one with her.

My little "siesta" ranged from an hour to an hour-and-a-half in my life, before I got up and started roaming the deck. I thought the swells were modest but they managed to rock this vessel. For those not of a sea-faring nature, some motion sickness was taking a toll, including Rob. My cabin companion was taking some medication that the ship provided and was sleeping quite soundly.

After being together for the better part of three days, I had met some unique travelers on board. The age ranged from the mid-sixties right down to the mid-twenties, and of the eighty to a hundred passengers, all seemed to be very adventurous people. Many of them planned to spend several years in

342

SOUTH AMERICA
EXPLORATION

South America. I was thinking of Sarah, the young lady on that ship to the Antarctic. She would be here for about eight months with her boyfriend and had planned wisely, taking advantage of some low airfares to swing through vast distances of South America. I admired her outgoing free spirit, and ability to cope with adversity and thoroughly enjoy the days of true adventure.

Another gentleman that I talked to had done a two-year stretch in the Antarctic. I enjoyed the diversity of these people's knowledge base and their openness to share their experiences. He had enjoyed the remoteness and the lack of government intervention. We talked for a couple of hours on technology and ecology and I thoroughly enjoyed his perspectives on it.

A young man from San Diego had brought two surfboards along and was going to surf the coastline of Chile. He was looking forward to the northern part especially, and he was committed to surfboarding as a true love. He was saying that because the shelf in California goes out for such a long distance that the waves start to dissipate. He was hoping to experience a new perspective here because the shelf was shorter on the Chilean coast and he should be able to get more "big surf".

I also spent many hours talking to a man (of German descent) from Kenya, who worked for the Citibank. Because of my time spent in Africa, I could relate to his background and stories of growing up in that country. He was telling me, in his opinion, how the African was such a forgiving person but didn't have any long-term focus. They would welcome Europeans to develop their natural resources, (i.e. oil, or diamonds) and the government of the day seemed to allow them to take over the economic agenda of the country. In return, these companies realized that if they were to explore, let alone extract any of these rich rewards of the land, that they would have to build roads and bridges to at least get the equipment in. He was telling me that when he was a boy of thirteen, that he traveled all through Uganda and the mid-West of Africa and the roads, bridges and cities had the European influence and were in very good condition. He had returned about five or six years ago, and he said the bridges were gone. They used ferries now to try to commute back and forth; sometimes they worked, sometimes they didn't, sometimes the rivers were too high. When he did get on the roads, they were almost impassable because of the deterioration.

He was explaining the problems that Africa was having as not so much tribal wars or hostility. He said these did exist, but the biggest single factor seemed to be an African attitude of living for the moment. He relayed an example. In South Africa a man had invented a portable device to compress mud to form a durable brick because a lot of Africa did not have access to cement. A lot of the homes made of the traditional brick would get washed away in the rainy season, and there was no stability in the dwellings. This particular device was able to compress mud into a form that would endure those climatic conditions. He introduced this device into a village in Zimbabwe after the government and some business people approved it for this village to use as a test market. This gentleman spent time showing the villagers how to operate it and, and motivated them on the benefits. He left the piece of equipment, and returned about two months later. He saw a big pile of bricks, and asked why things had not progressed further, and they said the piece of equipment was broken. When he examined it, the huge compression screw had been removed. He asked what had happened; I guess one of the villagers had seen this screw, saw the possibilities that it could be used for, either to jack up his vehicle or repair some immediate problem. The compression rod was beyond hope of being reassembled into the piece of equipment. He was not saying this with contempt or anger or disenchantment with the African. He was just explaining how they looked at the immediate problem rather than the long far-reaching ramifications that would impede the progress of not only their own quality of life but also the surrounding communities. This seems to be prevalent throughout Africa as a continent.

SOUTH AMERICA
EXPLORATION

He was also saying that his own company had built more than commendable shelters for their employees, only to return and find them in complete squalor and need of repair. He then got paint, materials and the tools to repair them, and even paid them for days that they would normally have worked in the factory to put them back into condition. The people would do it willingly, he said, and without any resentment. But they just didn't have the attitude to be motivated to maintain, let alone improve the situation.

It was interesting spending the afternoon with him, learning about some of his experiences and his comparisons on life in general. He said that he wanted to go to Canada and visit some of the northern parts and up into Alaska. He had a keen interest in wild life in general, and especially birds. I'd seen albatrosses and he was telling me that although they were prevalent here, they were almost an endangered specie because with the fishing vessels, the bird would scoop down to pick up the bait and of course, that was fait accompli for the albatross. Once it swallowed the hook, it was a victim, just as the fish that was being lured by the bait. He described how beautiful the bird was, how it never touched land, only to nest and then continued its voyage in the skies, only dipping down to take on nourishment. He inspired me to not only pay more attention to the fair-feathered friends of the skies, but to have more enthusiasm for this bird with its love of the sea. Also, we talked about the condor and its huge wingspan, over fifteen feet from tip to tip. I had the good fortune of seeing a condor (in captivity at the Melbourne Zoo), and all these years later, would send a cold shiver down my spine just thinking of the actual size of this creature of the skies. There was little doubt in my mind that this great bird was actually more of a scavenger or vulture.

The afternoon progressed on more mundane subjects like economics and capital flows. Being a banker and now having his own company, he was more than conversant with, and it was enlightening to talk to somebody on those subjects that were dear to my heart.

Robert F. Edwards

I was excited to recognize on board the young girl that had spent two years in the Antarctic. I had first met her in Torres del Paine Park and was again thrilled by some of the experiences that she shared. We talked on other subjects, she liked singing and playing the guitar and I asked her what kind of music she liked. She said, "Well, I really do like folk music," and we discussed English ballads and my limited knowledge of Gaelic folk songs. She reminisced with tales of when she and her father had been in Wales. The men would gather in a pub and after a few pints would break into song, almost in a chorus group.

In sharing these anecdotes, I told her about myself writing bedtime stories for my grandson and she was enthralled, which gave me encouragement. When she was in the Antarctic a magazine had approached her to write a monthly article on her experiences, thoughts, and what scientific achievements the station was making. For a young person in her mid-twenties, she had already really done so much, and I admired the diversity she had in her life.

Many of these people I met were not afraid to jump into a new adventure or different lifestyle. The purser, another interesting man, had started off as a mechanic, then moved to teaching children and finally ventured into working as a guide in the Patagonian area. Now he was planning to spend four or five months up in Dawson City in the Yukon with some other company.

Jim (the man from Wyoming) had spent two years doing research and was driving his BMW motorcycle across these terrains, working his way up through Central America into Mexico and then on through the United States back home. This same man had already crossed the United States and through Canada to Halifax. These were some of the people that sat at my table and not only shared a meal with me but fed me with their adventures. A rich gourmet meal of the mind.

It was almost lunchtime again and it would be the last meal that I would be served on this ship. The food had been very good, and I commend the chef for providing both variety and nourishment on a cargo ship rather than on a pleasure cruise. It had been a restful day and I relaxed in the camaraderie of my fellow passengers. The movie that night was "Father of the Bride" with Steve Martin. It wasn't something that I enjoyed and the people were talking in the rest of the eating area, so we had a hard time hearing it.

About eleven o'clock, Rob had already retired for the day and I thought I'd follow suit. So, another day passed on this adventure, enjoying a bit of R&R and letting the crew look after me rather than foraging for myself.

Goodnight, my beautiful little wife. One day closer to you. This part of the world reminds me of our camping experiences and how much I enjoy being with you. What a great life we have together and right at this very moment, I am thinking of us camping and little Buttons sniffing around in the forest and just how happy my life is when I'm with you, sweetheart. Goodnight, my beautiful wife.

Robert F. Edwards

March 26th, Monday
Enroute to Puerto Montt, Chile

Well, another first has happened. I actually slept in. Over the loudspeaker, they were announcing breakfast at eight o'clock and it was quarter-to before this sleepy munchkin stirred. I was amazed that I had to be woken up by the speaker. One thing about my cabin, being in total darkness, it did help me sleep throughout the night. We had still maintained a course in the open channel and with the rocking motion for me was the best sleep that I could possibly get. Many times I would go down on my own little sailboat just to achieve a good night's sleep in 'my cradle in the ocean'.

For breakfast, I got another gift from the Chileans to my Scottish heritage – porridge, and their porridge was good. Along with this was a ham and cheese sandwich. I found their sliced bread to be somewhat dry. For a few reasons, one obviously was it's their preference; and secondly is a lack of preservatives. Not one of my favorite breads but the rest of the food was more than commendable. I thoroughly enjoyed the fruit salad that they have for breakfast. These last months have changed my eating habits, which I hope to continue when I return to my daily routine in Vancouver.

It was just one of those mornings, I was more than lethargic. Not only did I sleep in, I could have slept longer. I made some conversation and socialized for most of the morning, and spent a couple of hours writing. Before long, lunch was being served, which to my delight was potato salad and again, a delicious salmon. If anything, this cook had a way with fish and because I come from coastal waters with a large variety of salmon, I knew it was not the easiest fish to cook. It's inclined to, if overdone, become very dry and in my opinion dis-

348

tasteful. The sauce was a buttery-lemon with chives, which complemented the fish and enhanced the flavor.

We were arriving earlier than the designated time of six o'clock in Puerto Montt. Our now anticipated arrival was at three and as I was enjoying the last moments aboard, I noticed that for the first time since we left Puerto Natales some small fishing vessels. I mentioned to Rob that we must be close to our port of entry, as I saw a person using his cell phone. The terrain was more lush and I was seeing some buildings for the first time in two or three days.

Even though the day was overcast, it was much warmer than what I had experienced further south. In keen anticipation of our arrival, I had all my belongings packed and ready for disembarkment. Even the cattle seemed to have rallied to the cry of more space, if not freedom. I had thought some would be dead by the morning, but they all survived the night.

As the afternoon passed and we were getting closer to the port, more and more people were enjoying the outdoors. They were either looking over the deck, gazing at the shoreline for birds or making conversation. It was gratifying to see that though I hadn't talked to every one of the eighty to a hundred passengers on the voyage, I had managed to meet and talked to the lion's share of them. At about two o'clock, I was one of the first to spot the shoreline indicating the presence of Puerto Montt. It was quite misty, so the distance was  deceiving. It was rather intriguing, as the ship started to sight land, the landscape unfolded like a slide at a time.

Robert F. Edwards

As the bow kept breaking the water, we got a better view of the harbor. This seaport had a population of ninety thousand in this sheltered harbor. As we got closer, I was getting excited to continue on with the last part of my adventure, which would be coming to a close in the next few days. The ship started to veer off to the portside and in my puzzlement I realized we were not heading towards the harbour channel. Before our very eyes, we dropped anchor and the land lovers thought that this was some kind of nautical procedure, but I assured them that we were anchoring, and not going anywhere beyond the circumference of the anchor.

Shortly thereafter, we were informed that we would not be going into port until six. The more pessimistic people were now predicting a midnight disembarking. Disappointed, but nothing that could be done about it, so I spent most of the time up on deck, as the ship pivoted in one direction or another. The hours moved quickly and the purser informed us that we would be lifting anchor and going into port. Sure enough, a little before six, the engines started up and we started to sail into port.

It was a smaller harbor than I thought at first. As we approached through the narrow neck, there were smaller vessels beached on the shoreline, indicating the tide was out, which didn't seem to assist in our docking maneuver. However, I was informed later that there was another ship occupying the berth and that was the reason why we couldn't enter ahead of schedule. Once we got through the narrow neck and near the wharfs, I could comprehend there was only room for one vessel at a time. Maybe at high tide, our vessel could have gone through the other passage, which would have made it more accessible to dock. As it was, it took a huge tug plus two small ones to accomplish a difficult maneuver to bring the ship into dock. The procedure took the better part of an hour and it seemed painstaking. The docks were somewhat antiquated for the size of this particular vessel and the tonnage that it was carrying, but the docks were built long before this boat was commissioned.

SOUTH AMERICA
EXPLORATION

The port was five or six kilometers from the downtown core of Puerto Montt. The city was much nicer than I anticipated, quite a colorful port and much more vibrant than Puerto Natales. This boat trip had been a pleasurable one, well orchestrated and the purser kept everybody well informed. The crew showed their pride in being commissioned to a newer vessel. For myself, it was a very restful and enjoyable period of my journey, and gave me a chance to reflect on the events of the previous weeks. Also, it was a golden opportunity to meet many people with interesting agendas, and to relive vicariously some of their experiences.

We began to gather up our gear, and I as lugged my heavy pack, even Eric the fellow from Switzerland said he couldn't believe how heavy it was, and he was only twenty-one. Rob, and Eric, and myself were planning to go on to a smaller place after we got off the ship and our first requirement was to get to a taxi.

It was about seven-thirty. Our port of call for the first night was going to be Puerto Varas. It was about twenty kilometers north of Puerto Montt and once we got there, it was love at first sight. It was very Bavarian, with a completely different appearance from most of the places I had seen in South America. I had read that the Lake Area had a strong Germanic presence, and the city resembled an Alpine village in Switzerland. I didn't see any beer gardens, but did notice a gothic church that was supposed to be a replica of one of the churches in the Black Forest in Germany.

351

Robert F. Edwards

The three of us made our way to a residential hotel and were greeted by the landlady, a woman probably 6'1", just a big beautiful blonde. It was so odd to hear her speak Spanish. She showed us the rooms and I almost expected her to yodel at any minute. Though the place was old, probably closer to the turn of the century with wood construction, it had that German touch of perfection to it. Everything was spotless, and comfortable with chesterfields in the sitting areas, and the kitchen had little cupboards in it. The room had three beds, all with puffy down comforters to sleep under. I was impressed that the three of us could stay there for nine thousand six hundred pesos, and she also had the Internet.

We got our gear unloaded and decided to go out and enjoy the town. There were two main streets, and as we were pointing out different buildings, we noticed one that was even built like a lighthouse. A very modern hotel with a huge casino in it overlooked Lago Llanquihue, one of the largest lakes in the area. We promised each other, sooner or later, that we would make our way there, not that any of us were highly motivated when it came to gambling.

We were all enjoying the different structural designs, and the Bavarian atmosphere. Even the sidewalks, of a tiled design, were in excellent shape. There was a strong feeling of pride and maintenance was a priority, regardless how old or new the buildings were. We noticed a restaurant that Hansel and Gretel would have been lured into, and we were no exception. We looked over the menu, and both Rob and Eric were on a tighter budget than I, but we all agreed to go in and have a meal. As we entered through the curve-topped wooden door, I felt I was in Switzerland. I am sure that Eric felt a lump in his throat being homesick.

As we sat down, the waitress approached us, a young lady in her mid-twenties who spoke very good English, and could have been Heidi's sister. She was blond, of course, and dressed in the typical Bavarian outfit, white blouse, and the high jumper with embroidery, and dirndl skirt. The tables were made to look like huge slices of wood from mammoth trees, and there was a large barbecue pit where they prepared the meats. Since I entered this town, I had a strong desire to have some Bavarian food and the other two were receptive also. However, when "push came to shove", Rob and Eric ordered some pasta dishes that were quite inexpensive. We shared a pitcher of local beer and the other two being more connoisseurs than myself, said that it was very good beer compared to what they have been drinking. Myself, I just enjoyed the atmosphere.

I satisfied my cravings with sauerkraut and wieners schnitzel, potatoes, and spaetzle, little dough twisters so prevalent with German food. Oh, and some applesauce. I wanted dessert, but they did not have any apple strudel or ice cream. We saw a restaurant across the street that would satisfy any sweet tooth, with chocolates and a huge variety of cakes. Eric was motivated by this and we ended up buying a piece of black forest cake. Rob bought a couple of chocolates. They said that it was cheaper if we bought it as a 'take-out'. Unfortunately, when we got back to the room, and started eating it, the cake was quite dry. I am sure it was a couple of days old and it had lost all flavour. Fortunately, Eric had some red wine to wash this dry dessert down with. It was about eleven o'clock and off to bed the three of us went. We said goodnight to each other and I'll say goodnight to one and all.

Well, my darling dearest little wife, it's not long now. It's a matter of days before I'll be in your arms and I can't tell you how much I'm looking forward to being with you. I've missed you dearly and goodnight, my beautiful wife.

Robert F. Edwards

We all got up at about seven-thirty and looked out the window to see the volcano and no, we couldn't, but the skies looked promising. They were overcast, but with a few patches of blue skies. So highly optimistic, we all started to prepare ourselves to visit some of the surrounding areas of this community. The first thing we did was get out on the street and go over to the lake.

Puerto Varas was the gateway to Lago Todos los Santos. There were a lot of boats and bus crossings to Bariloche Argentina. Some of the popular activities in this delightful place were mountain bike riding and trekking, climbing, bird watching, rafting; anything to do with lakes, from swimming to wind surfing, etc. We were here in the off-season, so we were seeing mostly the local population. No, they didn't wear Bavarian short pants with the big straps on them. They were dressed conventionally, and the school kids wore uniforms.

We walked to the lake and this was one large lake, believe me. Of course, like every enthusiastic photographer, whether the volcano was in good form or not, we were not taking any risks. We settled with taking pictures instead, and there was some cloud formation midway through it. So, it looks like a layer cake in some ways, but very majestic.

The volcano itself was Volcán Osorno, about twelve hundred and fifty meters from sea level. It could be climbed with the proper snow and ice gear, but none of us had the time. Instead, we decided to see the surrounding areas in Parque Nacional Vicente Pérez Rosales. This was Chile's first national park, established in 1926 and had interesting green lagoons in the scoured glacial basin below the volcano. The mini-bus took us to the park, which was 50 km east, for five hundred

354

pesos (about fifty cents U.S.) We walked up to the lagoons and they were ample, but quite small. It was nice to be with somebody else that was disappointed as well.

We originally had planned to spend the entire day there but now decided to take in a few more events. So, we continued to head over to one of the falls and en route we visited a small town called Ensenada. From here was a good view of the jagged crater of the volcano Calbuco, which erupted during the Pleistocene Period. As there really was not much to see in this town, the adventurers headed on towards the falls.

We passed through a small village called Peulla, and here the blue waters of the lake changed to emerald greens. The waterfalls we were heading towards, called Cascada de los Novios, cost us a thousand pesos to enter through a walkway. Unfortunately, my previous experience at the Iguazú Falls of Argentina with its massive cascades diminished the beauty of these falls somewhat, just because of the sheer comparison of size. The falls were still attractive, with the waters spilling down the deep gorges into dark blue lagoons. The three of us were eager to continue on, completed the entire circuit and were back out in record time to catch the next bus. I think the gate warden figured that we had spread wings to fly over the falls.

By now, Eric wanted to head on to Puerto Montt, to fly home later that night. My bus did not leave for Santiago until ten that evening. The three of us returned back to Puerto Varas on the bus, and this was where our directions parted. Eric left to catch his flight and Rob and I were on our way to Frutillar about seventy kilometers south of Osorno. Believe it or not, it was two French Canadian schoolteachers that told us about this place. We decided that we had the time, so off on the bus again, and the trip was only seven hundred pesos.

The scenery in this part of Chile was primarily agricultural, with little farms all well maintained. The German influence was very evident in this area. The lake region was a popular area for Chileans during the summer months, which I could comprehend only too well. Its beauty was a lush green, but was more cosmetically manicured than the rugged natural beauty of the Patagonians. Just a pleasant European countryside.

Once we got to this small hamlet, it consisted of a main street; and on the opposite side, was a beautiful lake, Lago Llanquihue. To both Rob's and my delight, the clouds had burnt off and the volcano was now exposed in its full beauty and it looked like it was planted right on the lake. Some people said that it looked cone shaped. To me, it almost looked like Mount Fuji, at first glance, that had been relocated to South America. This one had that same beautiful snow-capped top and a large black base below it.

The lava base on a volcano has a unique type of rock formation. It felt like walking on foam taffy, but with a great strength and endurance. It has a honeycomb appearance, whether it was in small pieces or large formations. The largest volcano, flanked on either side by smaller ones, dominated the skyline. It was a very beautiful part of the world for me and the Chilean people were justifiably proud of it.

SOUTH AMERICA
EXPLORATION

As we walked along the shoreline, the buildings on the adjacent side were dramatic in design. Most of them dated back to the early part of the century, and many had been converted to Bed & Breakfast establishments or hostels. We noticed a small Lutheran Church, and Rob asked, "Do you want to take a look at it? And I said, "Sure, why not?" The fellow there was doing maintenance work, and I got talking to him. It was remarkable how I managed to get so much information without having the language to assist me. The church had a bell tower, and I learnt that he was the bell-ringer; one being five hundred kilos, and the other three hundred kilos. I expressed my interest in seeing inside the church itself, which was not as ornate as a Roman Catholic Church, but peaceful and serene. The big surprise came when I saw a huge pipe organ. This generous fellow took me up to the loft to get a close up look at this mammoth organ, which had been brought over from Germany in 1954. The company that made this organ was established in 1868. I would have loved to have been there on Sunday to listen to that remarkable instrument. It must have been overpowering in that small church that it commands.

I couldn't help but comment to Rob, "You know this is really the only way to travel and see things, forgetting the price and the collectiveness of tours." With a tour, I would lack the opportunity and the freedom. There were always limitations with a preordained itinerary and large groups. If there were only two of us, then there were only two ideas, compared to twenty different opinions on what to see or do. The way that tours function with any kind of success was as a rock skipping across the water. At best, they could only make slight indentations on the cultural basis of the area. I much preferred this type of vagabond backpacking and the true adventure of the unexpected and the ability to deviate plans quickly.

We continued our tour, and came across an Internet in a modern building with very good computers. Both Rob and I took advantage of the opportunity to catch up on some of our

Robert F. Edwards

mail, and then decided it would be prudent to return to Puerto Varas. By now, it was six o'clock and without too much anxiety we enjoyed the bus trip back.

Once back at our home base, Rob wanted to book a bus tour for tomorrow, and I checked out my flight tomorrow, back to Vancouver, Canada. With all that administration out of the way, and sunset fast approaching, we decided to get a few last pictures of the glow over this beautiful volcano.

Rob and I were unanimous in our decision to have our last meal together at the "Hansel and Gretel" restaurant that we enjoyed so much yesterday. It was still rather early, about quarter to eight. In South America, nine o'clock to ten o'clock was usually when people decided to take on their evening meal. So, we were one of the first there. Our delightful waitress brought us a pitcher of beer and hot bread to start off with. We ordered a large casserole dish to share and we ate as much meat as we could possibly handle. It contained anything from steak to big ribs to sweet breads, tripe, blood sausage, and pork chops. We ate until we felt uncomfortable and the waitress even reheated our dish on the fire. It was an interesting way of barbecuing and this clay type pot kept the meat in its juices, succulent and hot. I still felt that the Argentineans excelled with their meat, and the Chilean expertise lay in the fish and seafood of their region.

As we said goodbye, I had a little lump in my throat. I would always be glad that I came here to finish my last days in Chile and South America. At quarter after nine, I was at the bus stop, which was just outside the hostel where we were staying, and by ten o'clock, was on my way to Santiago, my final destination in Chile.

Another wonderful day in this part of Chile. I was so glad that I got to see the Lake District, which I was hoping for but wasn't really counting on. Now, I had some wonderful memories of it. Goodnight, one and all.

Goodnight, my beautiful wife. Last day in Chile, last night in South America. Goodnight, my beautiful loved one.

SOUTH AMERICA EXPLORATION

I woke up after a hard night in an upright position, but I managed to catch some rest through the night, and it was seven o'clock in the morning. It was very overcast and we had come into some fog. My breakfast consisted of instant coffee, some little wafers, and the highway was my table. We were making good time and should arrive some time around eleven or twelve in Santiago, which would allow me the better part of an afternoon and early evening before I had to make my way to the airport.

The scenery had changed and was much drier as we headed north. We were now into quite arid terrain and the mountain ranges had little foliage on them. The farms had regressed back into small dilapidated-looking structures. It was a far cry from the Lake District, with its lush vegetation, beautiful green grass on the boulevards, and flowers prevalent everywhere.

Now, as I continually make my way toward Santiago, the weather has become pleasant, and I have seen many fruit trees amidst the heavily agricultural, truck farming areas. This valley is a fertile band for growing produce nestled amongst the mountains. The skies have become a clear blue, such a difference from the overcast clouds just a few hundred kilometers south.

I was conscious of the very long narrow corridor that Chile covers in South America, with a huge variation of latitude from the northern end to the southern tip. Chileans must experience some of the widest ranges of weather conditions in the world. I have been told that Santiago enjoys a very stable weather condition, with little variance, due to its position on the coastline.

Robert F. Edwards

By ten o'clock, we had been served our coffee and biscuits, and I was enjoying the warmth of the day. I had noticed the "Dole" name on quite a few warehouses as we passed, so am sure the products that I enjoyed back home have found their way up from this area. I had also been told that many of the best wines produced in the country are shipped out, but not being a connoisseur, I had enjoyed the ones that I had tasted here. I knew for sure that coffee didn't get a high rating, and had experienced the "Nestle" instant coffee more than I cared to say.

By ten-thirty, we enjoyed a small break off the bus, and were already reaching the perimeter of the city. In a short time we had reached our terminal, and I managed to find a locker to store my luggage, for 1000 pesos for the day. I located a washroom, and for 150 pesos entry was able to clean up, and felt like a new man to start the day. As I made my way towards Centro, I walked past a few shops and bazaars. I still hadn't fulfilled my mission to purchase a gaucho hat, and regretted not getting one in Salta, but the thoughts of carrying it for two months wasn't practical.

I found an Internet spot, and was a bit disappointed not to have received one from Marietta as a going away present. However, I punched one out to her and Wendy to let them know I was here, on my final day before leaving tonight. I happened by chance to enter one of the coffee shops that Mandy and Caroline had been telling me about, where the girls were scantily dressed. They were supposedly quite popular, but this was my first experience of one. The girls wore a type of fishnet costume, with only a small black bikini bottom. I got a good view of the breasts as they served my espresso and sandwich, and surprisingly the price of a cup of coffee was as competitive as the fast food joints.

I continued my walking and came to a learning centre with many of the buildings named in honor of John F. Kennedy, primarily for the learning of English. Along this corridor, I saw the students mostly in their teenage years, and again dressed in uniforms. I had learnt now that though most of the kids wore the same uniform, you could distinguish the school by the different crests. The girls' skirts were short, and many wore thick knee-highs, or nylon stockings, but the style of shoes was the same for all. The thick heavily soled shoes that all the girls wore reminded me of properly shoed Clydesdale horses of old. An observation of the girls, they struck me as a bit chunky, quite sturdy little kids, although the boys didn't seem to pack on as much weight.

I came to a church, and had thought to go in, and give my thanks to 'our Father, who art in heaven', but unfortunately the doors were locked. I often wonder what Christianity is all about, as the places of worship are sealed off like tombs of the Apostles. Throughout this journey, I had seen in the small towns, where people had taken time during their daily activities to go kneel to their God and say a few prayers. To me this is what the House of God should be; open 24 hours a day, 7 days a week, not just for a short ceremonial ritual. Here in the capital city, this church is locked up tighter than Fort Knox. I walked over  to the Basilica, which was locked also, but in fairness, they were in the restoration phase, and repairing walls.

I actually took my first subway ride, 150 pesos, to go just about anywhere, and it was very clean. There were three lines heading out, and all the cars were clean, and efficient.

Again, I tried another church. I was determined to do a bit of worshipping, but then like baseball, three strikes and you are out. So I finally gave up this quest. I covered a fair amount of the city, and enjoyed passing by the many parks, even in the residential areas. It seems these were a popular spot for

361

courting. I had a chuckle when I noticed a lady walking her dog, a poodle just immaculately groomed, and she looked like she had just rolled out of bed.

The street cleaners were out in force, and yes, they really do sweep, with brooms, and none of this standing around looking for something to do. They were kept busy picking up litter, even with the garbage containers all around.

The weather was great, neither too hot, nor too cold, just the perfect Goldilocks porridge weather. For my last lunch in South America, I went for some fritas, chicken and a beer, 2300 pesos. I made my way over to the railway station by two-thirty, and to my delight the train was in. This is the only running passenger train in Chile, and it eventually works its way down to Puerto Montt. It was just six cars, and a modern fiberglass sterile construction. I took a few pictures of the older nonfunctioning trains, and it seemed a shame, with their beautiful ornate ironwork being disregarded. It was an attractive station, and a section had been converted over to a shopping mall.

The wrought iron work was very prevalent throughout the city, as most of the residential areas had gates, and high fences, whether for security or the style, I wasn't sure.

I also noticed a lot of graffiti, and earlier that day I had observed a group of kids with paint on their faces and clothes. I had thought they were asking for handouts, but later learnt that these ambitious kids were painting over the graffiti. I have to commend their efforts, and the pride they were taking in their city, in trying to keep ahead of the vandals.

362

SOUTH AMERICA
EXPLORATION

With luck, I found a few shops on the mall that carried the full gaucho outfits, hats to boots. Even though they were more expensive than in Salta, they were still only a third of the price of the Ushuaia hats. I found a shop that accepted Visa, so bought myself the sombrero, bolero jacket, and sash, as a fond reminder of the gaucho I so admired.

I made my way back to the bus station and picked up my belongings. I wasn't able to get a bus to the airport, so took a cab to arrive by five o'clock. I got my large bag checked in, and had my boarding pass ready, even though I still had five hours to wait. I dressed up in my new outfit, and settled myself down with a book. I had a limited amount of Chilean pesos, and so governed the last moments accordingly.

It was a warm evening, so I sat out and enjoyed the last moments of this beautiful country and the memories of this adventure as I watched the sun go down over the Andes. I had a modest meal to while away the last few hours, and was able to get an airport attendant to take a picture of me. So many moments of my life have been spent waiting for an aircraft.

I enjoyed strolling around the airport, and watching the cosmopolitan activities. I had a feeling of nostalgia when I no-

Robert F. Edwards

ticed some nuns dressed in the formal habits of the past, and children wearing their Sunday best, waiting to travel somewhere exciting.

A few hours passed, and I cleared through Customs into the duty free section of shops. I spent some time browsing in the bookstore with my eye constantly on the monitors, watching the arrival/departure times. Eventually boarding began, and we left without any delays. We were served an evening meal, and the wings of the plane pierced the night sky towards my destination of Los Angeles. The movie we were entertained with was finishing just as we made our descent into Lima, Peru.

My port side window gave me a good view, and as with so many cities, the night-lights give the appearance of a larger circumference than the day would indicate. This was a short stopover, and after reloading a few more passengers, we continued on through the night.

By the morning light, I was able to spot the shores of North America. I was feeling apprehensive clearing customs now in the United States, and catching my final flight, with Alaska Airlines. I should have had a three-hour window, but for reasons untold, this flight was now an hour late. I had to get to another airport, and had hoped that with this transfer, my luggage would continue on.

Wrong. I was quite adamant that it had been tagged for transfer to carry on, and Customs was equally as adamant that it had to be picked up here. Thank goodness I listened, and after grabbing it off the carousel, I quickly got directions to the other airport, which was some distance away. I got there with room to breath, and again made my way towards the gate. Now after boarding, this is my final flight homeward bound.

I enjoyed the scenery coming up the coast and took a few pictures on the way, and an interesting crater-lake was clearly visible.

At last, we touched down, and my beautiful wife is there to greet me, 'the gaucho from South America'. We were both

SOUTH AMERICA
EXPLORATION

happy and grateful to see each other. My daughter and grandson were there waiting for me at home, with a celebration of balloons and banners, and more pictures were taken. The traveler, the adventurer, had returned and the stories of this part of South America have come to an end.

I hope that, in some small way, those who take the time and effort to peruse these pages find some measure of enjoyment and fulfillment as I, the writer, have had in experiencing them.

Adiós, amigos.

ISBN 142512402-X